World War II and Mexican American Civil Rights

World War II and Mexican American Civil Rights

EDITED BY RICHARD GRISWOLD DEL CASTILLO

University of Texas Press ⟡ Austin

Requests for permission to reproduce material from this work should be sent to:
    Permissions
    University of Texas Press
    P.O. Box 7819
    Austin, TX 78713-7819
    www.utexas.edu/utpress/about/bpermission.html

⊗ The paper used in this book meets the minimum requirements of ANSI/NISO
Z39.48-1992 (R1997) (Permanence of Paper).

Library of Congress Cataloging-in-Publication Data
World War II and Mexican American civil rights / edited by
Richard Griswold del Castillo. — 1st ed.
        p.   cm.
Includes bibliographical references and index.
ISBN 978-0-292-71738-1 (cloth : alk. paper) —
ISBN 978-0-292-71739-8 (pbk. : alk. paper)
1. World War, 1939–1945—Mexican Americans. 2. Mexican Americans—Civil
rights. 3. United States—Ethnic relations. I. Griswold del Castillo, Richard.
II. Title: World War Two and Mexican American civil rights. III. Title: World
War 2 and Mexican American civil rights.
D769.8.F7M48 2008
940.530868'72073—dc22
                                                                    2007014877

Dedicated to the memory of Richard Steele, a friend and colleague who had the vision to begin this book

Table of Contents

Introduction   1
BY RICHARD GRISWOLD DEL CASTILLO

1. Mexican Americans in 1940: Perceptions and Conditions   7
    BY RICHARD STEELE

2. The Federal Government Discovers Mexican Americans   19
    BY RICHARD STEELE

3. Violence in Los Angeles: Sleepy Lagoon, the Zoot-Suit Riots,
    and the Liberal Response   34
    BY RICHARD STEELE

4. The War and Changing Identities: Personal Transformations   49
    BY RICHARD GRISWOLD DEL CASTILLO

5. Civil Rights on the Home Front: Leaders and Organizations   74
    BY RICHARD GRISWOLD DEL CASTILLO

    Epilogue: Civil Rights and the Legacy of War   95
    BY RICHARD STEELE AND RICHARD GRISWOLD DEL CASTILLO

Appendix A: Ruth Tuck, "The Minority Citizen"   108

Appendix B: Statement of Carlos E. Castañeda before the U.S. Senate
Regarding the Need for a Fair Employment Practices Commission,
March 12, 1945   135

Appendix C: Executive Order 8802 Establishing the Fair Employment
Practices Committee, June 25, 1941   143

Appendix D: The "Caucasian Race—Equal Privileges" Texas House Concurrent Resolution, 1943 145

Appendix E: Manuel Ruiz, "Latin-American Juvenile Delinquency in Los Angeles: Bomb or Bubble!" 148

Appendix F: Raul Morin, excerpts from *Among the Valiant: Mexican-Americans in WW II and Korea* 159

Appendix G: Affidavits of Mexican Americans Regarding Discrimination in Texas during World War II (Collected by Alonso S. Perales) 189

Notes 207

Selected Annotated Bibliography 227

Index 231

World War II and Mexican American Civil Rights

Introduction

RICHARD GRISWOLD DEL CASTILLO

World War II was a turning point in the experience of many Mexican Americans. Within four years, 1941 to 1945, hundreds of thousands of Mexican Americans left segregated urban barrios and rural *colonias* in the Southwest and, for the first time, experienced a kind of equality with white Americans within the military, sacrificing their lives for the cause of democracy and freedom. Other hundreds of thousands of women and men found new factory jobs working in urban areas where, also for the first time, they earned wages equal to those of Anglo-Americans. After the war, as a result of their experiences on the home front and in the military, Mexican Americans were less willing to tolerate a second-class citizenship, having proven their loyalty and "Americanness" during the war. They had come to believe the rhetoric of patriotism, and they wanted to have the civil rights they knew they had earned.

The Mexican American struggle for civil rights predated World War II. In the prewar years, countless labor union activists and community organizers fought against inequality, and many of them continued to do so after World War II. Zaragosa Vargas, in his book *Labor Rights Are Civil Rights*, has shown how the working-class organizations in the prewar period contributed to an expanded definition of civil rights for Mexican Americans. He argues that in these years, "Mexican Americans initiated a labor and civil rights movement of the postwar years, which formed the foundation of the modern Chicano movement."[1]

Mario T. García, in his pioneering study of the Mexican American generation, *Mexican Americans: Leadership, Ideology, and Identity, 1930–1960*, has also shown how leaders and organizations from the 1930s were important precursors to the civil rights movement of the 1950s and 1960s. In his words, this Mexican American generation that came of age during the war "gave a high priority to the achievement of civil rights for all Mexicans in the United States."[2] Biographies of Mexican American leaders like Bert Corona reveal the evolution of their activism in the 1930s and how the war served to influence their careers.[3] Important regional histories of Mexicans and Mexican Americans by David Montejano, Arnoldo De León, and Rudolfo Acuña indicate how an awareness of civil rights and the growth of organizations developed over a continuum.[4] Thus, although World War II was certainly an important watershed event, it should not be seen as the cause of a new civil rights movement among Mexican Americans.

The importance of the U.S. government's role in shaping a dialogue with new terminology about Mexican Americans and their rights has not been examined by contemporary scholars, although it was a topic of much discussion by some Mexican American leaders during the war years and immediately thereafter.[5] Largely as a result of changing federal priorities, Mexican American leaders began to expect the government to take a more direct interest in the problems of the people of Mexican origin in the United States. During World War II, the nation at large discovered Mexican Americans as an ethnic minority, and simultaneously, federal and state officials began working to address issues that targeted this population.

On the eve of the Second World War, Mexican Americans were one of a number of immigrant groups that had come to the United States in large numbers over the previous half century. Each, to varying degrees, suffered from poverty, discrimination, and the larger public's indifference. But no immigrant group experienced these to a greater degree than the nation's 3.5 million Americans of Mexican descent. Of course, a large number of Mexican Americans were not immigrants at all, but descendants of some of the first non-Indian families to settle in Texas, New Mexico, Arizona, and California. In the popular mind, however, these Spanish-speaking citizens were considered foreigners.

To breach the walls of ignorance and hostility and achieve their rightful place in American society, Mexican Americans had to command a new level of political force. "Mexicans," which is how they were known in the United States at least until the 1940s, had long constituted a community in the sense of a people united by a matrix of social and cultural ties—preeminently a common heritage and language. What they lacked in 1940 was a corporate sense of their ethnicity that linked them to others of similar background. European immigrant groups in America, and their offspring, have found it expedient to subordinate regional and class differences that divided them in their countries of origin in order to present America with a common front. If Mexican Americans were to find relief from their problems in government action, they would have to follow suit by constituting themselves as a self-conscious, unified political community that gave at least the appearance of sharing common interests and speaking with something approaching a single voice. The first step to reform was the recognition that persons of Mexican descent had needs specific to them that government officials had an interest in addressing.

As the Second World War approached, Mexican Americans began to think of themselves in these terms, but it was the events that accompanied American preparations for participation in a global conflict that first significantly advanced this goal. The impetus came from the government itself, but the groundwork was simultaneously being laid for a new era in civil rights consciousness by many Mexican American organizations. In the early 1940s, as the nation prepared for war, policy makers looked for ways to strengthen the nation's capacity for the impending struggle for national survival. Success, they concluded, required encouraging each of the groups that constituted America's multiethnic society to believe that victory was in its interest. As part of their effort to unite and motivate all Americans, officials "discovered" Mexican Americans. The former were concerned lest a sense of grievance or disaffection on the latter's part undermine their willingness to work and sacrifice for the common effort. Washington was also concerned that the mistreatment of Spanish-speaking Americans might adversely affect sensitive relations with the nations of Latin America in general, and Mexico in particular. Officials concluded that the treatment of Mexican Americans had a bearing on national security. A people hardly known to American officialdom before 1939 was now given a name—indeed several names. They were called "Spanish Americans," or "Spanish-speaking Americans," or "Mexican Americans." A select few individuals emerged as unofficial representatives, and a variety of programs and reform initiatives were introduced at all levels of government to deal with their needs. The basis for Mexican American political power and future reforms at the federal level had been laid.

But the war's effect on Mexican Americans was not only, perhaps not even primarily, political. The vast majority of Mexican Americans were unaware of and little affected by the petitions of their leaders, the calculations of government officials, or the implementation of high-minded reform programs. Nevertheless, partly as a result of emerging government efforts, but largely as an unintended consequence of the necessities of war, opportunities for mobility and economic advancement did become available, and those who were able to take advantage of them found that the war improved their lives. Exposed to wartime experiences, many of the sons and daughters of Mexican immigrants found a sense not only that they belonged in America, but that they should raise their voices in the struggle to secure for themselves and their children the benefits that life in the United States could entail. The veterans of the war, whether they wore uniforms or not, were no longer content with second-class status. This personal transformation paralleled and fed the emergence of a political community after 1945.

These are the themes of this book: how World War II encouraged government and society to recognize and deal with Mexican Americans, and how Mexican Americans themselves were affected personally and politically by the wartime experience, which led them to work on their own agenda of social and political advancement. As was true for another U.S. "minority," the African Americans, World War II was a watershed in the mobilization of new energies to combat segregation and racism and was instrumental in shaping a new kind of ethnic identity—one that refused to accept second-class status while striving for acceptance and inclusion.

Despite the seeming importance of World War II and its impact on Mexican Americans, little attention has been devoted to these years and to how they shaped a new cultural and political environment for Mexican Americans. Only a few books have been published that specifically deal with the World War II experience of Mexican Americans. In 1963, Raul Morin's *Among the Valiant* was a pioneering account of the heroic actions of Mexican and Mexican American soldiers during the war. It provided important information about the military contributions and sacrifices of Mexican and Mexican American servicemen.[6] Mauricio Mazón has written a social-psychological study of the so-called Zoot-Suit Riots, which took place in Los Angeles in 1943. This penetrating study of scapegoating and racism in wartime dramatized the contradictions inherent on the home front for Mexican American youths. The only other book-length treatment focusing on the war and Mexican Americans, *Mexican Americans and World War II*, an anthology edited by Maggie Rivas-Rodriguez at the University of Texas, was published in 2005. This pioneering book has excellent essays about life on the home front and the complexities and contradictions of the Latina and Latino experience during the war.[7] Other important articles and portions of books discussing local organiza-

Figure 0.1. Héctor P. García, one of the founders of the GI Forum, which was composed of Mexican American WWII veterans, is seen here marching alongside Chicanos in a "Marcha for Justice" in Corpus Christi, Texas, April 8, 1977. This was a protest of a local judge's racist remarks in court and a demand for his removal. This photograph illustrates the continuity between generations of civil rights struggles. Dr. Héctor P. García Papers. Courtesy of Special Collections and Archives, Mary and Jeff Bell Library, Texas A&M University, Corpus Christi, Texas.

tions and workers during the war have been published, but by and large, there has not been a synthetic study of Mexican Americans and the many changes they experienced during the war. With the exception of an important chapter by historian Zaragosa Vargas, no one has yet studied the evolution of civil rights consciousness during this conflict.[8]

This book provides an introduction to what is known about the emergence during World War II of what has been called the Mexican American generation by looking at the process by which they changed their ideas about their place in America and formulated ideas about their right to equal treatment and respect. As an introduction to the relationship of World War II to Mexican American civil rights struggles, this book is a starting point for deeper study and research. The five chapters and epilogue explore the issues touched on above and provide the historical narrative to understand the documents that follow in the appendices. This collection of key essays and documents from the World War II period gives a first-person understanding of the civil rights struggles of Mexican Americans. An annotated bibliography lists works that help place the World War II experience in the context of the social and political history of Mexican Americans.

Although this is a collaborative book, most of the writing and inspiration for it came from Richard Steele, Professor Emeritus of History at San Diego State University. Richard's long career as a historian focused on American civil liberties during World War II, and he authored two important books interpreting this era, both of which provide insights into how the U.S. government changed its policies and perceptions regarding ethnic minorities. He became intensely interested in Chicano history after his retirement in 2000 and in conversations with me. He read most of the important books that had been written by Chicano scholars. His passion for history and, most importantly, his demanding search for the truth have shaped the tone and direction of this book. My assignment was to research and write about how this war affected the Mexican American communities in shaping their sense of civil rights. Richard passed away before we could finish our work together. His widow, Elaine, graciously agreed to allow me to proceed with the then incomplete manuscript. She also acted as an important editor of the final drafts. The result of our collaboration is this book, an effort that is by no means exhaustive, but one that may suggest avenues for future research and writing. Our hope has been that besides serving as a catalyst for others, this book will be a valuable teaching tool for future generations.

CHAPTER I

Mexican Americans in 1940: Perceptions and Conditions

RICHARD STEELE

Few Americans in 1940 knew their compatriots of Mexican origin first-hand. What most did know was a creation of the popular media that portrayed them, no matter which side of the border they lived on, either as peons with eyes averted and faces buried in oversized sombreros, or as treacherous, grinning, bandoleer-draped *bandidos*. This mélange was leavened with the occasional appearance of a lighter-skinned but nonetheless indolent and irresponsible *caballero* vaguely associated with Mexico but more likely identified as "Spanish."[1]

In the Southwest, where millions of Mexicans (as all people of Mexican extraction were known) lived, familiarity produced a slightly different image, but little enlightenment. To most white Americans (or "Anglos," as they were referred to by the Mexican community), the term "Mexican" commonly conjured up images of the bent figures in a distant cotton field or the swarthy common laborers encountered in the region's towns and cities. In either case, they were assumed by white Americans to be members of a ragged race of inferiors provided by providence to do the region's most unpleasant work.

The pervading ignorance and hostility were reflected in a poll conducted in 1942, which asked a cross section of white Americans to rate the qualities of a list of "people[s] or races of the world . . . in comparison with the people of the United States." The question was unexceptional in this era of ethnic stereotypes, an era before the concept of race had been questioned and before Americans were discouraged from making invidious comparisons between peoples. Those who responded predictably categorized the English, Dutch, and Scandinavians as being "as good as we . . . in all important respects"; ranked the Irish, French, and Germans as somewhat inferior; and placed the Greeks, "South Americans," "Jewish refugees," Poles, Russians, Chinese, Spaniards, Italians, and Japanese, in that order, as more clearly alien and inferior to Americans. At the very bottom of the list, below the Japanese, with whom the United States was at war, were Mexicans, who were identified as being "as good as Americans" by only 12 percent of those surveyed, and as "definitely inferior" by a startling 59 percent.[2]

Official and informed opinion in the early 1940s was less judgmental but hardly more positive. Those who took an interest in America's Mexicans saw them as suffering social and economic disabilities so intense and demoralizing that their resultant disaffection threatened national security. Reports commissioned by two federal agencies in 1942 described the Mexican immigrant and his progeny as constituting "probably the most submerged and destitute group in the United States"; employed in the "lowest paid and least desirable jobs"; plagued by illiteracy, juvenile delinquency, criminality, and disease; despised by the people among whom they lived; and presenting "perhaps the most striking need for economic rehabilitation and cultural assimilation in the entire United States."[3]

These conclusions were certainly not valid for every Mexican American (the term used herein for convenience to designate all persons of Mexican descent in the United States regardless of nativity or citizenship). Nor can they even hint at the full range of personal stories subsumed under the generalizations. Yet both the stereotyped views of the general public and the more thoughtful, though culturally biased, assessments of the government investigators suggested that Mexican Americans confronted a problem compounded by their poverty and by the ignorance, hostility, and discriminatory habits of those around them. This chapter, then, explores the Mexican American condition and its social, political, and ideological contexts on the eve of World War II.[4]

Observers have estimated that approximately 3.5 million persons of Mexican descent lived in the United States in 1940.[5] The vast majority had come since the turn of the century, the last of a number of immigrant groups that had arrived in the United States in the four decades after 1880. Like other immigrant groups, most had embarked on the challenging journey to the United States for material reasons—to earn enough to return to their native land and start anew, or to make a better life for themselves in the new country. Unlike the others, they found themselves strangers in the very lands that were part of their patrimony. Texas, California, and the American Southwest, where most settled, had been part of Mexican territory until 1848, and although the region was, with the exception of New Mexico, now dominated by Americans of European descent, or "Anglos," it still bore traces of its past in the Spanish names of its towns, cities, and topographical features.

The Mexican American Social-Economic Caste in 1940

Only a handful of the descendants of the original pre-1848 settlers remained in Texas and California in 1940. Many had integrated into Anglo society, and they maintained a distant relationship with the far more numerous and impoverished immigrants. In New Mexico, there were more than 250,000 persons descended from the Mexican colonists who had settled in the northern borderlands of old Mexico from the sixteenth through the eighteenth centuries. They still lived in relative isolation, with their inherited culture largely intact. Preferring to be called Hispanos, Nuevo Mexicanos, New Mexicans, or Spanish-speaking Americans, they had maintained the Spanish language and colonial customs by minimizing their contact with the English-speaking people who settled among and around them in the nineteenth century. They, too, had little sense of identity with the Mexican immigrants whose language they shared.[6]

Most of the persons of Mexican descent in the United States in 1940 were not the offspring of early settlers, but rather immigrants and the immediate progeny of immigrants who had been driven from their homeland by poverty and revolution and drawn north over the past half century by the opportunity to work. The attraction was jobs provided by Anglo miners, farmers, and entrepreneurs who, having displaced the native population and pushed aside the early Mexican settlers, were feverishly exploiting the resource-rich land in the West. The major obstacle to the seemingly limitless bounty the region offered was a chronic shortage of labor, which they sought to remedy by recruiting workers from around the world. Foreign labor was preferred because the more "foreign" and more desperate they were, the harder working and less demanding those who came were likely to be, and the less likely to get a fair hearing for any grievances. Racism, the belief in a biologically determined hierarchy of peoples, helped serve the economic interests of employers, who could comfortably treat Mexicans—as they had Asian Americans—as an alien, transitory workforce, not worthy of a decent living or commanding the rights customarily enjoyed by "white" Americans. Employers promoted and used racial prejudices to ensure that Mexicans and others played their designated role in the economic scheme.[7]

Figure I.I. Cañoncito school before World War II, San Miguel County, New Mexico—an example of the kind of neglect and poverty that was common for rural Mexican Americans. George I. Sánchez Papers, University of Texas, Austin. Courtesy of University of Texas at Austin Libraries.

For a time, the Mexicans provided an ideal labor source as they moved into and out of the United States as the economy dictated.[8] When there was work, they came in numbers that outstripped the need. When the economy slowed and they were no longer needed or welcome to stay, they were likely to return to Mexico. But over time the arrangement gradually faltered as the immigrants, their dreams of returning to Mexico fading, chose to remain in settlements (*colonias*) north of the border.[9] Having raised children and nurtured a uniquely Mexican American culture in the North, they were reluctant to move on at the first sign that American prosperity was ebbing.[10]

With the onset of the Great Depression in the 1930s, Mexican immigrants saw opportunities wither and hostility increase, but these were now not enough by themselves to force many Mexican Americans to leave. State and federal authorities, abetted by Mexican officials, undertook to repatriate the now "surplus" Mexican families whose labor was readily replaceable by the many destitute Anglo-Americans who roamed the countryside. Many expendable Mexicans, and their American-born dependents, were hustled out of the country to relieve bankrupt state relief resources in an often cruel campaign of expulsion. Although over a million immigrants of all nationalities left the United States in the 1930s, only the Mexicans were the objects of a systematic coercive expulsion.[11]

The repatriation effort was tacit recognition that the one-time migrant Mexican population had put down roots in the United States. Indeed, by 1940, large numbers had settled in Texas, mostly in small towns along the border and as far north as San Antonio, and in Southern California, chiefly in Los Angeles County. From both areas, a portion migrated throughout the Southwest and beyond, following the crops and returning in slack seasons. Perhaps half the Mexican American population toiled in agriculture, most as migratory workers cultivating and picking various crops.[12] A few established themselves as shopkeepers and professionals serving the Mexican American communities. Most of the rest worked as day laborers or in the low-paying jobs maintaining the railroads and working in the mines of the Southwest. At a time when more than a third of American workers were unionized, few Mexican Americans were. As they were competing with an endless supply of desperate workers from Mexico and elsewhere, their incomes were kept barely above the subsistence level and well below that paid to Anglo workers for comparable work.

Poverty was generally the lot of unskilled, especially migratory, labor in the United States; one need only recall the plight of the so-called Okies, poor white migrants (many from Oklahoma) who came to California in the late 1930s in search of work. Their plight was dramatized in John Steinbeck's novel *The Grapes of Wrath*. But economic problems for Mexican Americans were compounded by the disposition of Anglos to see them as part of a permanent underclass and to discriminate against them accordingly. Color prejudices were common throughout the United States, but Mexicans settled in areas where racial prejudice was deeply rooted and particularly strong. Darker on average than Anglos and stigmatized by name and language, the Mexicans were natural targets of the "race"-based discrimination that victimized American Indians, African Americans, and Asians. The fact that they were mostly unskilled, illiterate, and forced into subsistence living reinforced the assumptions concerning their supposed innate inferiority.[13] It was easy to stereotype them as unclean, unmotivated, slow, dishonest, able to live on less, and not fit to associate with "whites."

In Texas, a state that had been part of the slave-holding Confederacy during the American Civil War, Mexicans encountered a racial caste system that operated on the principle that denying some people (principally African Americans) rights legitimately enjoyed by whites simply enforced the natural order of things. In California, the political system had long been dedicated to obtaining and controlling an exploitable workforce through race-based legal distinctions and selective law enforcement.[14] Historically, in both places, where these faltered, vigilantism could be counted on to enforce the caste system. By the time Mexicans arrived in the state in large numbers, employers were accustomed to carefully discriminating between their workers on "racial" grounds, and most workers had internalized the prevailing mores. Such attitudes undercut working-class solidarity and encouraged a sense among Anglos (of all ethnicities) that better wages and working conditions for them depended on the subordination of Mexican Americans.

The vagaries of racism produced anomalies such as these described by Charles S. Johnson in a survey of industrial employment in Los Angeles in 1926:

> In certain plants where Mexicans were regarded as white, Negroes were not allowed to mix with them; where Mexicans were classified as colored, Negroes not only worked with them but were given positions over them. In certain plants Mexicans and whites worked together; in some others white workers accepted Negroes and objected to Mexicans; still in others white workers accepted Mexicans and objected to Japanese. White women worked with Mexican and Italian women but refused to work with Negroes. Mexicans and Negroes worked under a white foreman; Italians and Mexicans under a Negro foreman.[15]

Living conditions for most Mexican Americans were substandard, even by the low expectations of the time and place. Those who resided year-round in the cities or retreated to them in the off-season typically lived in densely populated run-down barrios where they were denied services (garbage collection, sewers, access to potable water) available to other urban residents. Rates of tuberculosis and infant mortality, indices of destitution, were high.[16]

Segregated and inferior school systems in both Texas and California reflected the Mexican Americans' second-class status. In Texas, although no law established them, "Mexican schools" were the rule, particularly in the lower grades. This humiliating social policy failed to deliver the instruction it was presumably intended to provide, and despite a state law mandating compulsory education, Mexican American children on average received fewer months of instruction during the school year than their Anglo counterparts and fewer years of schooling overall. Indeed, according to an official survey done during the war, 42 percent of Mexican American children of school age received no education at all. The

Figure I.2. A sign like those that appeared in many restaurants and public facilities in the Southwest during the 1930s and 1940s. Segregation was enforced by local ordinances, in real estate covenants, and in the practices of local businessmen. Dr. Héctor P. García Papers. Courtesy of Special Collections and Archives, Mary and Jeff Bell Library, Texas A&M University, Corpus Christi, Texas.

instruction they did receive was inferior, helping perpetuate the cycle of poverty for the children trapped in the system.[17]

In California, the situation was very much the same. The state had a history of separating students of different cultures. Unlike in Texas, African Americans could attend schools with whites, but school districts might exclude the children of Asian and American Indian background. Although the law did not mention children of Mexican descent, in town after town in Southern California, school districts provided "Mexican schools." The separation was not uniformly or rigidly imposed, and the children of middle-class Mexican American parents were often admitted to Anglo schools if their parents insisted. Nevertheless, on the eve of World War II, most Mexican American children in California attended classes apart from other children.[18]

The social stigma attached to segregation was sometimes noted and its pernicious effect in perpetuating an ill-educated underclass recorded. But despite one or two challenges to its application,[19] the practice was generally accepted.[20] Segregation was seen as a solution to the problem of educating Mexican Americans, not as a problem to be overcome. Mexican children, it was argued (perhaps with some justification), needed a special protective environment where they could be instructed in the English they were not exposed to at home. But little was done to give them the special instruction they needed. The "Mexican schools" were underfunded, often served as a dumping ground for less-competent teachers, and were usually inferior to the Anglo schools. At the base of these conditions were the convictions of school officials and the Anglo community that second rate was good enough for Mexicans.[21]

It was an attitude that readily applied to other areas of Mexican American life. Restrictive covenants prohibiting the sale of homes to members of a variety of ethnic and racial groups were commonly found in property deeds throughout the country. In California and the Southwest, these legal agreements invariably named people of Mexican descent as among those ineligible to buy. Although many Mexican Americans preferred life in the friendly, if poor, precincts of the barrio, the covenants prevented those who chose to move out and up from doing so even if they were financially able. They thus tended to ghettoize Mexican Americans by denying them a principal vehicle of social mobility.

Persons of Mexican heritage were deprived of other civil rights as well. Those born in the United States or naturalized here were citizens and had a constitutional right to participate in electoral politics. But in Texas most were excluded from the Democratic Party primaries, whose outcome usually determined who was elected, and the vast majority were discouraged from voting in the general election by a poll tax that kept poorer citizens from the ballot box. There was no equality before the law for Mexican Americans. Officers of the law and representatives of government acted in ways that impressed upon Mexican Americans the not-too-subtle notion that this was not their country. In fifty counties where they constituted a significant portion of the population, one investigator reported that "persons of Mexican descent have never been known to be called for jury duty."[22] This meant that Mexican Americans involved in legal proceedings did not enjoy the presumed benefit of a jury that included their ethnic peers. Their second-class status was driven home in encounters with police, border officers, and other officials who adopted attitudes that ranged from disrespectful to humiliating. Police brutality was often visited upon Mexican Americans accused of crimes.[23]

The most obvious reminders of what was essentially a caste system—the demarcation of social status by race—were announcements posted on restaurants and other places generally open to the public indicating that persons of Mexican descent would not be served. Movie theaters often segregated their Mexican American customers, confining them, with African Americans, to the balcony. The use of public toilets was also frequently denied to people identified as "Mexican," and they were barred from or assigned special times for their use of public parks, swimming pools, and other recreational facilities.[24] Such practices were not dictated by law, nor were they universal. Sometimes a person of Mexican descent learned of an establishment's policy only after an employee (sometimes on their own authority) ignored him, ordered him around back, or denied him service entirely.[25]

The impact of such practices was obvious. Mexican Americans were deprived of services to which they were entitled and were daily reminded of their inferior status. In 1934, Emory Bogardus, a University of Southern California sociologist, wrote that such practices made Americans of Mexican lineage disheartened, resentful, and despairing of ever making a decent life for themselves or their children north of the border. Six years later, conditions and prospects for Mexican Americans remained much the same. Mexican Americans remained largely rural, disproportionately illiterate, mostly very poor, physically isolated from their Anglo neighbors, and deprived of the full potential of life in the United States.

Other racial and ethnic minorities have faced similar predicaments. In most instances, they organized and joined self-help and advocacy groups, demanded changes in public attitudes, and pressured politicians for changes in government policies. The efforts of African Americans and the National Association for the Advancement of Colored People are exemplary in this regard, and their successes in California (for example) are notable.[26] But in 1940, such organizations and initiatives among Mexican Americans had not yet been successful in creating a sustainable national focus on civil rights.

A prerequisite was lacking in the greater Mexican American population. No such group consciousness, on a national level, was manifest in 1940. There were many Mexican communities in the United States, united by a common language and memories of a homeland with its recent revolutionary history. Although a growing number of Mexican Americans had begun to think of themselves in national terms, most as yet did not identify beyond their family, friends, barrio, *colonia*, and parish.

Creating group consciousness and providing it with direction is often the function of a minority group's elite, and one might have expected the descendents of early Spanish-speaking settlers, some of whom were well placed socially and economically, to play this role. But many of these older families had little in common with Mexican immigrant populations and, in any case, sometimes sought to distance themselves from these impoverished newcomers.[27] Nor did the clergy fill the vacuum. Most Mexican Americans were nominally Roman Catholic, and the Church had been a force in America for helping other immigrant groups achieve cohesiveness, status, and power. But the clergy that served the Mexican Americans, anticipating that their temporal salvation would be found in a return to the mother country, not in the United States, tended to align themselves with Mexican consular officials in promoting Mexican culture in the United States. It was a stratagem and an attitude that while attuned to current realities, neither fostered development of an indigenous leadership nor encouraged full participation in American life.[28]

It is true that there was no shortage of social clubs and *mutualistas* (mutual aid societies) serving the Mexican American communities located in the Southwestern states, and those who read Spanish had access to approximately forty newspapers (almost all weeklies) in their native language.[29] But neither the aid societies nor the newspapers were apt to address larger issues of life in the United States,[30] and, in any event, they represented and reached relatively few. The San Antonio–based League of United Latin American Citizens (LULAC) and a few others had the potential to serve as a national advocacy group, but in 1940 no organization had yet been able to register the specific grievances or press the claims of a national Mexican American constituency on an ignorant and indifferent political establishment.

One reason for this lack of representation was that the voting potential of the Mexican American rank and file had yet to be realized. Throughout the 1920s and 1930s Mexicans resident in the United States were among the least likely immigrants to take the steps necessary to secure American citizenship and hence the right to vote. Even on the eve of the Second World War, as other aliens flocked to immigration offices to take out their first papers or complete their naturalization, Mexicans, many of them long resident in the United States with apparently no intention of returning to Mexico, held back.[31] Officials explained their reluctance to move to the threshold of political power on the Mexicans' attachment to their homeland and a reluctance to forswear allegiance to Mexico.[32] Poverty and a lack of education also played a role in keeping people from citizenship and the polls, as did the relative isolation and transience of many farmworkers. Many were also, with good reason, suspicious of American authorities, disillusioned with life in the United States, and convinced that citizenship conveyed no protection against discrimination. Perhaps, as David Gutiérrez has suggested, many Mexican Americans were trapped in the transnational Hispanic culture of the *colonias* and found political involvement tangential, if not irrelevant, to their lives.[33] Whatever the reasons, both contemporaries and recent scholars have noted that Mexican Americans lacked the singleness of purpose or the effective voice, on the national level, that was being mustered by other American minorities.[34]

The Mexican Americans as an Ethnic Group

It was easy for the American public to overlook Mexican Americans, and the group remained relatively unknown to government officials and those who championed the rights of minorities in the 1930s.[35] A handful of academic studies shaped informed perceptions, but these did not deal with Mexican American civil rights per se. The older works by Paul S. Taylor, of the University of California, and Emory S. Bogardus, at the University of Southern California, focused on the group dynamics and social pathology of the Mexican American.[36]

In 1940, George I. Sánchez, one of a handful of Mexican American academics, added to the slim body of works on the Mexican American an influential book on the plight of *his* people: the Spanish-speaking community of New Mexico. Significantly, Sánchez's study focused on the New Mexicans' cultural isolation and their propensity to live in the past, rather than on the racial prejudices they suffered at the hands of their Anglo neighbors.[37] Like the experiences and outlook of the New Mexicans themselves, the work was only distantly related to the lives of Mexican Americans in California and Texas, and like most discussions of Mexican Americans, it barely mentioned civil rights. Partly as a result of these kinds of studies, Mexican Americans were seen as an ethnographic/anthropological curiosity, or as a dysfunctional subculture. Thus, when public officials spoke of the "Spanish-speaking" people of the Southwest, their minds turned to the colorful natives of New Mexico. And when they spoke of the "Mexican problem," they referred not to the difficulties confronting the Mexican Americans in the arena of civil rights, but to the threat that Mexican American poverty posed to public health and the welfare of the larger society. Even Carey McWilliams' popular *Factories in the Field* (1939), which dealt in part with Mexican American migrant workers, described their problems (like those of other

agricultural laborers) almost exclusively as the product of economic exploitation. And it is perhaps not surprising that in an era before the concept of civil rights was fully articulated, commentators failed to see the
problems of Mexican Americans in these terms.

Although most Mexican Americans in 1940 had not reached the point
where they thought of themselves as an American minority, their attitudes were changing. With the steep decline of immigration in the 1930s
and the repatriation of hundreds of thousands of Mexican-born residents,
the group came to be made up more and more of those born in the United
States—people who harbored no illusions of returning to Mexico. Recognizing that life in the United States was what they would have to make of
it, a growing minority were more interested than their parents had been
in challenging the status quo through politics. By 1940, a small number
had gone, or were going, to college, and a middle class of merchants, lawyers, and other professionals was emerging. Historian Mario T. García
argues that by the onset of the Great Depression, a "Mexican American generation" was adopting American values and expectations. More
conscious of their rights as Americans, they were more sensitive to the
gap between the promises and realities of life in America.[38] On the eve
of World War II, García argues, a U.S.-committed, genuinely Mexican
American leadership, inspired by the political and social reform activism
of the New Deal, had begun to form. Nevertheless, that leadership, according to this view, would not mature until after the war. For the time
being, Mexican American political power was not even commensurate
with the group's locally concentrated numbers.[39]

National reform initiatives would not come from San Antonio or Los
Angeles, where the largest concentrations of Mexican Americans lived,
but from Washington, D.C. Not long after the Japanese attack on Pearl
Harbor thrust the United States into war, federal officials suddenly developed a strong interest in the Mexican American population. This concern was not a response to group-generated pressures, or a reflection of
official conscience. Learning more about Mexican Americans, and perhaps even addressing their problems, had become a matter of national
security. Several federal agencies undertook studies based on what little
had been written about the group and on observations and interviews
gleaned from brief tours of Mexican American communities. The effort
signaled a new national interest in the group and suggested that things
were about to change.

CHAPTER 2

The Federal Government Discovers Mexican Americans

RICHARD STEELE

On the eve of World War II, Mexican Americans suffered from a grinding poverty stemming from hostile and indifferent public attitudes and institutionalized racism. There were few signs that these conditions would soon change, but within months of the onset of hostilities, government officials felt obliged to acknowledge the community's existence and address its complaints. Authorities began to speak of a "Spanish-speaking," Hispanic," or "Latin American" community—in effect constructing, for political purposes, an ethnic group out of the diverse elements of Mexican and Latin American origin. At the same time, they acknowledged Mexican American spokesmen, from whom they would learn of Mexican American needs and through whom they could effect the changes the situation seemed to demand. Three-and-one-half million people were suddenly "discovered" and their wants made part of the national security agenda.

The War's Impact on Mexican Americans

Benefits began to accrue to Mexican Americans even before the United States became involved in the war. In the two years before the Pearl Harbor attack (December 1941), the military had begun to open its ranks to volunteers, and Congress authorized the nation's first peacetime draft. Eager young Mexican Americans jumped at the enlistment opportunities, while others among them found themselves swept up in the draft. Military service offered an honorable, even adventurous, alternative to a hardscrabble existence, and soon large numbers of Mexican Americans had been transported to a new life with new opportunities and challenges.

It appears that a larger percentage of Mexican American youth than that of any other ethnic/racial group served in the military during World War II. There were disproportionate numbers of Mexican Americans of draft age, and relatively few held jobs that would earn them deferments.[1] Mexican American youth soon distinguished themselves on the battle-field by both the many military decorations they earned and the casualties they suffered.[2] Whatever their motives for joining, if they survived, most profited from the experience. Military service, because of its emphasis on performance rather than class or ethnicity, provided opportunities for achievement and recognition not found in civilian life, and taught atti-tudes and skills that could prepare barrio and *colonia* youth for successful engagement with the larger society to which they would return.

Even as some began their military training and proceeded to military posts around the world, opportunities at home expanded. From 1940 on, as the likelihood of American involvement in the European war increased, the nation began manufacturing munitions to supply Hitler's enemies. Plants and facilities that had been idled by depression economics opened and expanded, creating unprecedented industrial growth—and jobs. In 1940, unemployment nationwide was still at 14 percent; three years later, it was close to zero. Real wages increased by about 25 percent in the same period.[3]

Discrimination Continues

Boom-time opportunities, however, were not equally available to all Americans. The first jobs generated by the military-procurement-driven economy went to members of the most favored groups in America, and discriminatory practices continued to keep Mexican Americans and other traditionally excluded minorities from fully sharing the bonanza created by war.[4] Even on the eve of hostilities, defense contractors, violating the administration's stated policy, continued to stipulate racial preferences in seeking employees. The requests they submitted to the U.S. Employment Service, which the Service honored, typically demanded "Americans only," "Nordics," "North European stock," or "Anglo-Saxons." African Americans, Italians, and Jews were often specifically excluded by eastern employers. In the West, the list of "undesirable types" included "Mexi-cans."[5] California aircraft manufacturers reported that they preferred to recruit among white (Anglo) Texans, even though some of them had difficulty documenting their citizenship, but at least "looked American."[6]

Sometimes the government was responsible for the discrimination. Federal legislation made aliens ineligible for certain types of security-sensitive employment, and confusion about the application of this provision encouraged defense employers to exclude noncitizens. The large number of aliens who resided in the Spanish-speaking community were among the provision's victims.[7] The exclusion of persons of Mexican descent, regardless of the reason, contributed to the labor shortage, and officials at the Justice Department worried about the effect such practices were having on the loyalty of the victims of discrimination.[8]

In June 1941, President Roosevelt issued Executive Order 8802 establishing the Committee on Fair Employment Practices (later called the Fair Employment Practices Committee [FEPC]).[9] The agency's staff was genuinely committed to ending discrimination,[10] but its authority was limited, and getting justice from the FEPC depended a great deal on the pressure that affected groups were able to bring to bear.

Lacking a Congressional mandate, the Committee could not command changes. It could only expose unfair practices in the hope that targeted industries would respond appropriately to public pressure. In practice, the FEPC's limited powers of persuasion were used only in circumstances that literally cried out for remedy—that is, in those instances in which spokesmen for the victims of discrimination demanded remedies so loudly that their clamor for justice threatened the shaky edifice of domestic unity. This unstated practice worked to the disadvantage of Mexican Americans, who did not have national organizations that were vocal enough to fully avail themselves of FEPC influence.

The interests of Mexican American workers were represented by a number of labor organizations that were particularly active in Southern California.[11] For a time, just before the war, these were united in a formidable organization called El Congreso del Pueblo de Habla Española (The Congress of Spanish-Speaking People).[12] Including some members of the Communist Party of the United States (CPUSA), El Congreso was able to mobilize considerable support from outside the Mexican community and seemed for a time to offer a promising vehicle for pushing a broad Mexican American agenda.[13] But by the time the FEPC was created, the organization was in decline, partly as a result of the CPUSA's policy. Following the lead of party officials in Moscow,[14] the CPUSA had decided that its first priority was victory in the international war against Fascism, not domestic revolution or change. In certain circumstances, this meant abandoning its militant labor stance in favor of cooperating with government to secure industrial peace and all-out war production. The radically inclined El Congreso may have fallen victim to this decision. Additionally, as the war erupted, the energies of its member organizations turned toward the war effort rather than toward the pursuit of civil rights at home.

The first public hearings conducted by the FEPC were held in Los Angeles in the fall of 1941. Southern California was home to much of the nation's military aircraft industry, and the hearings were crucial to the Mexican Americans who constituted a sizable portion of the labor pool in the area. But neither El Congreso, which disappeared entirely shortly thereafter, nor other representatives of Mexican American interests were represented before the committee.[15] The community seemed unable to fill the vacuum left by El Congreso's default.

In any event, the result was that the FEPC hearings in Los Angeles were dominated by the concerns of African Americans, who were well organized and vocal.[16] Indeed, the transcript reveals that the committee heard no testimony from witnesses speaking as representatives of the Mexican American community. Bert Corona, a Mexican American official of the International Longshoremen's and Warehousemen's Union (ILWU) and an El Congreso activist, did testify, but only as to union hiring practices, which, he assured the Committee, did not tolerate discrimination. "If a brother objected to working with a black, his card was lifted."[17] The plight of the Latino worker on the West Coast remained largely unexamined.[18]

Industrial mobilization provided many Mexican Americans, particularly women, with opportunities they would not have had in the absence of war. For example, by 1944, Mexican Americans represented 10 to 15 percent of Lockheed Aircraft's workforce.[19] But, overall, Mexican Americans gained less from the wartime boom than other racial and ethnic minorities. Those who worked in or aspired to employment in the defense industry were unable to fully utilize the potential that the FEPC had for improving their lives. The demands of war could, and often did, work for Mexican Americans, but, as we will see, it could also work against them. It depended in each instance on the administration's calculation of what was to be gained and lost by serving the group's immediate interests. This was particularly apparent in developments in Texas, where U.S. concern for Mexican government sensibilities worked to both the advantage and the detriment of Mexican Americans.

Mexican Americans and the Good Neighbor

The fate of reform initiatives affecting Mexican Americans revolved around the government's understanding of how various undertakings might affect the Good Neighbor policy. For decades, the peoples of Central and South America had had reason to fear the imperialistic colossus to the north. Although unilateral intervention in Latin American affairs had declined in recent decades, the memory of past incursions and humiliations lingered. Soon after his inauguration in early 1933, President Franklin D. Roosevelt, seeking to dispel latent hostilities and establish the basis for a new era of international cooperation, announced that his administration was committed to a "policy of the good neighbor." His concern at first was principally to ensure American investments, promote trade, and forestall increased European—particularly German—commercial penetration of the region. However, by the eve of World War II, the Good Neighbor policy reflected pressing security concerns as well.

Significant numbers of Latin Americans were among recent immigrants from Germany, Italy, and Japan, three nations that shared grievances against the Western democracies and would eventually form the Axis alliance against which the United States would fight in World War II. There were also right-wing nationalistic political movements in Mexico and elsewhere that were thought by American officials to threaten U.S. interests in the region. According to one historian, "Few issues gave Roosevelt more concern in the summer of 1940 than the threat to Latin America."[20] In this regard, relations with Mexico were particularly problematic. Many Mexicans sorely resented American imperial airs and remembered well Uncle Sam's aggressive intervention in the Mexican Revolution.[21] Although FDR succeeded in developing cordial relations between the two governments,[22] he could not erase the Mexican public's hostility and suspicion. The war, which Mexico formally joined in May 1942, was not popular. Anti-American/antiwar feelings were exploitable by President (Manuel) Ávila Camacho's opponents and by those elements on both ends of the Mexican political spectrum that wished to disrupt relations with the United States.

A critical issue in shaping attitudes toward the United States was American racial practices, particularly evidence of the contempt many Anglos in the Southwest had for Mexico. Mexicans, including members of the political elite, boasted of their Indian heritage and proudly proclaimed Mexican culture free of racial prejudice.[23] They were sensitive to the fact that in some parts of the United States a person of Mexican descent, regardless of class or station, was apt to be insulted and discriminated against because of his race.[24] Mexican diplomats and businessmen traveling in Texas often saw and experienced firsthand the contempt with which Texans held all their compatriots. Although equal access to restaurants was probably not high on the list of priorities of the average Mexican American, it was a matter of considerable concern to Mexican officials.

As the United States prepared for war, Mexican officials began to register their dissatisfaction. Early in 1941, the Mexican Foreign Office called its consular officials in the United States to an emergency meeting in San Antonio to discuss what it described as "humiliations, as unjust as they are cruel, which have been imposed for years on Mexican elements."[25] It is not clear why the Foreign Office chose to press the issue at that time. When they notified the U.S. State Department of the meeting, the Mexican officials pointed to an increase in anti-Mexican discrimination in the Southwest since the onset of American mobilization, but the offenses listed were consistent with traditional Texas practices. It may be that pending negotiations between the United States and Mexico over the implementation of the Bracero Program had made this a good time to raise the issue. The observations were certainly timely, given the enlivened U.S. interest in the Good Neighbor and U.S. wartime propaganda insisting that the nation was the champion of democratic values. The Mexican ambassador to the United States, Francisco Castillo Nájera, pointed to the fact that "Mexicans" were often denied access to places generally open to the public, and that in theaters, and even in prisons, they were often placed with African Americans, a practice which, in his eyes, was a particularly degrading form of discrimination. He also called attention to restrictive covenants in housing, and criticized the arbitrary arrest and abuse of Mexicans by local police.[26] The ambassador pointedly noted that in the coming months his government would be using a group of Americans of Mexican descent to document specific instances of discrimination.[27]

The resentment evidenced by this advisory was a matter of considerable concern to federal and state officials in the United States. Not only did discrimination undercut the Good Neighbor policy; it also threatened negotiations between the two nations on the crucial issue of whether, and under what conditions, the government in Mexico City would permit Mexican nationals to work in the United States.

The Politics of the FEPC

In the spring of 1942, the National Union of Mine, Mill, and Smelter Workers, which represented a large number of Mexican American mine workers in West Texas, New Mexico, and Arizona, urged the FEPC to look into discrimination in the mining industry in the Southwest.[28] Lawrence Cramer, the Executive Secretary of the FEPC, welcomed the prospect, believing that the announced inquiry would demonstrate that the U.S. government genuinely sought to ensure opportunities to all its minorities, including Mexican Americans. This, he argued, would favorably impress the Mexican government.[29] But news that the FEPC contemplated hearings in Texas produced consternation at the State Department, where Under Secretary of State Sumner Welles, chief architect of the Good Neighbor policy, warned President Roosevelt of the harm the hearings were likely to do to that policy. Exposing the grievances of the mine workers, he argued, would do little to improve the Mexican American standard of living or improve race relations (these, he said, required long-range programs). Instead, the revelations of systematic discrimination that were certain to emerge, would be used by Axis propagandists against both the United States and Mexico.[30] The prevailing wisdom in official circles held that the interests of Mexican Americans had to be sacrificed to the need to preserve the nation's democratic image and the Good Neighbor policy. There was a certain irony to a policy that dictated cultivating good will in Mexico by denying a venue for Mexican American protests, but Roosevelt ordered the proposed hearings abandoned.[31] Further efforts were made to secure hearings in the Southwest, but the latter never materialized.

Government expediency ruled the day, but the policy was made politically feasible by an apparent lack of Mexican American organizational action. As Carlos Castañeda, a history professor at the University of Texas and a driving force behind the effort to use the FEPC on behalf of Mexican Americans, commented in another context, "Not one percent of the population of the Southwest knows or understands what FEPC is or means to them." He faulted, in particular, the Spanish-language press for its failure to make the communities aware of this avenue for protest.[32]

The administration would do what was necessary to placate adversely affected ethnic groups when they howled, but as long as the war effort did not suffer critically from discrimination, and the offended group did not threaten to turn the situation into a political liability, the White House would not venture into controversial territory. Ethnic and racial harmony were important objectives for the government, but they were goals that competed with more pressing matters, including, apparently, relations with Mexico. Here, ironically, an asset enjoyed by Mexican Americans, Washington's desire to satisfy the Mexican government's concerns about conditions in the Southwest, worked to the group's disadvantage.

The demands of the war could work for Mexican Americans, and often did. But they could work against them as well. It depended in each instance on the administration's calculation of whether the "national interest" was best served by addressing the group's immediate interests or ignoring them. The duality of the national security issue was particularly noticeable in the effect that the administration's relations with Mexico had on its attitude toward the treatment of Americans of Mexican descent. This was apparent in the issue of the proposed FEPC hearings in the Southwest. It was even more evident in the struggle for Mexican American civil rights in Texas.

LULAC Lobbies for Civil Rights

The effort to fight for Mexican American civil rights in Texas was spearheaded by the Texas-based League of United Latin American Citizens (LULAC). Although one scholar notes that even at its height of influence, LULAC represented only a small percentage of the Mexican American population, and another suggests that public accommodations issues that preoccupied LULAC were of marginal concern to Mexican Americans at the outset of World War II, a number of its leaders were able to exploit the cooperative relationship they enjoyed with Mexican officials to gain significant, precedent-making concessions from the state.[33]

LULAC was founded in 1929 in Texas as an umbrella group for a number of local Mexican American civic organizations.[34] Its members were small businessmen, lawyers, and educators and included at least one newspaper editor. A few had political experience as diplomats, and one was a former state legislator. Several had graduate degrees, mostly from the University of Texas. Most subscribed to the precepts and values of the American middle class and, without sacrificing pride in their Mexican origins, sought to foster personal initiative and other qualities and attitudes they associated with succeeding north of the border.[35] In the 1930s, the organization was the most prominent of a number of groups that had been working to end the segregation of Mexican Americans in education, and to secure from Texas recognition of the minority's civil rights.[36] By 1940, it had succeeded in Texas only in gaining unofficial designation of

Mexican Americans as "white,"[37] a concession to white supremacy that would be unacceptable today, but which at that time constituted a significant victory, since no politician in the state would approve of any law that undermined the state's staunch commitment to its Jim Crow policy. Despite any objectionable implications, by being classified "Caucasian," Mexican Americans were in a position to escape the galling system of denial, discrimination, and segregation.

Benjamin Márquez, in his history of LULAC, contends that with the onset of the war, many of the organization's members entered the military, local councils closed, and the League fell dormant.[38] However, while LULAC as an organization may have languished, a few of its leaders took advantage of the increased interest in Mexican American problems to press the organization's civil rights agenda. Two lawyers, both U.S. citizens who had been instrumental in founding LULAC, took the lead: Manuel J. Gonzales, who also served as legal advisor to the Mexican consulate, and Alonso Perales, who at the time was Nicaragua's Consul General in the United States and who has been described as one of the most important Mexican Americans in Texas. U.S. officials were looking for the voice of Americans of Mexican descent. Thus, regardless of how representative Gonzales and Perales really were, they could, largely because of their contact with the Mexican government, plausibly claim that role. When official interest in Mexican American affairs expanded later in the war, they were joined in various dealings with federal and state authorities by a few others, most notably George I. Sánchez and Carlos Castañeda, both professors at the University of Texas.[39]

Although virtually unknown outside of Texas at the beginning of the war, within a year these men had been grudgingly accepted by officials in Austin and Washington as spokesmen for Mexican American interests. Some federal officials, reflecting the melting-pot hope (that this was a country in which immigrants eventually lost their sense of ethnic identity),[40] feared that government recognition of the LULACers would promote creation of a "protection [i.e., advocacy] group" among Mexicans.[41] Others saw the LULAC leaders as opportunists seeking to build personal power by exaggerating and agitating Mexican American grievances.[42] But the LULACers prevailed because they constituted the only window for Anglo officials into the unknown world of Mexican Americans, they were able to document a real and disturbing situation, and they enjoyed the support of the Mexican government. In turning to them, officials helped create an apparent political unity among Mexican Americans that did not really exist. LULAC, a head without a body, could not exert pressure on

Figure 2.1. The convention at which the League of United Latin American Citizens (LULAC) was established, Corpus Christi, Texas, May 17, 1929. Courtesy of University of Texas at Austin Libraries.

behalf of Mexican Americans comparable to other ethnic/racial advocacy groups, but the peculiar circumstances created by the war ensured that its spokesmen would get a hearing.

Beginning just before the war, Perales and Gonzales had begun to agitate for civil rights in Texas, particularly equal access to public accommodations. They were indirectly supported by the Mexican consuls, who passed along evidence of discrimination to the Mexican government, which in turn presented it to the State Department with diplomatically couched demands that the United States do something. Federal officials then cautiously took the issue to the Texas governor while Gonzales and Perales lobbied state officials.[43]

Late in 1941, Under Secretary of State Sumner Welles commissioned Consul General William P. Blocker, a Texan with extensive contacts in the state, to undertake a covert investigation of discrimination in Texas.[44] Blocker spent almost two months in early 1942 traveling throughout the state on this confidential mission. Not overly sympathetic with the plight of the ordinary Texas Mexican, he tended to see reported incidents of discrimination as isolated and relatively insignificant, and he noted, with no sense of irony, that persons of Mexican descent were no more discriminated against than "Negroes, Jews, Syrians, Italians and other [dark-skinned/obnoxious?] minorities." Most of the problems blamed on racial prejudice, he found, were really the result of class concerns—the understandable reluctance of Texans of the better sort to associate with what he called "sandal-foot peons." School segregation was also partly the result of the reluctance of Anglo parents to send their children to school with lower-class (termed "dirty and unhealthy") Mexicans, and partly the need to provide these children with special instruction. Although he conceded that some provincial Texans were guilty on occasion of discriminating against higher-class Mexicans, all in all, he thought race relations were improving. He cited as an example the fact that an Army base at Abilene had recently been named for a World War I veteran of Mexican lineage. (The dead hero's "wrinkled and brown mother," he observed, had been cheered at the dedication.)[45]

While Blocker tended to minimize problems between Anglo- and Mexican Americans, his observations suggested to his superiors in the State Department that race relations in the state, if not as bad as the Mexican government suggested, were still in need of improvement. The desire for better relations with Mexico encouraged state and federal officials to take notice of racist practices in the Southwest and to seek resolution of the most egregious cases. It was a promising start, but the drive to promote racial justice in the name of the Good Neighbor was circumscribed by the "national interest"—that of both Mexico and the United States. Frank Warren thought the initiative should come from Mexican Americans, but that they should seek gradual change within the system. Although militant unionists and African Americans had pioneered the use of aggressive pressure tactics in recent years, government officials, even the reform-minded ones, were unsympathetic with this approach, and not even liberals advocated aggressive confrontational tactics to secure civil rights.[46] The consensus was that demands for justice would be difficult to realize without disrupting the war effort, and this fundamental fact would seriously undermine what was attempted on behalf of Mexican Americans and other minorities during the war.

Officials in the highest levels of the federal government were in basic agreement: "Spanish-speaking Americans" were victims of poverty, prejudice, and discrimination that excluded them from the mainstream of American life. These conditions, they recognized, were an affront to basic democratic principles and a threat to wartime unity. Something

Figure 2.2. Schoolhouse, Mathis, Texas, 1946. One of the photographs documenting conditions in schools for Mexican American children as part of "A Study of the Educational Opportunities Provided Spanish-Name Children in Ten Texas School Systems" (1948), http://www.lib.utexas.edu/photodraw/sanchez/study.html by Virgil E. Strickland and George I. Sánchez. This study preceded a successful District Court decision, *Delgado v. Bastrop Independent School District,* that led to the desegregation of Texas schools. George I. Sánchez Papers, University of Texas, Austin. Courtesy of University of Texas at Austin Libraries.

had to be done, and by the first summer of the war, a number of reform programs were under way. The initiative was taken by the federal government, which proceeded on several fronts, each the responsibility of a separate army of bureaucrats guided by a mandate derived almost entirely from war-related necessity, and each convinced that human nature and the political system ensured the futility of efforts to effect dramatic changes in the status quo.

Those who took an interest in Mexican American problems tended to focus on one of two major issues: poverty and civil rights. Early reform concerning the former depended on the activities of the Fair Employment Practices Committee, whose struggle to achieve equal job opportunity seemed to promise Mexican Americans access to job skills and elevated incomes in the burgeoning war industries. Civil rights were the particular concern of LULAC and of other middle-class Mexican Americans who worked, especially in Texas, for laws that would ensure Mexican Americans equality before the law and equal access to schools and public accommodations. Everyone agreed that discrimination rested on anti-Mexican assumptions and stereotypes that endangered a wartime collaboration with Mexico and Latin America. Hence this problem attracted considerable attention from public service organizations as well as from local, state, and federal government agencies.

The Limits of Federal Concern

Some officials, recognizing that the scattered and uncoordinated nature of current efforts was inadequate, proposed the creation of an office of minority affairs devoted exclusively to improving conditions among the nation's racial and ethnic populations.[47] Nevertheless, no such agency was created. Most officials appear to have believed that the American people were, or at least should be, an amalgam of disappearing ethnic groups and that national policy should do nothing to interfere with that process. Such feelings seemed to preclude any official recognition that there were problems attached to a specific minority group or that warranted a targeted response.

Moreover, even indirect assistance was limited by a national ideology still strongly influenced by British social philosopher Herbert Spencer and American writer Horatio Alger. Judging from the official analyses of Mexican American problems, people in positions of authority saw self-help, not government paternalism, as the solution to many Mexican American problems. Thus the extreme poverty noted by all observers was treated as a function primarily of the inadequacies of the Mexican Americans themselves: their (self-imposed) isolation, the transient nature of their presence in the United States, and their failure to organize or participate in the political process. The implication, rarely stated directly, was that the remedy lay in Mexican Americans pulling themselves up by the bootstraps, organizing their community, and integrating themselves into the larger society. Such attitudes were well represented in a resurgent Republican Party in Congress during the war years. Programs that undertook to seriously address the social and economic needs of Mexican Americans were apt to meet a cool reception from a Congress and a public that knew little of the group, and were showing signs of fatigue with New Deal activism. Consequently, efforts to help the Mexican American would be undertaken through existing programs or agencies and only insofar as they could be justified by the necessities of war.

A relatively benign strain of racism also played a role in limiting the efforts to improve conditions for Mexican Americans during the war. This was the belief, even among enlightened people, that making invidious distinctions between people based on their race or ethnicity, while reprehensible, was a deeply engrained human trait that could be changed, if at all, only through considerable reeducation. Thus, State Department officials worried about the dislocations and discontents in Latin American communities, but confessed that "racial friction" seemed both inherent in the human condition and based on economic disparities, which government was not in a position to address.[48] Official caution not only was a product of conservatism in social matters but reflected a widespread sense that the status of American minorities was not an appropriate subject for affirmative governmental action, but rather a problem that would have to be solved at the initiative of its victims. Vice President Henry Wallace, a leading administration liberal who was sympathetic with minority rights and an optimist concerning the potential for effecting progressive change through government action, sounded the commonly held sentiment. In June 1941, a Texan complained to Wallace that discrimination against Latinos in the Lone Star state was undermining the spirit of hemispheric solidarity that the government so earnestly sought to cultivate. The Vice President agreed, but noted that "under our Federal form of government there is no authority for dealing with a situation of this sort. Neither, I suspect, is there any authority in the state government. . . . It does occur to me, however, that if there were local organizations of the Mexican people that could use in a quiet way the methods which have been used by other minority groups, good results might be obtained. . . . It is my observation that matters of this kind are usually handled better quietly and privately."[49] These recommendations were far removed from the strategy that would bear fruit twenty-five years later. But this was 1941, and although militant unionists and African Americans had pioneered pressure tactics, in these years, government officials, even the reform-minded, were unsympathetic with this approach. Not even liberals were active in organizing action. Commenting on wartime race riots, the liberal press pointed to sources of racism and argued the need to eliminate it. But liberals themselves offered no "sustained organized action" toward the laudable ends they described.[50] The government's reformist imagination was limited by basic assumptions concerning the restrictions on realistic initiatives. This left officials, even those in deep sympathy with Mexican Americans, with only the war-necessity rationale for tackling the problem of race. The plight of Mexican Americans (and other minorities) was seen as a threat to wartime unity and efficiency, not as an issue of human rights. The war effort, not the group's welfare, was the ultimate justification for any policy initiative. And that would seriously undermine what was attempted and accomplished.

The government's preoccupation with military efficiency was at the heart of what was potentially the greatest boon to Mexican Americans. Insofar as the government wanted access to the largest manpower pool, the expansion of war industries offered enormous possibilities for Mexican Americans. But even here the demands of wartime expediency ultimately vitiated the good the war might have brought to the group. The war generated job opportunities, but they were not equally available. Racism was as deeply rooted in the workplace as it was in other areas of American life, and the fact that workers were needed did not mean that marginalized workers, including Mexican Americans, would share equitably in the opportunities the war created.

CHAPTER 3

Violence in Los Angeles: Sleepy Lagoon, the Zoot-Suit Riots, and the Liberal Response

RICHARD STEELE

Although Mexican Americans had been discovered by government early in the war, their problems had failed to register strongly on the consciousness of political and social reformers whose support was a prerequisite to change. The eastern literati and the nation's liberal political activists and commentators were sensitive to the abuses suffered by America's minorities and were in the forefront of efforts to expand their civil rights. But while the members of this influential group waxed eloquently and often about American prejudices as they affected African Americans, Jews, Indians, and even the European foreign born, they had little to say about the segregated schools, restricted public accommodations, and denials of rights suffered by the Mexican Americans of the nation's Southwest. Hollywood and Los Angeles had not yet assumed the centrality in American political and popular culture that they would a generation hence, and the region in which most Mexican Americans lived remained terra incognito for those who set the nation's reform agenda.[1] Perhaps, as Carey McWilliams suggested in another context, the intellectual compass of liberals did not stretch much beyond the East Coast.[2]

Without the support of those who normally championed civil rights, it seemed unlikely that the discovery of the Mexican American would be followed by an outpouring of public sympathy or official commitment to change. A dramatic event was necessary to move officials to action. Such publicity-attracting events did in fact materialize at the end of 1942 and the following spring, and by mid-1943, Mexican Americans would at last register on the national consciousness.

The Sleepy Lagoon Case

Since the beginning of 1940, the press in Los Angeles had become increasingly preoccupied with evidence of "delinquent" behavior among Mexican American youths as manifested in the growth in gang membership and the violent, sometimes criminal activities associated with it. Journalists and local officials took this as evidence of the widely anticipated juvenile rebellion against parents, institutions, and common decency. Anxieties of this kind had been growing since at least the turn of the century when the term *juvenile delinquency* first came into vogue, and public figures assumed that the social upheaval attendant on the onset of war would be accompanied by an outburst of youthful defiance in which children would turn on their elders. Primed to expect a breakdown of morals and authority, many people in Los Angeles found proof of its occurrence in reports of gang activities in the city's streets and alleys. Apocalyptic fears of a collapse of societal norms and community morality were no doubt intensified by the tendency of newspapers to sensationalize incidents that they depicted as chiefly emanating from "alien," that is, "Mexican," elements in the community.[3] Head shaking and finger wagging by the public, including some influential leaders in the Mexican American community, were given expression in a municipal policing policy that emphasized control through intimidation and brutality.[4]

In the spring and summer of 1942, a number of minor incidents involving youths identified as Mexican gang members culminated in the death of a young Mexican American from wounds sustained in a fight the night before at an East Los Angeles gravel pit used by locals as a swimming hole. The press picked up the story, dubbed the locale "Sleepy Lagoon" after a popular song of that time, and suggested that the incident exemplified a growing plague of lawlessness perpetrated by Mexican American youth. The police first arrested twenty-four young Mexican American gang members and charged them with murder, and then attempted to sweep "Mexican" gang members from the streets. On the nights of August 10 and 11, approximately six hundred persons were detained.[5] For the first time, Mexican Americans were drawing media attention,[6] most of it hostile, prejudicial, and unfair.[7]

A significant segment of the population responded to the Los Angeles gang phenomenon differently. Made up principally of social workers, reformers, leftist activists, and members of the Mexican American community, this group saw the outbreak of violence as a natural manifesta-

Figure 3.1. The Sleepy Lagoon defendants in jail during their trial in 1943. *Los Angeles Daily News* photo. Courtesy of UCLA Special Collections, UCLA Library, Los Angeles, California.

tion of the youths' rejection by the larger society. The antisocial behavior of Mexican American youths, who were disparagingly referred to as pachucos, was no different, they argued, from that exhibited historically by the youth of other ethnic minorities. They were the actions of the widely written-about "second generation," that is, the offspring of immigrants to the United States. This group-in-between, lacking the consolation provided their elders by the culture they carried with them from the old country, now found themselves rejected by the larger society in which they were coming to maturity. Alienated from one world and unable to fit into the other, they sought to create a subculture for themselves by "hanging out," bonding with others similarly situated, and adopting various cultural affectations of dress and language that, in setting them apart from the larger society, attested to their belonging.[8] Those familiar with social-scientific thought saw gang membership and related behavior as the normal, if regrettable, way in which Mexican American youth sought to compensate for the sense of isolation and worthlessness created by racism and discrimination. Those who viewed the issue in this way were more likely to attribute extremes of youthful antisocial behavior to the larger society than to fault the young people themselves. From this perspective, both the gang activity that produced the death at Sleepy Lagoon and the community overreaction were parts of a familiar story of society's exploitation of immigrants, the shunning of their offspring, and its indifference to the resultant social and economic consequences.

The conclusions of the grand jury investigation into the affair were quite different. In early October, the panel issued a report that emphasized that juvenile delinquency among Mexican Americans was a sign of basic social and economic conditions in their community, recognized the need for "drastic" corrective action, and urged the federal government to help local authorities in addressing the problem.[9] The report was sent to a number of federal officials, some of whom responded positively. The war, an official of the War Manpower Commission declared, "has now forced upon us the necessity for doing what we have . . . been indisposed to do in the past." We must "raise the economic level [of Mexican Americans] to approximate parity," provide job opportunity, end school segregation, supply better housing, etc.[10] Many officials were worried that dissatisfaction among Mexican Americans over the way officials had handled the Sleepy Lagoon affair was severely undermining the community's morale. They feared that the publicized injustices associated with the trial of the Sleepy Lagoon defendants cleared the way for Sinarquistas — members of a Mexican Fascist organization — or other fifth columnists to make converts in the community.

It fell to Alan Cranston, an official in the Office of War Information who had ties to California, to prevent the current situation from getting out of hand. In November, Cranston went to Los Angeles, where he found officials and community leaders concerned and cooperative. His efforts centered on cooling the inflammatory press rhetoric. Among his prized accomplishments was an agreement he secured from local newspaper publishers, who promised that in exchange for a higher allocation of rationed gasoline for reporters' cars, the press would (1) stop identifying persons involved in gang activities as "Mexicans," and (2) run "Mexican" stories of a positive nature. Seeking to minimize the sensational and provocative character of the Sleepy Lagoon prosecution, he got the local district attorney to agree to keep publicity about the case to a minimum, narrow the murder charges to two of the youths, request a general reduction in the charges for the others, and ask the judge to go easy. All in all, an optimistic Cranston concluded, the morale of the Mexican American community, which had been hurt by the affair, was now much improved, and a "critical situation has been overcome completely."[11]

He was wrong. The Los Angeles district attorney apparently concluded that it was more important to teach the youths a lesson (and satisfy Anglo opinion) than to serve justice and preserve the uneasy calm. In the fall, twenty-two young men between the ages of fifteen and twenty-two, almost all born in the United States of Mexican heritage, were indicted for the murder of José López at Sleepy Lagoon. In mid-January 1943, after thirteen weeks during which the case was well covered in the local press, an all-Anglo jury acquitted five on all counts and found five others not guilty of murder, but guilty of the lesser offenses arising out of the melee that surrounded the victim's death. The remaining twelve were convicted of all charges, including murder in the second degree.[12] There is little to suggest that the prosecutor or the judge attempted to prevent the affair from becoming a celebration of anti-Mexican sentiment and prejudice. The verdict guaranteed that the Sleepy Lagoon case would become a cause célèbre for the liberal and radical communities. In any event, the absurdity of convicting so many for a death to which no one individual could be directly tied provoked an immediate public outcry. The heated political climate and the conduct of the trial confirmed the worst suspicions in the community concerning the administration of justice in Los Angeles as it applied to Mexican American youth.

Within a short time, however, Carey McWilliams, a lawyer and writer on civil rights, reported that "the local Mexican situation [was] out of hand again."[13] Mexican Americans felt betrayed, and local activists helped mobilize their anger. A number of citizens formed a Sleepy Lagoon Defense Committee and began raising funds to publicize and rectify the miscarriage of justice. Officials had inadvertently conspired to make the Sleepy Lagoon a rallying point for those dissatisfied with the treatment of Mexican Americans in Los Angeles. But the defense committee's makeup would ensure that much of the ensuing discussion would be less about Mexican Americans and more about what was wrong with Los Angeles and the United States.

The outlook and associations of those most active in this defense effort shaped much of the ensuing controversy. The most vocal protestors were not Mexican Americans, but Anglos and African Americans who had a history of involvement in civil rights causes. Several were active members of the Communist Party.[14] For most of them, the Sleepy Lagoon defendants were victims of the fundamental problems plaguing American society: racism, exploitation, discrimination, and reactionary interest-group politics. This was a constellation of evils they called "Fascism." The term, most accurately applied to the corporate state ideology associated with the nationalistic, dictatorial regime of Benito Mussolini in Italy, was also used to denote the extreme racist totalitarianism of Nazi Germany. However, for some time, the American Left had been accustomed to blurring distinctions between what was happening in Europe and the injustices and inequalities endemic in the United States. "Fascism" in the late thirties came to be used to identify the source of almost everything that was wrong with America, from the Great Depression to the nation's failure to stand up to Hitlerism. For the Left, American Fascism was manifest in the anti-labor activities of industrialists (like Henry Ford), in the racist rhetoric of southern politicians, in the printed word of reactionary newspaper publishers like William Randolph Hearst,[15] in the isolationism of Charles Lindbergh, and in the anti-Semitic demagoguery of Father Charles Coughlin. To many who viewed the world in this manner, the plight of Mexican Americans in Los Angeles was evidence of the Fascist conspiracy at home—a conscious effort to create and maintain conditions that not only exploited Mexican Americans but made them susceptible to foreign intrigue.[16] The mistreatment of the Sleepy Lagoon boys was cited as proof of the rise of the Sinarquista conspiracy and of the malicious power of Hearst, whose xenophobic Los Angeles newspaper had sensationalized the city's gang activity. A spokesman for the Communist Party, in discussing the harassment of Mexican American youth a few months later during the so-called Zoot-Suit Riots, ascribed it to the activities of the enemies of the Soviet Union: "the Pacific First crowd, William Randolph Hearst and all those [Fascists] who want to see the country divided and hampered in its war effort."[17] Few Americans, much less Mexican Americans, appeared to have been convinced by this analysis.

Government investigations turned up no evidence of significant Sinarquista activity among the Mexican Americans of Los Angeles, and little likelihood that the barrios and *colonias* of the Southwest would turn against the war effort. Indeed, examination of the subversion issue by the FBI and others concluded that the situation was being exaggerated by the American Communists in order to gain a following among Mexican Americans. Thus, from the federal point of view, the problem was not the need for immediate and dramatic reforms, but a restoration of the racial truce that had existed before Sleepy Lagoon.[18]

The Sleepy Lagoon defense effort was both a success and a failure. Thanks largely to the committee's legal efforts, the California Court of

Appeals, pointing to the absence of admissible evidence of guilt on the part of each of the twelve defendants, reversed their convictions.[19] On the other hand, the leftist character of the Sleepy Lagoon Defense Committee leaders, and their insistence in the face of the facts that there was a fifth-columnist plot afoot, inclined officials to dismiss committee demands (justified though they were) as Communist grandstanding. Nor did the Sleepy Lagoon aftermath generate the kind of indignant interest nationally that would have served the Mexican American cause. Carey McWilliams, who was a major presence in the Sleepy Lagoon defense movement, later claimed that the case and the work of his committee attracted "nation-wide attention."[20] In fact, even in the liberal press, the episode generated very little comment outside of Los Angeles and California, and it certainly did not turn out to be another Sacco and Vanzetti affair, as some had hoped.

Whatever its effect on the Mexican American community, and this is difficult to establish, the case did not have a dramatic impact on the status of Mexican Americans in the country at large or even in Los Angeles. Despite the official promises of a new attitude and reforms, and the creation of a large number of well-intentioned committees, only the first steps toward addressing the problems confronting Mexican Americans were taken. A number of locally initiated investigations and community action programs were instituted, but the best-funded of these had a membership that represented the Anglo establishment, contained not a single Mexican American, and was largely ineffective.[21] City officials stated that vocational training and job opportunities would be increased as well as recreational facilities and counseling for young persons of Mexican descent. The civic action committees that sprang up improved communication between the Mexican American community and local authorities and provided a training ground for future leaders.[22] However, once the FBI convinced officials that there was no danger of a Sinarquista-led rebellion, and that social problems and political unrest were being blown out of proportion by the Communists, they felt free to limit their activity to encouraging improved communication between the Anglo and Mexican American communities on reforms in the juvenile justice system. All in all, Sleepy Lagoon produced a slight shift in governmental attention from Texas to California, but left undisturbed the basic disposition to do nothing.

Potentially more important than the official reaction was the response of reform elements nationally. McWilliams and others hoped that the affair would demonstrate to America that the mistreatment of Mexican

Americans was at the heart of the gang phenomenon and that ending juvenile delinquency in Los Angeles required a national commitment to reform, starting with "an affirmative federal program designed to improve living and working conditions and eliminate the prevalent social and economic discriminations."[23] Such reforms required dramatic evidence that conditions in the Mexican American community demanded profound changes in public policy. Despite the efforts of those who championed the cause of the Sleepy Lagoon defendants, their victimization was not seen in this way by those who had the power to effect change. More provocative were the Zoot-Suit Riots that erupted in Los Angeles just as the furor over the fate of the Sleepy Lagoon boys was subsiding. This infamous episode marshaled the sustained drama and national attention that the Sleepy Lagoon affair lacked. If nothing else, it seemed to demonstrate that the racial tensions in Los Angeles could produce serious social upheaval.

The Los Angeles Zoot-Suit Riots

On the evening of June 3, 1943, gangs of sailors and other servicemen swarmed out of nearby military bases and began roaming through sections of Los Angeles looking for young people of Mexican descent. They were apparently drawn particularly to those wearing the "zoot suit," an outfit that had been popular among hipsters, particularly African Americans, for some time, and had recently been adopted by some barrio youth. Typically, it consisted of a flat-topped hat; a long, broad-shouldered jacket; and baggy trousers very narrow at the cuffs.

The sailors' motives are not clear, but probably included a search for excitement, revenge for earlier individual encounters, and resentment over the freedom and fun they may have found represented in the alternative "uniforms" of the pachuco youth. Hatred or disrespect for their victims because of their race was no doubt part of the mix for many. Over the next several nights, the marauding servicemen, sometimes accompanied by civilians, accosted youths of Mexican descent and occasionally African Americans on the streets, dragged them from buses and cars, flushed them from theaters and other assemblies, beat them, and often stripped them of their clothing. Large numbers were injured and humiliated as police first stood by, then dragged the victims off to jail.[24] At night, large areas of Los Angeles were given over to rioters and their curious (and sympathetic) civilian followers. Busloads of sailors traveled up to Los Angeles from the naval base in San Diego to participate in what military officials feared was a servicemen's riot. On June 9, the Navy declared particularly troubled areas of the city off-limits to military personnel. With the servicemen off the streets, the violence subsided.[25]

The events were dramatic and cried out for political meaning. What this would be was neither inherent in the episode nor self-evident, but would depend on how the episode played in the national and foreign media.[26] In a recent study of the almost contemporaneous violence in Detroit that pitted white against black, Karen Huck suggests that the public's perception of these events made the race riot a landmark event in the struggle for civil rights. Whether or not the riot produced any significant change,[27] she effectively argues, the coverage in the popular picture magazine *Life* communicated a message that changed the national debate over race and would be part of a future legacy for civil rights for African Americans.

Huck argues that *Life*'s photos and brief text depicted sympathetic, passive, well-dressed, apparently middle-class African Americans being assailed by frenzied mobs of lower-class white antagonists while the local police stood by. Their rescue, the story suggests, was ultimately effected by federal intervention. Huck contends that *Life* conveyed to its massive readership a clear sense of the moral meaning of events—evil assailing innocence—and provided an unwritten brief on behalf of a federal solution to the nation's racial problem. The analysis provides a framework for understanding the political implications of contemporary events in Los Angeles. If the dominant press image of the violence on the West Coast had been, as it would be in Detroit, of an unprovoked, racially motivated assault on innocent victims, the affair might have served Mexican American interests in advancing their recognition for civil rights.[28]

The political results of the Zoot-Suit affair, at least in terms of the Anglo-American liberal reformers, rested in large part on the pictures (and text) conveyed to the public by the press. But there were grounds for concluding that what happened in Los Angeles did not rise to the seriousness of what would shortly transpire in Detroit. Even putting the worst face on it, the Los Angeles riot did not stand out in the epidemic of interracial violence that swept the nation in 1943. In that year alone, there were an estimated 242 racial battles in the nation's cities and military bases, and the upheaval in Detroit claimed the lives of twenty-five African Americans and nine whites, left more than seven hundred injured, and caused over two million dollars' worth of property damage.[29] By contrast, in the Los Angeles rioting, no one was killed, only about 125 were thought to be injured, and there was relatively little loss of property. Nor was there prominent evidence of intense racial hatred of the kind that was palpable in Detroit. For the Anglo-American liberals, the scale and intensity of the violence did not cry out for public soul searching.

Nor did the Zoot-Suit victims evoke public sympathy. Photos of the young Mexican American victims of violence were not those of the soberly dressed adults displayed in *Life*'s story on Detroit. Many showed them being taken into custody by police or arrayed in police lineups, that is, in the role of criminals. Moreover, in an era preoccupied with the threat youth were assumed to pose to authority, even those lying in the streets, battered, their clothing torn, might easily be seen as youthful troublemakers, probably gang members, who had simply gotten the worst of the kind of hooliganism people expected of juvenile delinquents. It was easier to identify them as youthful rebels than as members of an oppressed minority. Indeed, this was the way many older Mexican Americans responded.[30]

Reports that appeared in newspapers around the nation were based almost exclusively on wire service dispatches and were very similar in content and imagery. They focused on the zoot suits that many of the victims wore. Outlandish to the conventional eye, the colorful "uniforms" were seized upon by grateful journalists who identified the nature and origin of attire as the event's preeminent newsworthy element.[31]

The tone of the coverage was anticipated by a series of *Li'l Abner* cartoons that, by coincidence, ran on the comic strip pages of many of the nation's newspapers shortly before the affair in Los Angeles. The popular strip by Al Capp was a satire on faddism purporting to show how Americans (the usual Capp characters) came to adopt and reject the zoot suit. Although the Capp series can be read in various ways, it seems likely that most readers read nothing into it, and that even astute readers saw it as depicting the slightly silly, infinitely gullible, and conformist nature of the average American. These lovable oafs come across as objects of amusement, perhaps of ridicule, but not of the hatred that historians have been apt to assign to the strip.[32]

Capp's amused contempt for the wearers of zoot suits was echoed in national press coverage of the violence in Los Angeles, but the universality of his message was lost. Violence and humiliation are common elements of humor, and the alliterative, slightly ridiculous name "zoot suit" lent itself to the none-too-serious coverage of events. The press treated the affair as a joke rather than as a jeremiad, and nothing in the coverage was likely to provoke readers to think about the racial implications of the riots. Seen principally as the wearers of bizarre clothing, the young victims of mob violence were portrayed as deviants whose dress seemed to demand rebuke. The outfits appeared expensive, indicating by implication that deprivation was no factor in the youths' behavior. On the contrary, their profligate use of materials in short supply suggested an unpatriotic disregard of wartime conservation imperatives. The apparel hid the humanity of the young victims of mob violence, and while it did not obscure their race, it tended to make it irrelevant.

Although the photographs established for most readers that "they" definitely were not "us," the newspapers avoided referring to the victims' ethnicity. Ironically, the subordination of their national origins to their outfits was encouraged by the deal that Cranston had reached with Los Angeles newspapers. In an effort to keep readers in the city from associating gang violence with "Mexicans," journalists had agreed to use terms that did not suggest the ethnicity of the accused troublemakers. Thus, those involved in the Los Angeles riots were described as "wearers of zoot suits," "zoot suiters," "pachucos," or "gangsters." Though it was probably vaguely understood by most readers that these were "Mexicans," the advisory discouraged the press from describing the victims as American-born citizens of Mexican descent, which they mostly were, or from presenting the wearing of the outfits, or the mob action, as a reflection of West Coast race relations. The preoccupation with zoot suits led to naming the rioting not for the locale or the perpetrators, but for the dress of some of the victims.[33]

Indeed, the question of who was the perpetrator and who was the victim was not clear. While those photographed on the ground, bruised and defrocked, were almost all Mexican Americans, press reports compromised any sense that they were unjustly abused, for interspersed with such pictures were accounts of a policeman ambushed and injured by zoot suiters and of an innocent (Anglo) woman attacked by female gang associates. One story featured an interview with a "pachuca" who in accented argot professed her loyalty to the gang. An accompanying photo showed a young gang-affiliated woman displaying her arsenal of crude weapons for the camera.[34] The female gangster was not well known in the 1940s, and such pictures and accounts, startling in their contrast to the commonly held ideals of true womanhood, no doubt evoked revulsion in the average reader.

But if the victims of violence were portrayed as starkly sinister and unsympathetic, their antagonists were almost invisible. Little was written about the servicemen and their allies. Although a few photographs showed uniformed personnel as part of mobs, none showed them engaged in violence or detained by authorities.[35] The servicemen remained a kind of offstage presence. What we learn of them does not suggest members of a hate-crazed mob of bigots, but merely exuberant youth—joyful, perhaps mischievous, but not mean-spirited. Members of the crowd were described as "servicemen," and often shown in military uniform, so readers might assume that they represented a cross section of the nation's (good) youth, blowing off a little steam as they awaited a chance to face the nation's enemies. The contrast with their zoot suit–clad victims was obvious—although perhaps more apparent than real. The reality was that many of these young men in zoot suits would soon be in the military, where they were likely to distinguish themselves in a different and more deadly kind of combat.[36]

Few in the media deviated from this stock dichotomous treatment of the rioters and their victims. *Life* duplicated the standard superficial coverage of the scene in Los Angeles. The text was short and the photographs few. The story noted that some observers attributed the attacks to racial prejudice, but *Life*'s pictures focused on zoot suits, and one caption referred to "sartorial feuding." The story obscurely alluded to unnamed "factors older and more complex than any single episode could reveal." The reference was not to race but to sex, since authorities commonly traced the conflict to the "zoot suiters'" jealousy over sailors "stealing their girls."

The visceral contempt that the zoot-suiter stories evoked is reflected in exaggerated form by a pair of editorials appearing in southern newspapers. One called the zoot suit, which the editor noted originated in Harlem, "an affront and a monstrosity," and thanked the sailors on behalf of "135,000,000 sane and sensible Americans." The other charged that the victims were "organized gangsters," high on marijuana,[37] who in "a new low in open debauchery," preyed on servicemen and ravaged their women.[38]

A significant exception to the generally superficial and hostile coverage was a balanced story run by *Time*, which wrote that the "zoot-suit 'gangs'" were the "equivalent of boys' gangs almost anywhere," and traced the warfare to incidents initiated by some suiters, but described the servicemen's response as an indiscriminate attack on "zooters, Mexicans or just dark-complexioned males." *Time*, however, played down the racial significance of the affair, highlighting not the attacks but the origins of the suit wearing. This and other behavior associated with some Mexican American youth, the journal insisted in the enlightened fashion of the day, was not a function of race but a reflection of "a basic American problem: the second generation . . ."[39] At bottom, as *Time* portrayed it, the episode was a tale of rebellious, alienated immigrant children—just another group of new Americans struggling to make their way in the sometimes inhospitable land of opportunity. The account, while sympathetic with the youth, in effect denied the saliency of racism or the need for community self-examination or political reform.[40]

In the confusion that marked the affair, responsible authorities were free to draw their own conclusions. Local officials were particularly adamant that what had happened was no race riot—that the targets of the attacks were not Mexicans, but American-born hoodlums.[41] According to the official version, it was a generational problem, not a matter of race. In this view, troubled children of hardworking and concerned immigrant parents had for some time been taking advantage of the restraint shown by an understaffed police force and the inefficiency and coddling they had experienced at the hands of the juvenile justice system to initiate disturbances, often involving local servicemen.[42] The official story was that the overreaction of the servicemen and others had been encouraged by irresponsible local press coverage and the whole issue blown out of proportion by the agitation of "Communistic influences."[43] The insistence of local officials that race played no role was in part their effort to preserve the city's reputation. The mayor and others were concerned lest outsiders think of booster-minded Los Angeles as a racist town (and hence prone to upheaval). On the bright side, this rejection of the race explanation was tacit acknowledgment that racism was a loathsome and dangerous thing—a landmark concession in California.

Dismissing the suggestion that racism played a significant role in the troubles allowed officials to ignore substantive issues attributable to prejudice. On the other hand, by identifying the problem as juvenile delinquency, officials tacitly committed themselves to programs that addressed the demoralized and alienated conditions among Mexican American youth. Of course, the problem of the second generation would presumably diminish with the passage of time, assuming that the influx of Mexican immigration remained low. But while time worked its healing ways, the pains of alienated youth could be ameliorated by ensuring them adequate economic opportunity, by looking a little more intently at living conditions in Mexican American neighborhoods, and, most immediately, by improving recreational facilities for young people. Equally attractive to city officials, given their understanding of events, were plans for enlarging the system of juvenile justice: creating more judges, correctional camps, work programs, and detention facilities.[44] Los Angeles had come to acknowledge its juvenile delinquency problem, to grudgingly and unofficially concede that it was particularly acute among Mexican Americans, and to accept the need to initiate programs that would address the issue. Modest at first, the remedial programs grew substantially over the years, although achieving the goals remained elusive.[45]

The response of federal officials was very much like that of the local establishment. In the days after the riot, they flocked to Los Angeles, where they consulted with the mayor, the police, the Mexican consul, representatives of local civic groups, and anyone else they thought could provide a "responsible" explanation of what was going on. Their overriding concern was to prevent the affair from turning into a full-fledged race riot or from being seen as one.[46] Once they were assured by local officials and intelligence experts that neither the Axis nor the Sinarquistas had a hand in the affair,[47] they awaited an end to the rampaging and then happily retreated to Washington, content to let local authorities deal with any residual discontents among barrio youth.[48]

Washington eagerly echoed the "no racism" mantra. Accepting the proposition that the violence in Los Angeles was a product of juvenile delinquency (and hence indubitably a local matter) meant that there was no need to question American unity or to apologize to the Mexican government. Describing the victims of the attacks as zoot suiters or pachucos played well in Mexico City, where officials were happy to go along with the explanation that this was not a racial matter (and therefore not an affront to Mexican honor), but simply a case of juvenile delinquency among troublemaking American-born youth. U.S. and Mexican officials cooperated in a largely successful effort to keep events in Los Angeles from becoming a serious political issue south of the border.[49]

Those more familiar with the Mexican American situation did not accept the official explanation. Robert Lucey, the Catholic archbishop of San Antonio, in a speech to the National Catholic Welfare Council, asked whether the United States could rightfully claim to be a "bulwark of liberty while we maim and mangle Mexican youth in the streets." George I. Sánchez, an official of LULAC and sometime consultant to federal authorities, argued that events in Los Angeles were not simply due to problems of inevitably alienated youth; instead, they had exposed the more general mistreatment of Mexican Americans. The "zoot-suited 'pachucos,'" he explained, had adopted their apparently bizarre dress and antisocial behavior as a dramatic response to the "discriminatory social and economic practices, . . . provincial smugness and self-assigned 'racial' superiority" that confronted all Mexican Americans, wherever they lived. An end to their alienation and to the violence against them, he suggested, lay in broad reforms, starting with ensuring all Mexican Americans their civil rights. He found hope, not in the response to events in Los Angeles, but in the unheralded adoption by Texas of a Civil Rights Resolution a month earlier. While pachucos battled sailors in the streets of Los Angeles, he suggested, a quiet revolution had begun in Austin that promised genuine progress for Spanish-speaking Americans.[50] How far that revolution would progress was still an open issue.

CHAPTER 4

The War and Changing Identities: Personal Transformations

RICHARD GRISWOLD DEL CASTILLO

During World War II, millions of people all over the world struggled with fears and deprivation, suffering and death. The effects of this worldwide cataclysm were to be felt for generations to come as the survivors of the violence and unbelievable cruelty shaped their futures and carried with them memories and lessons from the past. For large numbers of Mexican Americans and Mexicans in the United States, this war had many lasting consequences, probably the most important being the redefinition of self-identity from "Mexican" to "Mexican American." Young men and women left their homes and families for the first time and learned how to live closely with other Americans in an entirely foreign environment— one that challenged others to rethink who they were and the meaning of their lives. For all Americans, it became increasingly evident that this war, fought to eliminate racism abroad, also meant that discrimination at home was morally wrong. Mexican Americans refused to continue to accept their second-class status as a result. This chapter explores the effect of wartime experiences on how Mexican Americans thought of themselves in relation to the larger society, how they constructed their identities during these national crises, and how these identities had implications for a consciousness of civil rights.

The Mexican American GIS

More than 3.5 million persons of Mexican descent lived in the southwestern part of the United States when the Japanese bombed Pearl Harbor on December 7, 1941. Of that number, more than half were native-born U.S. citizens, and probably about one-third, or just less than one million, were men of draft age. While there are no exact statistics, impressionistic accounts indicate that large numbers of Mexican Americans either volunteered or were drafted into the armed services during World War II. Probably about 500,000 Mexican American men joined the armed services during the war.[1] They volunteered for a variety of reasons. Some sought to escape poverty and discrimination at home; some wanted adventure; some did so out of pride, a sense of manhood, family loyalty, duty, and/or patriotism; and some, because their friends or relatives had enlisted.

Why did Mexican Americans join the fight to save America in World War II when they were being mistreated at home? The answer to this question varied from individual to individual, and no blanket statement could capture the truth. Perhaps the sentiments of a Navajo soldier writing back to his tribal council were similar to those of many Mexican Americans: "I don't know anything about the white man's way. I never went outside the reservation. . . . I am proud to be in a suit like this now. It is to protect my country, my people, the head men, the chiefs of my people."[2] Substitute "family and children" for "head men and chiefs" and you might capture the kernel of the impulse to sacrifice that has been called "patriotism."

The Congreso del Pueblo de Habla Española, which had been formed (in 1938) to organize Mexican Americans to fight for civil rights before the war, issued a statement urging participation in military service based on the claim of native birth: "We are also children of the United States. We will defend her." Perhaps Mexican American leaders saw the war less as an opportunity to pressure Americans in order to gain equal rights and more as a credit to their honor that could be cashed in after the victory abroad. Another prewar civil rights group, the Mexican American Movement, took this approach when they said, "It [the war] has shown them what the Mexican American will do, what responsibility he will take and what leadership qualities he will demonstrate. After this struggle, the status of the Mexican American will be different."[3]

Because they were not segregated within the armed services, as were African Americans, many Mexican Americans saw the fight as a golden opportunity to prove themselves equal to Anglo-Americans. Raul Morin, who later wrote the first book about Mexican Americans' sacrifices in World War II, was himself a foot soldier. He wrote: "Most of us were more than glad to be given the opportunity to serve in the war. It did not matter whether we were looked upon as Mexicans; the war soon made us all *genuine* Americans, eligible and available immediately to fight and to defend our country, the United States of America."[4] Becoming *"genuine Americans"* meant proving yourself in battle and in the sacrifices your family was willing to make at home.

Victoria Morales, a war worker, voiced the patriotic sentiments of some when she recalled, "The Japanese had attacked our country. I say our country because I was born here. My generation went proudly to war because this country, despite the discrimination, had provided my family with a better life than my relatives had in Mexico."[5] For Mexican Americans, World War II involved a leap of faith: claiming the United States as your country even when it did not claim you.

In addition to the U.S.-born Mexican Americans, there were also hundreds of thousands of Mexican citizens who were residents in the United States, many of whom were eligible for the draft. Probably about 15,000 Mexican citizens served in the military.[6] After June 1942, when Mexico declared war on the Axis powers, Mexican nationals living along the border crossed into the United States to join as well. They, too, were willing to sacrifice in the common struggle, and their use of the term *patria* (country) could often be ambiguous, referring to both the United States, where they were living, and to Mexico, the land of their birth. In Colton, California, for example, where a good portion of the workers were Mexican immigrants, it was decided to postpone the celebration of Mexican Independence Day, usually celebrated on September 15 and 16, to Sunday, September 20. This was to help win the war by allowing war work to continue uninterrupted on regular work days.[7] Meanwhile, throughout the war, the Spanish-speaking press in places like Los Angeles (*La Opinión*) and San Antonio (*La Prensa*) published lists of those killed in the war, making no distinction between Mexicans and U.S.-born.

There are hundreds of stories that tell of the bravery and sacrifices of Mexican and Mexican American GIs during the war. As has been noted by many historians, collectively, Mexicans and Mexican Americans distinguished themselves for their valor, earning seventeen Medals of Honor—the nation's highest award for bravery—more than any other ethnic group. Many of the stories of the Medal of Honor winners have been collected in Morin's book. In addition to these accounts of unimaginable bravery and hardship are descriptions of the strength of friendships and *mexicanidad* (Mexicanness).[8] The family back home learned of the true experiences of their men folk only after the war, due to strict censorship of the mail. Even after the war, many veterans preferred to keep silent about their experiences, and during the war their families were given only brief descriptions of the realities of their contributions. Thanks to the

Figure 4.1. The Sánchez brothers were raised in New Mexico and orphaned in San Bernardino, California, after which they were raised by their older sisters. All had their lives changed by the war.

Top left, Emiliano (Elmer) Sánchez, 370th Medical Battalion in Europe; *top right,* John Edward (Eddie) Sánchez, U.S. Navy Seabees, Pacific; *bottom left,* Santiago (Jimmy) Sánchez, 27th Armored Infantry in Europe; *bottom right,* S. Sgt. Severo Sánchez, killed in action in Leyte, Philippines, October 21, 1943; *center,* Leonidas Nicolás (Leo) Sánchez, Civil Defense volunteer, San Bernardino, California. Courtesy of Rita Sánchez.

Figure 4.2. Three Sánchez sisters who worked as riveters in the war industries in Los Angeles: *top left,* Antonia (Tony) Sánchez Mehl; *bottom left,* Amalia (Molly) Sánchez Carpenter; and *right,* Angélica Sánchez Miller. Courtesy of Rita Sánchez.

Latinos and Latinas in World War II Project at the University of Texas, there is now an effort being made to salvage the memories of Latinos and Latinas who served in the armed forces or worked on the home front during World War II. This oral history collection is long overdue and, at this writing, well under way, with more than four hundred interviews having been archived and many of them indexed.[9]

Mexican and Mexican American GIS

Hundreds of thousands of young men with names like García, González, and Sánchez either volunteered or were drafted into the U.S. armed forces during World War II. The sacrifices they made involved not only the physical loss of life and limb but also the psychological trauma that many experienced as a result of the horrendous violence they lived through. Uncounted thousands returned from the conflict only to spend the rest of their lives suffering from drug or alcohol addiction and debilitating fears and memories. Those who were able to survive physically and psychologically were undoubtedly changed by their experiences. But many returned with a new confidence in their abilities to compete in a larger society. Some took advantage of the GI Bill to get an education and purchase a home. And others merely picked up where they left off, returning to the fields or the factories. For all, the trace effects of the war remained with them throughout their lives.

Later, when they were old men and women, hundreds of these individuals were interviewed and asked to tell stories about their lives during the war.[10] They related a variety of experiences in narratives that were more than just a collection of autobiographical details. Today, their stories tell us of the meanings of their lives in relation to the social and political world by which they were and are surrounded. In the words of Ramón Saldívar, who has studied Chicano narratives, "A text can thus be said to refer not to concrete situations so much as to the ideological formulations that concrete situations have produced."[11] In this sense, the narratives of Mexican Americans who fought in World War II emerge as stories told against the ideological formation of American empire in the post–cold war years. Told to interviewers in the 1980s and 1990s, the stories often subvert or counter the hegemonic assertion of Anglo-American dominance and triumphalism. They project a voice that modifies the mainstream ideology of the victory of democracy against totalitarianism, the last "Good War" that benefited everyone with the destruction of evil. Not all the war narratives are openly stories of resistance or of conflict with prevailing ideology, but one trope that emerges again and again is that of the suffering, poverty, and discrimination that existed before and after the war and tacitly is assumed to continue to exist. The following samples give an idea of the diversity of ways in which the war affected Mexican American identity.

Take the example of Antonio Campo, who was raised in Houston, Texas, during the 1930s. He recalled the discrimination this way: "If you

Figure 4.3. Navy recruits taking an oath in front of the Palace of the Governors, Santa Fe, New Mexico, in 1942. New Mexico Department of Tourism Photograph Collection. Image No. 1394. Courtesy of the New Mexico State Records Center Archives (NMSRCA), 1205 Camino Carlos Rey, Santa Fe, New Mexico.

wanted to get fed, you had to go in the back. Mexicans and dogs were in the back. You had to get a sandwich and go home."[12] As a child, Campos joined a segregated Boy Scout troop with second-hand uniforms, and he was forced into a Hispanic high school band after being rejected by the all-Anglo band. Volunteering for the Army in World War II, he served as a paratrooper and fought in France. When he returned, he went to college on the GI Bill and attended Baylor Law School. When he graduated, he organized a campaign to improve English teaching to Mexican and Tejano kids and ran for mayor and city council, but was defeated after a bitter contest. During the campaign, he recalled that one official told him, "If you don't like it, why don't you go back to Mexico?" Campo stood up and told them that "I was born here in Texas. I went overseas and put my life on the line so you people can make decisions." His new identity was that of a patriot who had earned the right to criticize Americans for their lack of respect. But he still had to prove his identity as an American to others. Even after serving his country, he was hardly valued, proving that his fight was not over. Later, Campos put his wartime confidence to good use and succeeded in leading a coalition to end discrimination in Baytown, Texas.[13]

Many Mexican American GIs expressed love of country and patriotism as a result of the war, and often this new patriotism mixed with a Mexican identity in complicated ways, as evidenced by the narrative of Moisés Flores. Moisés was born in Colonia Dublán in Chihuahua, Mexico. He crossed the border to join the U.S. Army and was then sent to the Pacific theater, where he was wounded in action. After the war, he settled in El Paso, Texas, where he summarized his changed identity: "I am very proud to be American. Sometimes I even call myself gringo, which I'm not. I'm still Mexican, but I'm an American first."[14] The *mestizaje*, or mixture of ideas, in this statement reflects the impact of a war that recast Mexicans as Americans and erased the difference between "gringos" and Mexicans.

For some, the war experience created a reservoir of anger that remained just below the surface. It may have been channeled by the war, but later it would have tragic results. Andrew Tamayo recalled a lifetime of seeing discrimination that made him angry about "helping the gringos" with their war. Tamayo was from San Antonio and was raised by a single mother. "I remember how they used to treat us over here [in San Antonio]." His mother was not able to get decent work because she was a Mexican. Tamayo, however, served with distinction in the U.S. Army, earning a Bronze Star, a Purple Heart, and eight bronze Campaign Stars.[15] His war experience turned him into a fighter who refused to accept bad treatment.

Some experienced the betrayal of the American dream as a result of the war and thus formed an identity that was critical of Americanism. Luis Leyva was born in Mexico and grew up in Laredo, Texas, as an adopted orphan. Since he had grown up in an all-Mexican neighborhood and gone to all-Mexican schools, he had never experienced discrimination. He was an undocumented resident and was not drafted; he volunteered, saying, "I know no other country . . . This is my country; this is where I live." Leyva enlisted in the Army right after Pearl Harbor. His first experience with discrimination came when he asked some African American cooks to come into his barracks to see a photo of his girlfriend and they told him that they were not allowed to enter. He recalled, "I couldn't understand it . . . I was in the U.S. Army, fighting for the freedom of people in Europe, and we were having the same problem here in the United States." Although promised citizenship as a result of his service in Europe, he never received it.[16] This was a bitter disappointment for him. For Luis, the war years changed his identity by giving him a sense of disappointment in and betrayal by the only country he had ever known.

For others, the war experience strengthened an identity that had been shaped by family and community—one that had struggled against discrimination for generations. Raymond Flores was born in the mining town of Miami, Arizona, and was one of seventeen brothers and sisters. His mother, a role model for him, encouraged him to fight for what he believed in and for equality. He and his mother fought for him and his brothers and sisters to integrate an all-white American class in the local elementary school. Later, in high school, Raymond led a walkout of Mexican students protesting discrimination in the taking of the class picture according to national origin. He remembered, "It was a period of racism to the extreme when I was growing up. If you get accustomed to it, it doesn't hurt as much. But we didn't want to be accustomed to that. It was just not our way." In the war, Raymond joined the Army Air Corps, where he encountered more racial discrimination. "I hate to discredit different parts of the military, but racism was rampant." He recalled that he was not promoted because of his race. When he returned home after the war, he continued his activism in opposing discrimination, leading boycotts by college students.[17] He used the GI Bill and became a teacher, one who continued to question inequality and injustice. Raymond Flores's war experiences developed his identity as a leader in the struggle for civil rights.

Mexican American "Double-Consciousness"

One of the themes running through Mexican American war narratives is that of the prewar struggle against poverty and discrimination. The Mexican Americans who lived through the Great Depression and World War II developed a life philosophy that enabled them to cope with the fact that, individually and collectively, they were treated as foreigners and outsiders who did not belong. During World War II, they were called upon to sacrifice for their country, a nation that stood for freedom, tolerance, and human dignity. This "double-consciousness" of considering yourself a patriotic American while experiencing "second-class citizenship" led to the formation of a tough and resilient worldview, one that would make Mexican Americans the backbone of what came to be called "middle America."[18]

Mexican American men and women later remembered their youthful experiences with racism and discrimination as an integral part of shaping their identity, one that incorporated patriotism and belief in the American dream with memories of discrimination and humiliations and with the desire to overcome or reconcile the latter. The construction of Mexican American consciousness was often filled with irony and conflicting memories.[19]

Despite their status as citizens and disparities of appearance, status, and regional affiliation, most were classified as "Mexican" by the U.S. government and by white public opinion. Their speaking of Spanish, their brown appearance, and a century of historical economic and political submersion resulted in widespread practices of discrimination and segregation. Suspected of being disloyal to the United States and of being foreign, most Mexican Americans lived in the shadows, in barrios and forgotten rural enclaves, hardly noticed except when they were needed for work or became the targets of the police. During the 1920s and 1930s, they had grown up to expect hard work, poverty, hunger, and rejection. Individually and collectively, they learned to survive.[20]

Notwithstanding this common reality, there were many different stories of how Mexican American youth emerged from the era of the Great Depression and formed a worldview that redefined themselves as Mexican American men and women who expected fair treatment and justice based on their proven patriotic sacrifices during World War II. To some extent, all of these narratives demonstrate the development of a "double consciousness."

María Elisa Rodríguez, born and raised in Waco, Texas, of Mexican immigrant parents, was one of nine children. Her father was a day laborer who encouraged her and her brothers and sisters to get an education because he believed that this would protect them from discrimination and prejudice against Mexicans.

María remembered, "Waco had lots of prejudice, and that's the reason my dad always emphasized education." She felt the discrimination as a little girl when she learned that she was not allowed to join the all-white Girl Scouts or swim in the public pool. She recalled, "We couldn't even belong to the Girl Scouts or anything like that. There was a lot of discrimination. So we couldn't even get into the public swimming pools."[21]

As a teenager, María decided to try to get a job as a secretary even though she knew that Mexican girls were usually not chosen; they were expected to be maids and cooks, not white-collar workers. When she applied for the job, they questioned her citizenship, making her feel like a foreigner, and she was forced to define herself for them as an American of Mexican descent.

> There were very few secretaries at that time. . . . In fact, I was the first secretary to come here and be hired . . . and they would see my name, and the patient would say, "What nationality are you?" I'd say, "I'm Mexican and I am an American of Mexican descent." And they'd say, "Well, I've never seen a Mexican in an office." And I'd say, "Well, you're seeing one now." Because most of [us] were working in clothing stores because that was as high as you could get. There weren't too many opportunities offered to Mexican American women.[22]

During the war, she worked as a civilian clerk for the Army. She felt the contradiction of the double identity, that Mexican Americans were being called upon to be loyal Americans and sacrifice for their country while, at the same time, they were being discriminated against at home.

> And that's why I couldn't ever understand that they'd see these boys go and fight for this country and they'd come back and they couldn't get good jobs. That's the only thing I felt bad about. That they didn't give us the opportunity. Because our boys went out and died on the battlefront, and I thought we were entitled to everything. But as it was, we weren't; discrimination still existed.[23]

María married a WWII veteran after the war and raised a family. She also continued working for the Army as a monitor for employment practices. She became active in Mexican American rights organizations such as LULAC and Incorporated Mexican American Government Employees (IMAGE), and in the GI Forum, and she also volunteered her time to teach citizenship classes in Waco. Her experiences as a little girl shaped her later life as an adult who was not timid about asserting her rights as an American.

About the time María was attending school in Waco, Andrew Aguirre was growing up in Otay Mesa on the U.S.-Mexican border south of San Diego. One of eight children of Mexican immigrant parents, Andrew recalls that his earliest memories were punctuated by poverty, hunger, and work. All the family worked in the fields or as laborers. Andrew attended school only up to the eighth grade and then dropped out to work. In school, he remembered fights and punishments because he spoke only Spanish at first and because he was Mexican. Asked if the troubles in school were "a racial thing," his response was one of stoic acceptance but also of self-criticism:

> Yeah, there was racial stuff involved; let's face it . . . we've been racially picked on since we crossed the border. That's why as you get older you learn to assimilate more . . . But I think that part of the problem was that the Chicanos were their own worst enemies . . . because everybody was in a barrio . . . You feel comfortable in your own language and your own culture. So when a person tries to escape the barrio and assimilate into the Anglos, he was picked on . . . we were our own worst enemies.[24]

Andrew's self-criticism was undoubtedly learned after seeing the benefits of fitting in and hearing his barrio friends criticize him for speaking English and working with Anglos.

In 1944, as he was about to be drafted, his uncle convinced him to join the Marine Corps. In the Marine Corps, he found the sense of belonging and pride he had been searching for. After basic training, he was sent to Okinawa. He became a career service marine and five years later fought in Korea, where he was imprisoned in a North Korean prison camp. Reflecting on his experience in the Marines, he commented:

> I joined the Marine Corps and I really loved it. At first, I hated it. I hated those robots, you know (hep, hup, hey . . .) They wore their hats down here . . . They brought their face right up practically spitting on you. But gradually you start to develop a sense of unity, a sense of importance because you're part of something big, you know . . . At first, you really hate it, then you start to take pride in yourself, your buddies, and your platoon. You get Gung Ho! In fact, when I got released, they asked me if the Chinese had brainwashed me, and I said no, the Marine Corps had beaten them to it.[25]

For Andrew, the Marine Corps became a way of making it in American society despite his poverty, lack of education, and Mexican heritage. He became a proponent of assimilation, but not at the expense of his identity as a Chicano—a term he used to describe himself in the 1990s. His Mexican American identity was one of quiet perseverance and a tough self-confidence. His message to the youth was: "To succeed, you need self-discipline and goals."

The last example of Mexican American identity as shaped by the war is that of Héctor Peña Jr. Raised in South Texas as the son of a small merchant, he excelled in school, graduating from high school in three years. Héctor's family life was not typical of most Mexican Americans. His father was able to provide a good living for the family, and Héctor was able to attend college. He attended Texas A&I in Kingsville, Texas, in the prelaw program. He graduated with a teaching certificate, but was not able to get a job as a teacher. Undeterred and still believing in the power of education, he went to San Antonio in 1937 and attended night school, receiving his law degree in three years. He became a lawyer and settled in Corpus Christi. He remembered the discrimination he encountered in Corpus: "When I came to Corpus in '37, . . . they would not serve us in any downtown restaurant. If we wanted to go to the movies, we went upstairs with the blacks. My brother was the first secretary of the organization. Later I joined LULAC."[26]

As an educated professional, Héctor did not feel that discrimination was right. He remembered that civil rights organizations like LULAC were active before the war in challenging discrimination. He knew some of the important Mexican American leaders in civil rights, such as Héctor P. García, a president of LULAC and then cofounder of the American GI Forum.

Héctor Peña was a member and future leader of LULAC, and he remembered two civil rights battles. One involved an ordinance that prohibited Mexicans from using a swimming pool in Cold Park in Corpus Christi.

> I recall two major projects I was involved in, and one of them was the
> city council would not permit any Hispanics to swim at Cold Park . . .
> So we went and appeared before them to do something about it. We were
> trying to improve their [Hispanics'] standing, to get them their rights.
> And they did open it up.[27]

The other LULAC project he was involved with was one that spearheaded opposition to a segregated African American–only school in the barrio. This project laid bare some of the ways discrimination polarized the races, pitting the Mexican American community against the African American community as each struggled to maintain a sense of self-respect within the bounds of segregation.

Due to a medical condition, Héctor Peña did not serve in the military during the war. Instead, he worked as a censor for the government. It is evident that his civil rights consciousness was developing before World War II. His activism was part of a developing consciousness nationwide as well as within the Mexican American professional community. His formation with regard to civil rights can be attributed to his association with other Mexican American professionals and his South Texas roots, which told him not to ignore discrimination even though he was relatively well off.

These stories are a small sample of the diversity of ways that Mexican American men and women developed their identities during World War II. But they all shared, to some extent, a common theme, that of coming to a greater awareness, because of their wartime experiences, of the contradiction of being a loyal American while being treated as an outcast. The contradiction was stronger in this generation than in any previous one because of the magnitude of Mexican American involvement in World War II and the proportion of individuals who were U.S. citizens by birth.

Women's Identities and a New Self-Confidence

During the war, hundreds of thousands of Mexican American women had their lives drastically changed by the national emergency of war as they went to work in jobs that had always been reserved for men, such as in aircraft factories and related war industries. While there is a great diversity of experience among these women, one generalization seems true: the war created new awareness of women's abilities outside of the domestic sphere. The experience gave them a new self-confidence and independence that would become important in later civil rights struggles after the war. In Richard Santillán's words, the war developed among Mexican American women a "political awareness, social independence, grass-roots leadership, and economic self-reliance — personal strengths which greatly enhanced the postwar civil rights movement."[28]

Some researchers believe that the experience of women workers during World War II laid the foundation for the women's movement in the 1970s. As Sherna Berger Gluck wrote in her anthology *Rosie the Riveter Revisited*, "The war hastened the process whereby the United States became a more complex and less homogenous society. By being pulled into war industries, women were active participants in that process."[29] Specifically, Gluck pointed to the fact that these wartime women were the mothers of those who participated in the women's movement of the 1960s and 1970s and thus were their role models. Perhaps the same generalization could be made with respect to Mexican American women.[30]

William H. Chafe, in analyzing the war experience for all women, concluded that the war produced what he called the "paradox of change." The war was definitely a turning point with regard to the permanent increase in the numbers of women in factory and service jobs, and for the first time in American history, more older married women worked outside the home than single females. At the same time, attitudes toward women working did not change; their wages remained below those of men, and men continued to view women as more suited to being homemakers. Thus, paradoxically, there was no movement toward greater rights for women as a result of their new economic roles.[31]

Karen Anderson noted that the war created changes in women's workforce participation that became permanent after the war. The proportion of women over sixteen years old working in jobs outside the home continued to rise after 1945, and the female workforce was dominated by older married women. Generally, the war speeded up a process that was already discernible before the war began. During the 1930s, women were increasingly entering white-collar jobs and the workforce in general.[32] Most women remained homemakers during the war, and their story is important and undervalued.

A question that emerges, then, is to what extent do the generalizations made in these studies of American women apply to Mexican American women? Did the ethnic and cultural differences of Mexican American women make the way they experienced the war different from that of white women?

One major ethnic difference was that before World War II, compared to married white women, proportionately fewer married Mexican and Mexican American women worked outside the home for wages. In other words, the labor force participation of married Mexican American women was less than for white women. This phenomenon was attributed to the strong ideals of patriarchal authority and the cultural limits put on married women socializing or working outside of their family. Lorinda Flores, a Mexican immigrant to San Diego in the 1930s, remembered her experience: "I really enjoyed working . . . I wanted to grow up and be a buyer in a store, but I married a typical Mexican male who said you're not going to work; you're going to have kids and stay home. So that was my jail; I was a housewife."[33] Furthermore, married women usually had small children and growing families to care for, and it was just not possible to hold down a full-time job in addition to being a mother. Countering this cultural and economic limit on Mexican American women working for wages was a long tradition of them working in part-time and occasional jobs in order to help support the family. This was especially true for migrant farmworker families in which the entire family worked to help make ends meet. As we have seen in the case of María Rodríguez, discrimination prevented many Mexican American women from being hired for jobs that paid well. Thus, in another paradox, while proportionately fewer Mexican American women were in the industrial labor force than was true for white women, Latina wage workers were crucial to the survival of many of the poorest families, especially those who were migrant farmworkers. The experience of Hortencia Carrasco, a farmworker in San Diego during the 1930s, was typical: "When I started working, I was about fourteen or fifteen years [old]. I started working at Van Camp in 1943. I went to work to help the family. I had no choice; I had to help my mother, my parents, and the younger kids."[34]

World War II changed these trends in several ways. First, it loosened the traditional control of fathers and husbands over women. The exigencies of the war and the appeal of high wages, patriotism, and new job opportunities operated to force men to make exceptions for their daughters and wives to leave the home and go to work or to socialize in new ways with nonfamily. Second, the war increased the economic status of the poorest women, who were now able to get good-paying full-time jobs in industrial occupations because their labor was needed. The high wages paid for work in war industries boosted family incomes and increased the importance of women in relation to the economy. It also moved some women and their families away from dependence on occasional part-time farm work.

It should be noted that the majority of Mexican American women during World War II were not "Rosie the Riveters." They contributed to the war effort in other ways, by raising families and taking care of others. Their prosaic story is one that includes the difficulties of making ends meet within the limits of rationing and scarcity; the continued discrimination in public services and in education; the grief over the loss of brothers, uncles, fathers, and husbands; and the heroic sacrifices made to keep families together and support the morale of loved ones. All these dimensions of life have yet to be the subject of social historians studying Mexican American women during the war. It was, however, the dominant experience for most adult Mexican American women.[35]

An analysis of some of the themes that emerge in the oral histories of Mexican American working women is illustrative of the complications that arise when trying to discern ethnic differences. One recurring theme in other interviews done by the University of Texas Latinos and Latinas in World War II Project participants—Elizabeth Escovedo, Sherna Berger Gluck, Richard Santillán, and Santiago Solís—was that the war provided working women the opportunity to experience a new kind of social life away from the strict supervision of family and kin. A loosening of traditional patriarchal control by parents and husbands was justified by the war emergency.

Margarita Salazar, a New Mexican woman who grew up in Los Angeles, was working as a cosmetologist when the war broke out. Because of the lure of higher wages in the aircraft industry, she got a job there. She noted that before the war, Mexican American girls organized social clubs where they sponsored dances. They had an adult sponsor who acted as a chaperone. Many of the young girls were already working before the war, but during the war the clubs stopped functioning. Young women were now permitted to go unchaperoned to dances with servicemen. Salazar remembered: "My mother thought it was all right, because her sons were in the service. She was so wrapped up in missing her boys that she didn't see anything wrong with the servicemen. In fact, a lot of us had boyfriends in the service and people we'd write to."[36] She and many of her workmates kept up a lively correspondence with servicemen overseas—without any particular romantic attachment—just to keep their morale up. Margarita recalled using five sheets of carbon paper to type the same letter to five different soldiers.

Emma López was a native San Diegan whose parents owned a small barrio restaurant. During the war, she quit high school to get good-paying jobs, first in the tuna canneries and then at Convair, an aircraft assembly plant. After the swing shift, there were big-band dances, and Emma and her friends had enough energy to go almost every week: "I'd go around picking everybody up. We didn't want dates. We wanted to dance with the guys from Texas or New York, New Jersey, New Mexico." She recalled lots of late-night parties, going grunion running, and going to all-night movies. All this had the blessing of her parents, who saw it as part of the war effort.[37]

One factor that dramatically increased young women's freedom and sense of independence was the increased money they had to spend on activities that had been considered frivolous during the Depression of the 1930s. Now they had permission to be extravagant. Hortencia Carrasco, another San Diego native with Mexican immigrant parents, recalled deciding to quit high school because she "had no clothes to wear." She started working at the tuna canneries rather than at the aircraft factories because she could earn more money through piece rates—up to one hundred dollars a week. To get the job, she lied about her age, saying she was eighteen. "A couple of times we worked the whole month without a day off." After such lengthy work periods, she felt she had earned the right to have fun without the strict supervision of her parents.[38]

Indeed, Escovedo noted that many women among those she interviewed felt that they had garnered increased trust and respect from parents because of their wage-earning contributions. Almost without exception, unmarried working women gave a sizable portion of the money they earned to their parents. Santillán found that many married women whose husbands were overseas depended on their parents as babysitters while they were at work. Even with these changes, Mexican American women's views of acceptable social independence did differ, ranging from having the freedom to smoke, wear lipstick, wear pants, and date without chaperones to expecting equality in decision making at home and the right to education. Some women commented that their independence during the war prepared them for being widows or divorced women after the war.[39]

Another theme that links the diverse remembrances of Mexican American women during World War II was that of Americanization. In general, the war had the effect of stimulating patriotism through the common bond of suffering and sacrifice. Beyond that, Mexican Americans, along with African Americans, felt more justified in asserting their rights as U.S. citizens who had fought and worked for the victory over totalitarianism and Fascism. This demand for equal treatment and an end to discrimination gained force because of the common affirmation of loyalty to flag and country. For Mexican American women, this meant voting for the first time during the war. It meant buying war bonds and volunteering for work in the USO and Red Cross. It meant gaining a new awareness of the injustice of unequal treatment. Santillán heard one woman say:

> During the war, there was a lessening of discrimination by some public places only because they needed our money, with so many Anglos in the service. After the war, some restaurants, stores, and taverns again refused to serve us on an equal basis with whites. We knew this was totally unfair because we had worked hard to win the war. My generation realized then that we had to do something to change this condition, not only for ourselves but for the next generation.[40]

These words would be prophetic as women became activists during the civil rights movement after the war.

Mexican American women encountered the color barrier a bit differently in employment situations. In many aircraft assembly plants, whites refused to work with African American women, so the employers assigned Mexican American women to work with them. The result was an education in how racism affected everyone and the formation of cross-ethnic and interracial friendships. Many Mexican American women reported that they had formed, for the first time, friendships with other women who were non-Mexican.

Elvira Esparza was born and raised in San Diego of Mexican immigrant parents. During the war, she worked at Solar, making B-24s. She got men's wages because of the quality of her work. She was the first Mexican American woman hired at Solar. She remembered men saying that they liked her but couldn't date her because she was Mexican. "They didn't understand that this person, because she had brown skin . . . had a head just like anyone else; she could do the work, sometimes better."[41]

The changes wrought on Mexican American women during the war were also dependent on their level of prior acculturation. For some, it was the first time they had been permitted to leave the barrio and the home and, as such, represented a revolutionary experience. For others, perhaps the majority, it represented one choice out of many subsequent choices leading their lives toward more integration with mainstream society. Gluck quoted one African American woman as saying, "Hitler was the one that got us out of the white folks' kitchen."[42] This was also the case for many Mexican American women who had worked before the war but mainly in occupations that were reserved for women, such as laundresses, seamstresses, domestics, cannery workers, and the like. Hitler got them out of these low-paying jobs and into new arenas. For the first time, they came into prolonged contact with African American and white women with whom they worked. And they began socializing with men outside their ethnic group.

Some men used this war experience to criticize women who wanted to continue interacting with other cultures and groups after the war, accusing them of being too Americanized. Santillán quoted one woman:

They said we were acting like white women because we wanted to work and participate in the community. Yet, some of these same men were speaking more English than Spanish, had more Anglo friends than we did, and were not participating as much with the fiestas. It was true that we were less Mexican than our parents, but so were the men our age. We felt we could be Mexican American and have equal rights as women.[43]

Of course, there were many other experiences that do not easily fit into the generalizations made thus far. Within the Sánchez family, for example, two married women whose husbands were in the Army had very different experiences in the world of work. Helen Sánchez got a job as a riveter in a defense plant before her husband joined the service. She worked the swing shift at Lockheed while Eddie, her husband, worked the graveyard shift at the shipyards in San Pedro. These plants were in full operation, working around the clock during the war. And so Eddie and Helen took advantage of the increased work, but only saw each other in passing. She got off work at 11:00 PM, caught the bus, transferred to a streetcar, and walked the rest of the long way home. "Sometimes I didn't get home until 1:30 in the morning." She got home just in time to see Eddie off to work. These were turbulent times, but Helen remembers them as memorable times, too. "We would have breakfast together. I liked it because Eddie made the tortillas."[44] But then she went to bed while Eddie went off to work.

Catalina Sánchez's husband, Emiliano, joined the Army in 1943. Catalina, called "Lena" by her family, decided to follow her husband while he was in training. To be near him, she took the train to his initial assignment. It was her first time away from home alone. In Salem, Oregon, she rented a room in a boardinghouse and got a job nearby. One day, Emiliano came to Lena and said, "It's over for you, dear. You've got to go home. They're sending us to Missouri." But Lena decided to follow him there, too. In Missouri, she lived in a small cabin near the base. When Emiliano was transferred to Pennsylvania, Lena followed him there as well and rented an apartment nearby, sharing a few more moments before Emiliano was shipped out. Soon enough it was all over, and he was sent to Europe, where he was stationed for the duration. Only then did Lena return to Los Angeles.[45]

There were other battles to be fought. Then, as now, Mexican American women had to confront negative stereotypes about themselves. During the 1930s, *pachuquismo* emerged as a cultural expression of some young people, and this added new negative views that young women had to combat. *Pachuquismo* was a style of dress, talk, and behavior that openly flaunted conventional Mexican as well as Anglo-American society. During the late 1930s and the war years, young Mexican Americans in the Southwest were usually called "Mexicans" by the media and by Anglo-Americans. The term "Chicano" was almost exclusively used by barrio residents to refer to Mexican-born youth.[46]

Many Mexican parents were shocked and outraged by the pachuco style and were especially critical of the pachucas, who were considered to represent sexuality and violence. Needless to say, the Anglo-American press also publicized the pachuca as a recent reincarnation of the "Mexican spitfire" stereotype popularized by Lupe Vélez in a series of films. For older Mexican Americans as well as Anglos, the pachuca represented a threat to the traditional roles of women.[47] Many Mexican American women who were working in the war industries had neither the time nor the opportunity to adopt the pachuca style. Elizabeth Escovedo reported that one worker, Rose Echeverría, thought of the pachucos and pachucas as "pathetic in their clown suits . . . I think they were just losers myself. And they brought a bad name to a lot of people who really didn't deserve it."[48] In another interview, Escovedo recorded Margarita Salazar as remembering that "we didn't do those things [wear outrageous clothing]. So they were really, really different." In San Diego, Marcy Gastellum, who worked as a riveter at Convair, thought that the threat of the pachucos was much exaggerated. "The pachucos used to stand in front of the Cornet Theater, but they were harmless, they never hurt anybody, they just wanted to be the little tough guy . . . show off their clothing and the way they did their hairdo. . . . No one was afraid of them. . . . We never heard of any incidents where there was violence, or killings."[49] There were also some pachucas who worked in the war industries. During the aftermath of the infamous Zoot-Suit Riots, pachucas became scapegoats in both the Mexican and the Anglo press, where they were accused of being pot-smoking prostitutes who were cultural traitors. As reported by Vicki Ruiz, a group of pachucas wrote a letter to the editor of the *Eastside Sun* to confront these allegations. The letter said, "[We] . . . are young girls who graduated from high school as honor students . . . who are now working in defense plants because we want to help win the war, . . . who have brothers, cousins, and sweethearts in all branches of the American armed forces. We have not been able to have our side of the story told."[50] Perhaps the pachucas represented the extreme in the liberation of Mexican American women from the traditional confines of their roles. Their dress style proved to be transitory, and many young women affected only elements of the style. *Pachuquismo* was a youth culture, and as women became more mature, they graduated out of the style.

The oral testimonies gathered by researchers reveal that after World War II, most Mexican American women did not overtly challenge men's roles or advocate more egalitarianism in relation to men. Many Mexican American women wanted to retain their femininity and their special roles as mothers and women within the culture. Margarita Salazar, a war worker, put it best, speaking from the vantage point of the 1970s: "Be a woman. Push for rights, but be a woman first. Some of them think they have to be more mannish to get what whey want instead of getting where they want to as a woman. Fix your hair and fight like a woman—but get what a woman should have."[51]

Marcy Gastellum remembered that "a lot of women preferred to be housewives. But many did work, because a lot of them had to. A lot of my friends quit school during my high school years to get married—most of them. The first thing on their mind was leaving school, getting married, raising a family, and letting the man go to work."[52]

Many Mexican American women were already working when the war began, but the war enabled them to get better-paying jobs. Mexican American women continued to be employed outside the home after World War II. The traditional expectations of putting family first did not change because of their wartime experience. Before the war, working had been seen as an extension of their family responsibility, supplementing the male wage earner. During the war, their work was also seen as supplemental: to help win the war and to fill in for the men while they were in the armed forces. During that time, many women reported more independence in their social lives despite very restrictive attitudes on the part of their parents. Indeed, Americanization, whether in dress, speech, expectations, or culture, progressed faster during the war than before. And pressures for Americanization would continue after the war as well. Many women, especially those who worked in industrial jobs for the first time or those few who entered the military, became more aware of their independence and abilities.

What is the relationship between Mexican American women's expanded and changed role within families or the workplace and civil rights? Naomi Quiñonez, in her study of women war workers, concluded that the wartime experience generally gave women a greater sense of control over their lives and laid the foundations for a more independent outlook: "The social agency they acquired during the war reinforced a sense of independence that held many implications as they entered the postwar period of the 1950s, when the framework for the Chicana feminism of the 1960s would be constructed."[53] As we shall see, there were many women who were activist leaders for civil rights and within home-front organizations during the war. Their experiences would continue to provide a model for civil rights activism after the war.

Remembered Identities

The war affected Mexican American men's and women's identities on many levels, and they remembered the changes in their lives as they grew old. Offering advice to the next generation, many of those interviewed by the Latinos and Latinas in World War II Project used key words like "discipline," "hard work," and "perseverance." These were values that had long been part of Mexican culture, and they were remembered as being important because they became useful as they negotiated the dangers of the war years, either as soldiers or as workers on the home front. Collectively, a new idea gained momentum, that of deserving respect for being a U.S. citizen: an American of Mexican descent. This pride in identity meant that encounters with segregation and discrimination after the war were met with a new confidence and assertiveness born of fighting and working during a momentous war.

Certainly, pride in being an American, along with the activist impulse among some men and women of Mexican descent to organize and confront injustices, predated this war. What was notable about World War II was the extent to which Mexican Americans were mobilized by the government and private industry to serve the noble cause of ending totalitarianism and advancing the goals of a democracy. Whatever identities Mexicans and Mexican Americans had constructed prior to the conflict were altered, if only by an increased awareness of the contradictions between the American promise and reality. For many, patriotism and activism went hand in hand.

Identities are never-ending constructions, elaborations of ideas and practices that are drawn from a historical culture as well as from contemporary necessities. It is evident that a monolithic Mexican or Chicano identity does not exist. It is more accurate to speak of many possible identities and to emphasize that these are in constant change. Regional, class, gender, and generational differences affected the impact of the war on Mexican Americans and the identities.

Mexican American identity may have its roots along the U.S.-Mexican border in South Texas. For Tejanos living there, the issue of loyalty and allegiance to the United States has long been a life-or-death issue. Beginning with the Alamo and then following the U.S.-Mexican War, Tejanos' national allegiance has been suspect by Anglo-Texans, who used these suspicions as rationalization to take Tejano lands, liberties, and lives. In a book published in 2003, Benjamin Johnson explores the origins of a progressive civil rights consciousness in South Texas among a small elite of Tejano businessmen and professionals who, during the years before 1920, were convinced of the need to "turn to the politics of American nationalism," mainly by accepting the goals of being loyal and educated Americans.[54] They were convinced of this strategy because of the violent repression following the Tejano uprising of El Plan de San Diego in 1915, when a group of Tejanos began an armed rebellion to reconquer the territories lost by Mexico in the U.S.-Mexican War. It was put down by the military and the Texas Rangers after many indiscriminate killings. Johnson traces the lineage of LULAC's Americanism to the leadership of middle-class Tejano progressives, men like J. T. Canales, J. Luz Sáenz, and the Idar brothers from Laredo, who all believed that they could best improve their people by embracing American values in the fight for full rights of citizenship. The defeat of the radical and separatist Plan de San Diego proved that Mexican nationalism was never going to be the salvation of people of Mexican descent in the United States. In fact, they viewed all radicalism, especially that which drew on ethnic Mexican loyalty, as being dangerous to reform efforts. This very real fear of violent repression, Johnson argues, led the progressive Tejanos to cloak their reform in 100 percent Americanism.

In Texas, the Second World War intensified the Mexican American middle-class leadership's commitment to seek legitimization and acceptance through civic involvement. In California, on the other hand, a different process was at work. California Mexican Americans did not have an established tradition of middle-class leadership, and the majority of the Mexican Americans were children of recent immigrants. For them, their identities evolved more in opposition to Americanization. In radical labor unions such as Luisa Moreno's United Cannery, Agricultural, Packing, and Allied Workers of America (UCAPAWA) and in political groups like Josefina Fierro de Bright's El Congreso, Mexican American leaders were less concerned with being accepted as Americans and more concerned with opposition to racism and economic injustice. The symbolic expression of this kind of oppositional identity was found in the pachucas/os, who were rejected by both the American and the Mexican middle class.[55]

New Mexico provided some of the first heroes of World War II. These *nuevomexicanos* prided themselves on their American identity, even while they constructed themselves as Spanish and had participated in the public celebration of their unique colonial heritage.[56] These Hispanos were proud of being descended from the first and oldest American settlers. For them, the war was a renewed validation of their loyalty to the United

States, a loyalty that they knew had been proven in the Revolutionary War, the Civil War, the Spanish-American War, World War I, and now World War II. During the 1940s, the New Mexicans joined the civil rights movements that were started by Tejanos and Californians, but they were careful to bend them to local purposes.

Outside the Southwest, where Mexicanos lived in large numbers, in other areas such as eastern Washington, the Midwest, and especially Chicago, Mexican American identities were constructed out of the past and present to give purpose and meaning to everyday life. In these places, large-scale intermarriage, a noticeable effect of the war on Mexican American family life, was a major factor complicating the evolution of Mexican American identities.

Whatever the complicated energy shaping individuals' ethnic identity after 1945, the shared experience of sacrifice and struggle during World War II, along with the belief in patriotism, formed a strong memory that could unite people who previously thought they had little in common. This became a core strength of the Mexican American civil rights struggle.

CHAPTER 5

Civil Rights on the Home Front: Leaders and Organizations

RICHARD GRISWOLD DEL CASTILLO

On December 7, 1941, Americans joined in a common struggle against the evils of Fascism, racism, and totalitarianism. The patriotic idealism of the war years pervaded everyday life, from war bond drives to United Services Organization (USO) dances; from black, white, and brown soldiers in uniform to gold stars displayed in home windows to indicate servicemen killed in action. Along with expressions of unity and patriotism, Mexican Americans and African Americans were reminded of their second-class citizenship as a nonwhite group. Public facilities like movie theaters, parks and pools, schools, and housing remained segregated. Mexican Americans were denied service at some restaurants and were victims of police brutality and miscarriages of justice, of which the Sleepy Lagoon case and the Zoot-Suit Riots were only the most dramatic examples. Wartime America contained many contradictions, and these would become more evident in the postwar period.

Mexican American activism in fighting against discrimination and segregation did not wait until after the war. Actually, protest and activism became more widespread and officially sanctioned because of the war. Before World War II, Mexican American civil rights did not have official recognition. Because of the wartime experience, more and more Mexican Americans came to realize that local customs and practices were more than hurtful and insulting to individuals; they were also part of a larger evil: racism—a malady that was being opposed by the U.S. government and many Anglo-Americans. The kinds of injustices that African Americans, Native Americans, and Mexican Americans had experienced for centuries were now interpreted by officials as damaging to the war effort, either by hampering the production of war materials or by providing propaganda points for the Axis powers.

This chapter is about the Mexican American organizations and individuals on the home front who fought to achieve fuller citizenship and participation in American life while their brothers and fathers were fighting against the same evils abroad. It is about changes that took place in people's ideas and practices as they developed a new level of civil rights consciousness, one that was shaped out of their personal experiences with racial prejudice and given new urgency by the rhetoric of the fight to save democracy.

The Discourse of Civil Rights

Mario T. García, in his book *Mexican Americans: Leadership, Ideology, and Identity, 1930–1960,* discussed the ways in which diverse individuals shared a common generational experience and outlook. This "Mexican American Generation," he proposed, "believed not only in achieving civil rights but in protecting and advancing them by engaging in a process of political integration."[1] This age group had been shaped by their experiences during the Great Depression and the Mexican repatriation drives in the 1930s, but World War II became the glue that held them together as a generation. That conflict gave them a collective investment in the American political system and provided them a future agenda with which to confront discrimination and prejudice. Their discourse, engendered by the wartime contradictions between patriotism and bigotry, formed the Mexican American civil rights movement of the 1950s as well as the Chicano civil rights movement of the 1960s. This new consciousness, which included a self-confidence and dedication to lasting change, was born in these crucial years. The diversity of changing consciousness and activity can be seen in the wartime stories of a sample of prominent Mexican American leaders.

Carlos Eduardo Castañeda and the FEPC

The war forced individuals into situations they would never have imagined and educated them in a new kind of reality, one they would never forget. This was the case for Carlos Eduardo Castañeda, a historian and professor who got his formal education in civil rights as an assistant director and then director of the regional office of the Fair Employment Practices Committee (FEPC) during the war. Castañeda was born in

Mexico but raised in the United States. During the 1930s, he became a naturalized U.S. citizen and earned a Ph.D. from the University of Texas. As a Mexican growing up on the border, and then as a librarian and academic, he had bitter experiences with prejudice. Referred to as "the Mexican" by his Anglo colleagues at the University of Texas, in 1933 Castañeda was forced to leave because of anti-Mexican prejudices. He subsequently took a job as superintendent of schools in Del Rio, Texas, a border town where one of the first battles against public segregation had been launched. Castañeda came to know the community leaders who, in 1930, began one of the first desegregation lawsuits in Texas. Although the lawsuit failed, it mobilized public awareness in South Texas and provided an impetus for the formation of LULAC chapters throughout the region. It also attracted many future important Tejano civil rights leaders from South Texas to the cause: J. T. (José Tomás) Canales, Manuel C. Gonzales, Alonso Perales, and Eleuterio Escobar.[2] Despite the failure of the court to outlaw segregation, the public discussion of the issue remained on everyone's mind. The need to placate the community's dissatisfaction with the segregated system in Del Rio may have been a factor in naming a Tejano, Carlos Castañeda, to the superintendent's job.

After a few years working as superintendent, Castañeda was able to return to the University of Texas Library largely because of his academic success in the initial publication of his multivolume work, *Our Catholic Heritage in Texas, 1519–1936* (Austin: Van Boeckman-Jones Company, 1936–1958). In this work and others, he pioneered a vision of American history in which the Spanish and Mexican contributions became much more important than previously.[3] While at the University, Gonzales came to know George I. Sánchez, a professor who in 1940 was the president-elect of LULAC and who published a book, *The Forgotten People*, analyzing the root causes of the poverty and lack of education of native New Mexicans.[4]

When the war broke out, officials in Washington offered Castañeda a job as the associate director of the regional office of the FEPC in Dallas. For the next few years, he spent a great deal of time traveling throughout the Southwest gathering evidence of employment discrimination. This was a formative experience, seeing firsthand and directly from the people the widespread and pervasive prejudice that kept working Mexican Americans in low-paying menial jobs.[5] He met with employers and union officials who, when confronted with complaints from their employees, stonewalled and delayed complying with the federal directives. Castañeda tried to resolve some of the complaints on an individual level but mostly failed. Over time, he grew frustrated with the federal bureaucracy, which delayed and then cancelled public hearings specifically focused on Mexican American workers. After investigating a Phelps-Dodge copper mine in Silver City, New Mexico, he wrote:

> Not a single Latin-American is employed in a supervisory capacity. It is the set policy of the company to employ only Anglos in the supervisory positions. Many Latin-American employees with long years of experience in the various departments, who could efficiently perform the duties of supervisors, are refused an opportunity and are not even given a trial.[6]

Castañeda came to see that the FEPC's policy of resolving individual complaints of discrimination ignored the larger issue, that of systematic racism and prejudice. He wrote in one report: "The settlement of individual cases may be made to give the appearance of a correction of discriminatory practices without in fact curing the illness."[7]

Another example of Castañeda's education in the limits of civil rights organizing was his work with oil company executives and union officials in Houston. Working with W. Don Ellinger, the director of the Dallas office of the FEPC, over a period of two years, Castañeda organized an attack on eight major oil refineries and their unions to force them to change their discriminatory policies, presenting scores of specific grievances, most having to do with employment, wage, and promotion inequities. After a great deal of work and numerous meetings, the result was negligible by the end of the war. One union and two oil companies did make a token effort to comply with the FEPC directives. In 1945, Castañeda was appointed the regional director of the Fair Employment Practices Committee, but within months Congress discontinued funding for the agency. This ended further federal involvement with civil rights compliance initiatives until the late 1960s.[8]

The war years taught Carlos Castañeda that the rhetoric of good intentions coming from the U.S. government could not be counted on to bring about changes in discrimination and segregation. In the testimony he gave before the Committee on Labor and Education chaired by Senator Dennis Chavez from New Mexico in March 1945, Castañeda offered his assessment of the future course:

> I would say that we in Texas are convinced that the solution to the problem is legislation . . . that can be effectively enforced so as to restrain

that small, but very aggressive minority, that, because of ignorance, perhaps, practice discrimination that brings shame upon our American democracy.[9]

In 1946, Castaneda returned to the University of Texas, where he devoted the rest of his life to teaching and writing, occasionally renewing his contact with his old LULAC acquaintances to help them with their various desegregation projects. He died in 1958 before seeing a rebirth of civil rights organizing in the next generation.

Luisa Moreno and the Labor Movement

Luisa Moreno was a labor activist for whom World War II offered new challenges and opportunities for change. A Guatemalan-born immigrant who came with her parents to Oakland, California, when she was nine years old, Luisa grew to identify with the underdog, especially women workers.[10] Though not of Mexican origin, she was an active leader in developing a consciousness of civil rights among Mexican Americans. She devoted her life to working for and with Mexican Americans as well as other ethnic groups and changed others by her example and commitment. Bert Corona, a labor activist who lived through World War II, remembered: "I admired the fierceness of Luisa Moreno's spirit, the strength of her will of granite and dedication as a community leader. She placed substance before style. Her behavior was simple, direct, and honest. She enjoyed the respect or the affection of political and labor allies and of her rivals alike."[11]

In the 1930s, Luisa lived in New York City, where she saw the sweatshops and horrible conditions endured by immigrant laborers. Soon Puerto Rican activists introduced her to Socialist ideas, and, at the beginning of the Depression, she joined the Communist Party, wanting to fight against economic injustices for all people. This was not unusual at the time. Many regarded the Depression as proof of capitalism's failure, and Communism seemed like a viable alternative. An additional attraction for Luisa was that in the 1930s the Communist Party was active in protesting segregation, police abuse, and deportations. It was here that she first became a committed social activist. In 1935, she got her first job as a labor organizer for the American Delegation of Labor.[12] Thereafter she worked in the Deep South, organizing African American and Latin workers in agriculture, and then in 1937 she became an organizer for

UCAPAWA (United Cannery, Agricultural, Packing, and Allied Workers of America), a union mostly of Latino field, shed, and cannery workers.[13] While in Texas, Luisa got to know Emma Tenayuca, a Communist who had organized a union to help women in the pecan-shelling industry in San Antonio.[14] Moreno spent three months in the Lower Rio Grande Valley, where she saw the harsh life of the farmworkers. She worked as a union organizer and made contacts with vegetable and fruit canning and packing industry workers. She also helped to organize the field workers who harvested beets, sweet corn, cabbage, spinach, and other vegetables for only fifty cents a day.[15]

In 1938, Luisa moved to San Diego, California, to help the fish and cannery workers organize unions in the tuna industry.[16] While still in San Diego, Moreno traveled to Los Angeles and met with Josefina Fierro de Bright to help organize the civil rights group El Congreso de Pueblos que Hablan Español (the Spanish-Speaking Peoples' Congress). This group planned to bring together Mexican American unions, mutual aid associations, political clubs, and other organizations to work for an end to segregation and discrimination at all levels. El Congreso met for the first time in Los Angeles on April 29, 1939.[17]

For the next few years Luisa lived in Los Angeles, where she joined the Anti-Nazi League and worked to organize rallies to mobilize people against the Axis (this was before Pearl Harbor).[18] Moreno was the chief organizer of UCAPAWA in Los Angeles and San Diego. She traveled constantly, trying to break the discriminatory hiring habits of canneries and factories. In San Diego, she was successful in getting nondiscrimination pledges from several packing companies.[19]

During the war, Luisa spoke out against the removal of Japanese Americans to relocation camps and worked with the Sleepy Lagoon Defense Committee. Speaking before the Los Angeles Grand Jury that was investigating the Sleepy Lagoon case, she warned that tensions created by the media's sensationalism would result in violence unless corrective measures were taken.[20] Her prophecy turned into a reality. In June of 1943, the Los Angeles Zoot-Suit Riots began, sparked by violence between soldiers and sailors on leave and young Chicanos.

Along with members of El Congreso and other Mexican American community leaders, Luisa was involved in forming a defense committee on behalf of the youngsters who had been arrested by the police even though they had been attacked by the servicemen.[21] She worked with San Diego officials to try to prevent a similar outbreak of anti-Mexican violence there.

Figure 5.1. Luisa Moreno in 1940. A labor organizer and activist during World War II, Luisa Moreno lived in San Diego, where she organized women cannery workers to gain better wages. She also protested the treatment of young people during the so-called Zoot-Suit Riots in 1943. Courtesy of the California Ethnic Multicultural Archives, Department of Special Collections, Donald C. Davidson Library, University of California, Santa Barbara, California.

After the war, Luisa seemed to settle down and stay away from labor organizing. She married a U.S. sailor, Gray Bemis, whom she had met in San Diego during the war, and they built a house there. While Bemis worked as a manager for the Consolidated Pipe & Supply Company, she wrote books and essays of an autobiographical nature and occasionally gave guest lectures in adult education classes about civil rights and labor organizing.

This domestic tranquility ended in 1948 when she was called before the California Un-American Activities Committee headed by Jack Tenney. Hunting for radicals and especially Communists, they found a ready victim in Luisa Moreno. At the time, she was awaiting approval of her citizenship application. Given the tenor of the time, this was denied and she was ordered deported. Awaiting her departure, Luisa gave a speech before the annual convention of the California Congress of Industrial Organizations (CIO) Council in 1949, in which she said:

> Strange things are happening in this land. Things that are truly alien and threaten the very existence of cherished traditions . . . Yes, tragically, the unmistakable signs are before us, who really love America. And it is we who must sound the alarm, for the workers and the people to hear and take notice. For it seems that today, as the right to organize and strike was fought for and won, as the new labor agreements were fought for and won, as the fight against discrimination is being fought but far from won, so the fight for the very fundamentals of American democracy must again be fought for and re-established.[22]

In the end, World War II cultivated a love of American democracy for Luisa Moreno. Her vision was of a country that was committed to social justice, and she wanted to work with others to mold a better society. Tragically, the U.S. government rejected her. She died in Guatemala in 1992.

George I. Sánchez and LULAC

George Isidore Sánchez dedicated his life to improving educational conditions for Mexican Americans. World War II gave him a new vision of the national dimensions of the fight against segregation and discrimination. Born in Albuquerque, Sánchez came from an old New Mexican family that had lived there since colonial times. As a Hispano, he grew up with practical knowledge of the effects of poverty and prejudice on Spanish-speaking children. Prior to World War II, Sánchez worked as an administrator and teacher at a small rural school, and he studied to get his B.A. degree from the University of New Mexico, an M.S. from the University of Texas, and an Ed.D. from the University of California, Berkeley. Before the war, Sánchez had developed a critique of the educational system's treatment of Spanish-speaking children. In published articles and speeches, he strongly attacked standardized tests, segregation, and unequal school funding for Hispanic students. As a result of his controversial positions, the University of New Mexico denied him tenure. In 1940, he was appointed as a professor at the University of Texas. That same year he was elected the president of LULAC and published a book, *Forgotten People: A Study of New Mexicans*, a study of the children in Taos, New Mexico, showing how discrimination had perpetuated poverty.

In Texas, the most visible and notable Mexican American organization during World War II was the League of United Latin American Citizens (LULAC), which had been founded in 1929 in Harlingen, Texas. This venerable organization was composed mostly of Mexican Americans who fervently believed in the American dream. They were led by middle-class leaders who believed that it was possible to work with the existing institutions to improve economic, social, and political conditions for Mexican Americans. They considered racism to be an aberration that would be changed through self-improvement and education.

LULAC drew on the ideas that were first articulated during World War I by the Tejano progressives who, in the words of Benjamin Johnson, "were as intent on the modernization of their own people, the fitting them with the skills and attitudes necessary to compete in the twentieth-century United States, as they were in confronting Anglo racism."[23] This vision of future reform and uplift was expressed in the formation of several organizations that preceded LULAC: El Primer Congreso Mexicanista in 1911, the Order of the Sons of America in 1921, and the Order of the Knights of America in 1927. With LULAC in 1929, the reformist impulses of a small but cohesive group of middle-class Tejanos continued the ongoing struggle to improve both Mexican American and Anglo-American society.

The LULACers believed that Mexican Americans should embrace education; learn to speak English; become full, participating U.S. citizens; and be loyal to the American government.[24] Their collective goal, acceptance and integration within America, was greatly advanced during World War II, as LULAC members volunteered or were drafted and LULAC chapters turned their energies toward patriotic endeavors. In El Paso, for example, the local chapter taught classes on civil defense and collected gift packages for servicemen overseas. As George Garza, one of the LULAC leaders, said, LULAC "gave unreservedly of its manpower to the service of its country."[25] Or, as the LULAC *News* reported in 1945, "The primary or general objective of the League, to teach Americans of Latin American origin to be better and more loyal citizens, has been accomplished by the war."[26] Before the war, LULAC expanded to have more than 150 councils in three states, but this number declined during the war when the male leadership joined the armed services. This gave new opportunities for people like George I. Sánchez to gain experience in civil rights actions.

The war gave Sánchez a forum to advance his critique of the inequities of American society and their impact on Mexican American youth, and he did so with great vigor, occasionally causing his more conservative LULAC associates some apprehension.[27] An example of Sánchez's forceful criticism was his 1943 essay, "Pachucos in the Making," in which he attacked the discriminatory policies and racial prejudices of the Los Angeles city government, school system, and police, blaming them for the creation of the idea that pachucos were juvenile delinquents.[28] Sánchez saw teenage violence among Mexican Americans as the result of segregation and poverty forced on them by a racist society. The pachuco was the result of a "cancerous growth within the majority group which is gnawing at the vitals of democracy and the American way of life."[29]

By 1943, the government appointed him Latin American consultant to the U.S. Office of Civilian Defense and Education and then a specialist-consultant to the Inter-American Educational Foundation. Using his contacts through these offices and his position as president of LULAC, Sánchez was probably the most powerful spokesperson in the nation for Mexican Americans. Led by Sánchez, the LULAC leadership sought to push white Texans toward integration in the schools by appealing to the need for wartime solidarity. In one speech, for example, Sánchez told the National Congress of Parents and Teachers that the continued segregation of Mexican children did "more harm to Pan-Americanism than a shipload of Nazi agents."[30] Working with the South Texas lawyer Alonzo Perales, Sánchez and LULAC helped gather affidavits from Mexican Americans and Mexicans who had experienced segregation and exclusion. Some of these testimonies were later published as part of Perales' 1948 book, *Are We Good Neighbors?*. Some of the cases of discrimination were published in *La Prensa*, the San Antonio newspaper, and those involving a Mexican citizen became part of formal actions by the Mexican consulate.[31]

In 1945, Congressional Medal of Honor–winner Sergeant Macario García, a native of Coahuila, Mexico, was attacked by a man with a baseball bat when he protested being denied service at a local café near Hous-

Figure 5.2. Alonso S. Perales, one of the founding members of LULAC, was a civil rights activist whose life spanned the period 1920 to 1960. During World War II, he helped draft the Texas bill that would outlaw discrimination based on race (see epilogue). His book *Are We Good Neighbors?* (1948) was an indictment of anti-Mexican racist actions that contradicted sentiments of the Good Neighbor policy. Courtesy of University of Texas at Austin Libraries.

ton, Texas. He was on his way to a ceremony honoring his war record. Other dramatic incidents mobilized the Mexican community. One involving a group of Mexican congressmen and a senator who were denied service in the West Texas town of Pecos in March 1945 because they were Mexican led to lengthy commentary in the Spanish-language press, both in Texas and in Mexico. Other cases of discrimination came from among the thousands of Mexican and Mexican American farmworkers who migrated across the state each year, following the crops. In November 1944, a group of Mexican workers refused to work for farmers in a region of West Texas because a local restaurant refused to serve Mexicans. A violent incident and near riot of one thousand farmworkers in Levelland, Texas, on October 30, 1943, illustrated that farmworkers were willing to protest discrimination. The governor of Texas, Coke Stevenson, ordered an investigation because of concern from Washington that this incident would damage Inter-American cooperation.[32]

Sánchez and other LULAC leaders actively used the Mexican consulate to pressure the U.S. government to do something about the conditions of segregation and discrimination. Sánchez worked with the Mexican consulate to promote a Texas civil rights law, the Spears bill, which was introduced in 1945. The proposal prohibited discrimination against persons of Mexican descent and imposed a penalty of $500 and/or thirty days in jail. It passed the Texas Senate but did not pass the House.[33] The bill was opposed by the Texas Good Neighbor Commission, composed of liberals who had supported the wartime rhetoric of equality and fairness but who now feared that this law would open up society for the integration of African Americans.[34]

After the war, Sánchez remained active in LULAC and returned to academia, becoming chair of the Department of History and Philosophy Education at the University of Texas. He was involved in several key lawsuits challenging school segregation, and in 1950, he persuaded the governor to create a Texas Council on Human Relations to suggest ways of improving race relations in Texas.[35] In 1952, with a grant from the Marshall Trust, Sánchez worked with other Mexican Americans to found a national civil rights organization, the American Council for Spanish-Speaking People (ACSSP). For the next ten years, under Sánchez' leadership, this organization worked with LULAC and the American GI Forum (AGIF) to advance the attack against segregation. Sánchez assisted in the landmark 1954 civil rights case of *Hernández v. State*, in which the Supreme Court ruled that Mexican Americans were a special class and that their exclusion from juries trying Mexican-heritage defendants was a violation of their constitutional rights.[36] Sánchez also involved the ACSSP in litigating *Hernández v. Driscoll Consolidated Independent School District* in 1955, in which a federal court ruled that segregation of Mexican American students as a group was "arbitrary and unreasonable" and in violation of the law.[37] These cases, along with others that LULAC was involved with, would support the Supreme Court's 1954 decision in *Brown v. Board of Education* that segregation based on race was a violation of civil rights.

World War II broadened George I. Sánchez's experience in fighting for the civil rights of Mexican Americans, schoolchildren in particular. His wartime experience enabled him to form new alliances and conceive of Hispanic issues with a national rather than a regional perspective. His activism and militancy made him the foremost advocate for bilingual education programs as well as modern civil rights organizations.

The Fight against Segregation in California

In 1930, the Mexican migrant community in Lemon Grove, California, organized to fight against the segregation of their children in the local school and won. The Lemon Grove case was the beginning of a long history of litigation supported by Mexican American communities and their leaders that would lead to the final prohibition of segregation of Mexican children in California in *Mendez v. Westminster* in 1946.[38]

During the war, the struggle against segregation continued. In Los Angeles, young Mexican Americans formed the Coordinating Council for Latin-American Youth, led by Manuel Ruiz Jr.[39] Together with participating liberal Anglo-Americans, Ruiz and the Coordinating Council were active in youth job programs, desegregation issues, defense against racial prejudice, and political action. The Council acted as a "spokesperson" for the Mexican American community in Los Angeles, advocating improved recreational facilities in the barrios and special job training programs for youth. Its members lobbied the local school board to stop the segregation of Mexican American students in the public schools and, working with high-level state and local officials, unsuccessfully sought to repeal Section 8003 of the California Constitution, which allowed for this kind of segregation.[40] The Council acted as a watchdog, filing complaints when they found evidence of violation of federal guidelines regarding employment and housing, and complaining to the Los Angeles newspapers that continued to publish derogatory and stereotypical portrayals of Mexican American youth as pachucos. In the political sphere, the Council formed nonpartisan action committees that supported the electoral campaigns of a number of Mexican Americans who were running for local offices.[41] While none of their candidates won office, their organization paved the way for the future electoral victory of Edward Roybal, the first Mexican American elected to the Los Angeles City

Council in almost one hundred years. As was true with some other organizations, the Coordinating Council for Latin-American Youth ceased to exist when the war ended, killed off by a postwar recession and the infusion of Mexican American GIs returning from the war who sought to create organizations that were more responsive to their needs than those of youth. The Council's leadership, men like Manuel Ruiz Jr. and Eduardo Quevedo, continued to be active and were later part of the group that helped to found the California-based Mexican American Political Association (MAPA) in the 1960s.

Another individual in Southern California who was an active leader in the fight against segregation and discrimination was Ignacio López, editor of *El Espectador*, a Spanish-language newspaper serving communities in San Bernardino and Riverside Counties. Ignacio López was well educated, having received two master's degrees, in history and Spanish, from UC Berkeley. During the war, his wife, Beatriz, edited the newspaper, which claimed to be California's largest Spanish-language weekly. López and his wife used his newspaper not only to help organize assistance for the war effort but also to keep people informed about civil rights issues.[42]

Before the war, López had been active in publicizing acts of discrimination against Mexican Americans, and he had worked with various Mexican American organizations to advertise boycotts and protests that called attention to racism. In 1939, for example, López rallied the community of Ontario, both Mexican American and Anglo-American, to protest racial discrimination against Pedro Tucker, who had been prohibited from sitting in the middle aisle of a movie theater. After a boycott of the theater and many angry meetings, the owner signed a no-discrimination pledge.[43] Throughout the war years, López, with his newspaper and the Unity Clubs—precursors of the Unity Leagues discussed below—also organized boycotts and protests against discrimination in public facilities and restaurants.

The pages of *El Espectador* during the war chronicled Mexican American concerns and reflected the activism of the period. They frequently reported cases in which the Mexican consul lodged protests with officials of the local government concerning discrimination against Mexican nationals. On August 11, 1942, for example, López reported that the Mexican consul had filed a protest against the city of Colton for discrimination at the municipal pool. The mayor of Colton referred this matter to his legal counsel and told Ignacio López that Mexicans were free to use the pool and public parks without limit, but that it was preferable that they use the pool located in the southern part of the city.[44] In October of the same year, *El Espectador* reported that a group of Mexican railway workers had visited the Mexican consulate to complain that the Santa Fe Railroad refused to let them use facilities reserved for white workers and that they had been told to use the changing room and bathroom facilities marked for the "raza negra" (black race).[45] And in December, he reported that the Club Cívico Latinoamericano had won a victory in its battle with the California Portland Cement Company, forcing the company to open up hiring of Mexican nationals. The company, through its union, had a contract with the government that specifically stated that it would only employ U.S. citizens. The Club Cívico, whose members included Mexican nationals with sons in the U.S. military, protested to the War Manpower Commission that this was a violation of the federal guidelines that stipulated that there could be no discrimination by color or nationality.[46]

López went beyond reporting the activities of others to actively organizing as well. In December of 1943, López and a group of Mexican American leaders filed a lawsuit against the city of San Bernardino because of discrimination practiced at the municipal pool. Ultimately, they won the case when the federal court ruled that the prohibition of entrance based on race was unconstitutional. The victory was due to López's assistance in forming a Comité de Defensa Mexicoamericano, which dedicated itself to fighting segregation and discrimination in public places. This case had been its first project.[47]

In 1944 López and a group of Mexican American defendants successfully sued the city of San Bernardino for illegal discrimination in its public parks and pools. The court ruled that the city's "conduct . . . is illegal and is in violation of petitioners' rights and privileges, as guaranteed by the Constitution of the United States of America, and as secured and guaranteed to them as citizens of the United States of America, as particularly provided under the Fifth and Fourteenth Amendments."[48] This decision was one of several that the Supreme Court cited as precedents in the landmark *Brown v. Board of Education* desegregation decision in 1954.

Encouraged by occasional victories, López continued to expose cases of discrimination. On August 10, 1945, after the end of the war, *El Espectador* reported a story about a Mexican American veteran, Angel Serna, and four other GIs who were denied service at a restaurant by an Anglo owner who told them that he did not serve "Mexicans, Niggers, or Japs." Several of the GIs denied service were descendants of the pioneer founders of

Pomona. The four immediately hired a lawyer and sued the owner of the café, the Redwood Inn, for violating the section of the California Civil Code that specifically prohibited discrimination by color or race in public facilities.[49]

After the war, López organized about fifty Mexican Americans in the Pomona and Ontario areas, most of them veterans of World War II, to form the Unity League, an organization dedicated to increasing Mexican American political power and awareness in advancing civil rights. Unity Leagues soon sprang up all over Southern California, helping to organize Mexican American political campaigns.[50] For the next few years, the Unity Leagues had some success in electing Mexican Americans to local offices.

Mexican American Community Organizations and World War II

As we have seen, during the 1930s Mexican American communities all over the Southwest had developed organizations to give a focus to their social, economic, political, and cultural concerns. When the war came along, almost all of these supported the war by reorienting their efforts. One example out of many was El Congreso del Pueblo de Habla Española, which had been founded in 1939 by Luisa Moreno and Josefina Fierro de Bright. The purpose of this organization was to attempt a national coalition of Spanish-speaking groups that would be dedicated to problems of discrimination, poverty, lack of education, and political disenfranchisement. By 1942, the leaders of this group, although they continued to work toward these goals, increasingly took on the war effort as a major focus. In April 1942, they organized a Victory Program, which brought together leaders of Spanish-speaking organizations, including labor unions, to "discuss one or two phases of the war effort that affects our people." The culmination of this meeting was the drafting of a program delineating how Mexican Americans could help the war effort. This was presented to all Spanish-speaking groups in California.[51]

In addition to being the catalyst for the reorientation of existing clubs, mutual aid societies, and religious groups, the war motivated many Mexican Americans to form new organizations dedicated solely to helping the war effort. Christine Marín, in researching Mexican American communities in Arizona during the war, chronicled the hundreds of ways that they actively responded to the national emergency. Many of the mutual aid societies, originally established to provide low-cost burial insurance for working-class members, shifted their efforts toward the war. The Club Latino Americana and La Sociedad Mutualista Porfirio Díaz, for example, helped recruit volunteer pickers to bring in the cotton harvest in the Phoenix area during a severe labor shortage.[52] Using the local Spanish-language press, they recruited thousands of Mexican American workers to harvest this vital commodity (cotton was used in making parachutes). Using their local organizations, the Mexican communities in Arizona had drives to gather surplus scrap metal, rubber, and other commodities for the war effort in addition to organizing war-bond drives.

One organization was composed entirely of women, the Asociación Hispano-Americana de Madres y Esposas (Spanish-American Mothers and Wives Association). Besides participating in the bond drives and other volunteer activities in the larger community, the women in the Asociación organized drives to collect scrap metal, promote Victory gardens, offer child-care services for women working in war industries, make donations to the Red Cross, and provide recreational activities for servicemen. The Asociación published a community newsletter called "Chatter," gathering news from the Mexican American community and the GIS fighting in Europe and the Far East, which they then sent to the servicemen to keep up their morale. This Asociación continued to be a community organization until 1976.[53]

In Tucson, Mexican American women members of the Alianza Hispano-Americana organized Red Cross drives and helped form a local chapter of the Asociación de Madres. They in turn cooperated with other ethnic organizations to organize fund drives and events to boost morale. One of the important missions of the organization was to console those families who had lost a son, brother, or husband to the war. They also assisted those who spoke only Spanish in filling out government forms associated with the war. Many of the Asociación members kept up a correspondence with lonely servicemen and prayed in special novenas and masses for men overseas.[54] After the war, the Tucson Asociación provided seed money to establish Veterans Clubs for Mexican American GIS.

There were many other organizations within Mexican American communities that provided the basis for community organizing during the war, but the details of their activities are lost to history. In the aftermath of the Los Angeles Zoot-Suit Riots, the Federal Bureau of Investigation sent a team of agents to the Mexican section of the city to research community organizations in Southern California.[55] The federal government feared that perhaps Fascists had infiltrated Mexican organizations and

Figure 5.3. The Asociación Hispano-Americana de Madres y Esposas (Spanish American Mothers and Wives Association), c. 1945. Founded in 1944 in Tucson, this organization of Mexican American women sought to keep up the morale of Mexican American servicemen. They raised more than one million dollars for war bonds and did other volunteer activities in the community. It lasted until 1976. Courtesy of the Arizona Historical Society, Tucson.

were behind the riots. As noted earlier, these fears proved completely unfounded, but in the survey process, the FBI compiled a fairly complete profile of most of the community organizations in Southern California in 1944. Unfortunately, the FBI has blacked out names of individuals and some details. This organizational matrix for Mexican Americans in Los Angeles and the surrounding communities was probably duplicated in other metropolitan areas with a high Mexican American population, places such as Albuquerque, San Antonio, and Tucson. In any case, the list of organizations suggests the degree to which Mexican Americans were actively involved in shaping their community life during World War II.

LIST OF MEXICAN AMERICAN ORGANIZATIONS IN LOS ANGELES IN 1944

A. Religious Organizations

Catholic Churches of predominantly Mexican American congregation (34 Catholic parish churches listed by name)

Protestant Churches of predominantly Mexican American congregation (6 churches listed by name)

B. Media

Spanish-language newspapers

Acción

Alianza

Artista

Cinelandia

Eco de México

El Antifascista

El Comercio

El Informador

El Nazareno

Heraldo de México

La Esperanza

La Nube y el Fuego en el Desierto

La Opinión

Las Noticias

Sports Page

Vida

Spanish-language radio stations

FWKW

KFOX

KGFJ

KMTR

C. Secondary Organizations

A la California Club—social club

Agrupación Leales Españoles—social club

Américas Unidas—international affairs

Asociación Católica de la Juventud Mexicana—religious social club

Beneficencia Mexicana—immigrant aid society

Cámara de Comercio de California—business association

Cámara Mexicana de Comercio de Los Ángeles—business association

Casa de España—cultural association

Círculo México—business association

Citizens Committee for the Defense of Mexican American Youth—Sleepy Lagoon Defense Committee

Club Olivera—social club

Congreso Nacional de los Pueblos de Habla Española—youth assistance, political organization

Coordinating Council for Latin American Youth—youth assistance
La Alianza Hispano-Americana—mutual aid society
La Sociedad Beneficia Hidalgo—mutual aid
Las Damas Católicas—religious organization
Los Angeles Youth Advisory Board—youth assistance
Madres del Soldado Hispano-Americano—assisting war effort
Movimiento Afiliado al Comité Auxiliar Pro-Huérfanos—charity
    organization
Sociedad Cooperativa Incorporada Frente Único—charity
    organization
Sociedad Española de Beneficencia Mutua—mutual aid society
Southern California Council of Inter-American Affairs—social action
Unión Nacional Sinarquista—Fascist organization
Woodmen of the World (chapters in East Los Angeles)—social club
(80 additional social clubs in East Los Angeles given by name)
SOURCE: "RACIAL CONDITIONS (SPANISH-MEXICAN ACTIVITIES) IN
LOS ANGELES FIELD STATION," FBI REPORT, JANUARY 14, 1944.

As can be seen by scanning the names and purposes of the various organizations listed above, there was a wide variety of formal associations within the barrios of Southern California, ranging from religious groups to social and political clubs. The diversity of interests and orientations suggests the challenges that federal officials faced in finding community representatives. The diversity also suggests the difficulties that political organizers faced in trying to unite the Mexican American people around issues of civil rights. During the war, the male leadership of these organizations was unstable because many were drafted or volunteered. As a result, women increasingly played more prominent roles in many of these groups. The preponderance of social clubs as opposed to politically oriented ones might be due to wartime needs for recreation and escape. The number of *mutualistas* and charitable organizations attest to the value of self-help within the communities. This sample taken from Los Angeles could be multiplied many times when considering the large Mexican American communities in the small towns and cities elsewhere in the Southwest.

Generally, organized labor was not very hospitable to Mexican Americans or Mexicans who wanted to challenge their unequal treatment. The FEPC investigations in New Mexico, Arizona, and southern Colorado showed that unions were generally opposed to giving equal treatment to Mexican workers. An exception to this resistance was the action of the CIO in Southern California, where the union worked to get public housing for Mexican CIO members and fought against racist housing restrictions.[56] The CIO also worked with Mexican American union members to protest job discrimination in war industries and to promote the opening up of job-training programs to minorities.[57] Historian Zaragosa Vargas has shown how Mexican Americans joined labor unions in California and used them to work for their civil rights throughout the war period. By 1945, large numbers of Mexican American workers had joined unions in California like the CIO, the International Longshoremen's and Warehousemen's Union (ILWU), the United Steel Workers of America (USWA), and the International Ladies Garment Workers Union (ILGWU). They also produced union leaders, such as the previously discussed Luisa Moreno, who led them in demanding their civil rights.[58]

Civil Rights Activism and World War II

The documentary evidence gathered by the FBI during the war to search for possible subversive activities—the manuscripts, letters, and documents of Luisa Moreno and Manuel Ruiz, and daily publications of *El Espectador*—attest to the activism of Mexican Americans in California during the war years. In Texas and New Mexico, emerging leaders like Carlos Castañeda and George Sánchez worked within organizations like the FEPC and LULAC and, with others, educated and politicized a new Mexican American constituency. Labor union leaders like Luisa Moreno mobilized multinational coalitions of workers to confront discrimination at home during the war. Thousands of Mexican Americans gained experience in demanding civil rights within the labor movement. Throughout the Southwest, new Mexican American patriotic groups sprang into existence for the sole purpose of supporting the war effort. Some organizations were established to work for civil rights and against segregation. Other established organizations reoriented their efforts toward helping win the war. Finally, some Mexican American organizations died out or remained inactive because most of their members were serving in the armed forces. Within the new and established groups, Mexican American leaders were creating a discourse about citizenship and rights. After the war, they would help lead a new kind of civil rights movement.

Epilogue: Civil Rights and the Legacy of War

RICHARD STEELE AND RICHARD
GRISWOLD DEL CASTILLO

In the early summer of 1943, the Texas Legislature adopted a resolution affirming its commitment to civil rights for Mexican Americans. It was an unprecedented step and one extolled at the time by George I. Sánchez, a professor at the University of Texas, as heralding a revolution in the status of Mexican Americans. In fact, revolutionary change was a long way off. The resolution and concurrent events marked only the beginning of a much larger advance in civil rights activism. The war years intensified the process by which Americans of Mexican descent organized, asserted themselves, gained recognition from government, and slowly made inroads in the institutions and attitudes that had relegated Mexican Americans to second-class citizenship.

The outcome was a complex interaction between the pressures that Mexican Americans could bring to bear, and the interest the established order had in facilitating change or clinging to the status quo. The House Concurrent Resolution of mid-1943 was an outgrowth of fear on the part of Texas' governing bodies that in the absence of signs of goodwill, the state would not share in the bounty of cheap Mexican labor upon which its prosperity was largely dependent.[1] But when that fear dissipated, the status quo regained ascendance. At the time of the resolution's passage, Texas had two hundred thousand fewer farmworkers than it had had two years earlier, largely the result of workers leaving the farms for the military and for jobs in the defense industry. While employers in other states had made up similar deficiencies by participating in the Bracero Program, Mexico had denied the growers of Texas this privilege because of the state's abysmal human rights record. That spring, the legislature adopted a Concurrent Resolution on the Good Neighbor, and in late June the governor, citing the resolution, declared that it was the public policy of the state to give "full and equal accommodations, advantages and privileges of all public places of business or amusement to Mexicans [including Mexican Americans] and other Latin Americans" and directed "the citizens of the state to observe the principle of the Good Neighbor Policy."[2] The proclamation was a victory for Mexican Americans, the first of its kind. In September, the governor established a Good Neighbor Commission to "promote the principles of Christ in human relations" while preserving "the honor and prestige" of the state. The state's leadership had been introduced to the problems and aspirations of its Mexican Americans, and the time was ripe for the reforms sought. But circumstances change, and Sánchez's hopes that the action in Texas had initiated a peaceful civil rights revolution in the state that might spread to the rest of the Southwest turned out to be overly sanguine.

Anglo Texans remained wedded to their racial institutions, and the incentive to change proved inadequate. The fact that civil rights had gotten as far as they had in the state was probably attributable to the state government's fear that if discrimination was not addressed, the Mexican government would keep its citizens from going to Texas to work. But economic pressures confronting Mexicans were so great that authorities could not prevent the emigration of those seeking work north of the Rio Grande. And although the Mexican government continued throughout the war to refuse to allow contract workers to go to Texas, a constant flow of undocumented workers entered the state, and they, together with patriotic high school students, prisoners of war, and resident Mexican Americans, met grower demands. Consequently, Texas could meet its labor needs without conceding meaningful reform to Mexican Americans.

The result was that the authority and capacity of the underfunded Good Neighbor Commission, which had no power to compel compliance with its lofty principles, was not expanded, and ultimately its largest contribution to resolving the problems confronting persons of Mexican descent in Texas was its de facto acknowledgment of their existence. The difficulty in legislating civil rights was apparent when, late in the war, in 1945, the Texas legislature refused to pass a bill prohibiting racial discrimination in restaurants, an act that would have constituted a serious commitment to racial justice.[3]

The Federal Government and Civil Rights in Wartime

Securing civil rights for Mexican Americans would require a civil rights revolution, one that was not likely during the war, or for some time after.

Changes of the kind and scale needed would require federal initiatives, particularly vigorous enforcement of existing statutes as they applied to states and the enactment of additional laws expanding the meaning and application of civil rights.

The foundations for such a revolution had been laid in the 1860s and 1870s, in the immediate aftermath of the Civil War when, in an effort to ensure the civil rights of the newly emancipated slaves, the nation adopted a number of civil rights statutes and the 13th, 14th, and 15th Amendments. These provided for federal intervention on behalf of persons deprived of the right to vote and other less well-defined "civil rights." However, over the next generation, the Supreme Court, reflecting a national reaction against African Americans and Reconstruction-era reforms, handed down a series of decisions that limited the federal authority to punish discriminatory state behavior and gave it almost no jurisdiction over the acts of private individuals. The climate of hostility persisted, and for seventy-five years the ideal of equality under the law, regardless of race, was generally ignored. This began to change in the 1930s as the Roosevelt administration sought to use the 14th Amendment and Reconstruction-era statutes to prosecute civil rights cases.

During World War II, the Civil Rights Division of the Justice Department had been run by a civil rights "crusader," Victor Rotnem, and enjoyed the support of Attorney General Francis Biddle, a well-known champion of racial and ethnic minorities. This department initiated a carefully conceived campaign on behalf of minority civil rights. But the department's good intentions and crusading zeal were circumscribed by the fact that in many states, particularly in the South and Southwest, juries, from which African and Mexican Americans were customarily excluded, were hostile to federal "interference" and unlikely to bring in verdicts favorable to the government. When confronted with this reality, the department proceeded timidly.

Carefully choosing those cases that might advance its mission, the Civil Rights Division would eventually win a landmark decision in *Smith v. Allwright* (1944) that extended federal protection to persons denied the right to vote in party-conducted primary elections—a decision that looks puny from today's perspective, but one that elated civil rights advocates at the time. Nevertheless, Attorney General Biddle refused to follow through on the decision, arguing that stronger public support was necessary to successfully enforce the court decision. The people of the South, he concluded, were not ready for racial justice and, recalling the activities of the Ku Klux Klan and the South's resistance to Reconstruction, he predicted that federal initiatives might produce a popular reaction that could "easily be fanned into a terrifying conflagration." The department would back away from the issue for some twenty years.[4]

This strategy, based on realistic fears and the limits of the law, also dictated the department's response to civil rights cases involving Mexican Americans. During the war, Justice Department officials received reports of incidents of discrimination that persons of Mexican descent had suffered at the hands of private citizens and officials in Texas. The department, in refusing to act, explained that the discriminatory actions of private citizens (restaurant owners, for example), did not constitute a violation of federal law, and that while those instigated by public officials might be prosecuted, local prejudices made an indictment impossible to obtain. In a report to the secretary of state explaining the department's inaction, the head of the Criminal Division cited two instances in which Texas grand juries had refused to return a bill of indictment. In one, he noted, although half the county's population was of Mexican descent, no Mexican Americans served on the panel. In these circumstances, the department preferred to pass on cases referred to it to Texas authorities, from whom federal officials and the Mexican government could usually expect assurances that state officials were examining the situation, or had approached the person complained about, or had secured the removal of a sign, or some other action. Fear of provoking the "conflagration" that worried Biddle played less of a role in limiting federal involvement in Mexican American civil rights cases than it did in cases involving African Americans. At the same time, the incentive to intervene was far less, since the violence done to Mexican Americans and their rights was not as extreme as that suffered by African Americans, nor were the demands for federal action anywhere near as insistent or powerful as those registered on behalf of civil rights for African Americans.[5]

The war promised great things to Mexican Americans, and delivered in a number of areas. They gained greater access to better jobs, their civil rights demands for the first time were being addressed (albeit inadequately), and their status as full contributing members of the American community was recognized. None of this was likely to have happened when it did without the pressures of war. On the other hand, advances premised on the conflict's demands were limited by the same wartime exigency that promoted them. The war exposed communities' problems and encouraged government to address them. But the high stakes and compelling demands of the war suggested that this was no time to undertake potentially disruptive reforms. The same expedience that demanded placating Mexican Americans also dictated surrendering to those who would keep them subordinate.

The civil rights revolution that Sánchez predicted in 1943 would not materialize for another quarter of a century. The problem was more than the failure of wartime events to dramatize the plight of Mexican Americans, or even the limited capacity of Mexican American leaders to press their case. It involved as well the limited vision and weak will of officials and reformers to seek civil liberties for minorities in the face of politically and ideologically fortified attitudes and practices designed to keep minorities from full citizenship. The war had speeded up the erosion of racist America, but it would take more than the demands of war to effect the revolution that Sánchez thought he saw in wartime developments. It would also take the activist leadership of a new generation that was coming of age in Mexican American communities, a generation that had developed a new consciousness of their rights and of the contradictions in American society.

Postwar Mexican American Civil Rights Leadership

Before the end of the war, on March 2, 1945, a group of five Mexican Americans filed a class-action lawsuit against four school districts in Orange County, California: Westminster, El Modeno, Garden Grove, and Santa Ana. The suit was the outgrowth of two years of community organizing and dialogue led by war veterans and their families. The *Mendez et al. v. Westminster School District* case would take two years to be decided by the federal and appellate courts in San Francisco. The final verdict, upheld by the Ninth Circuit Court of Appeals on July 18, 1947, ruled that the segregation of Mexican-origin students within public schools was a violation of the U.S. Constitution's 14th Amendment, the so-called Equal Protection provision.[6] This was only one of many legal victories won by Mexican Americans after World War II that were made possible by the dynamics outlined in previous chapters: a new responsiveness on the part of the federal government, a new public awareness of the injustices flowing from racism, and lastly, a newly confident Mexican American leadership that demanded equal treatment under the law.

The victory in the *Mendez* case was an indication of a new energy among Mexican American leaders, who were insisting on their rights to equal treatment as American citizens. The vigor of the returned veterans reenergized older organizations such as LULAC and La Liga Pro-Defensa

Figure 6.1. Schoolchildren at the Lincoln School in El Modeno, California, late 1930s. These were the students whose parents joined together to sue the Westminster School District in 1945, winning the landmark 1946 *Mendez et al. v. Westminster School District* case, which was a precedent for the later *Brown v. Board of Education* desegregation case. Courtesy of Yolanda Alvarez.

Escolar, and Mexican American men and women began a new era working for expanded civil rights. After the war, LULAC initiated a series of suits and actions against school districts in an effort to end segregation and improve the quality of education for Mexican Americans. LULAC helped the families in the *Mendez* case during the two years it took the courts to reach a decision. In 1948, LULAC, working with the GI Forum, raised funds and provided legal counsel in the *Delgado v. Bastrop Independent School District* case, which applied the *Westminster* decision to Texas and clarified and enlarged the legal prohibition against segregating Mexican and Mexican American children.[7] Altogether, LULAC, in alliance with other organizations, filed fifteen antidiscrimination lawsuits in Texas in the postwar years.[8] In addition to the lawsuits, LULAC officers, acting as watchdogs and advocates, monitored complaints and administrative actions throughout the state.

No other postwar organization typified the new energies being brought to civil rights action more than the American GI Forum, an organization that was formed by returned veterans specifically to gain equal treatment and to end unequal treatment. In Corpus Christi in March 1948, Héctor P. García, a decorated veteran of the war, called for an organization of Mexican American veterans to work toward getting equal treatment from the government. Under the determined leadership of García, they were successful in protesting racial discrimination in the administration of Veterans Administration (va) hospital and educational benefits. Soon the American GI Forum involved itself in a dramatic case of discrimination, that of Félix Longoria. In 1948, after Félix Longoria had been killed in action in the Philippines during the war, his remains were finally sent to his hometown of Three Rivers, Texas. When the local undertaker refused to hold services in his chapel because it was for "whites only," Texas Mexican Americans launched a campaign to have Longoria buried in Arlington National Cemetery. In January 1949, García called a special meeting of the GI Forum to address the Longoria issue. The Forum's constitution stated that one of their goals was to "strive for the procurement for all veterans and their families, regardless of race, color, or creed, the equal privileges to which they are entitled under the laws of our country."[9] After getting Senator Lyndon B. Johnson's assistance in having Longoria buried with honor in Washington D.C., the GI Forum launched a successful campaign to expose the segregated practices of mortuaries and cemeteries in Texas. During the late 1940s and 1950s, they worked with LULAC in filing many civil rights lawsuits. In 1954, for example, they were instrumental in helping to win the *Hernández v. State of Texas* decision before the U.S. Supreme Court, which challenged all-white juries.[10]

In California, Mexican Americans who had come of age during World War II joined the Community Service Organization (cso) to work on changing the political powerlessness that had characterized their history. The cso had been started in the 1940s by the Industrial Areas Foundation (IAF) in Chicago to organize grassroots political action among Mexican Americans. In California, the IAF targeted Mexican communities and sent Fred Ross to organize. The cso was concerned with issues that affected the urban barrios: civil rights, voter registration, community education, housing discrimination, and police brutality. In Los Angeles, Ross, along with Tony Ríos, succeeded in getting more than twelve thousand new voters to turn out in a 1949 election—enough to give a victory to Edward Roybal, the first Mexican American member of the Los Angeles City Council since 1881. After this, Ross decided to expand the cso base by establishing chapters throughout California. In 1952 he recruited a young laborer named César Chávez in San José, California. Chávez,

GRAN JUNTA DE PROTESTA
AHORA En La NOCHE En La ESCUELA LAMAR

Ubicada en calles 19 y Morris a las ocho de la noche habra una **Gran Junta de Protesta** debido a que se le han **negado** los servicios de una casa Funeraria en Three Rivers, Texas, a los Restos de un **Soldado,** llamado Felix Longoria de Three Rivers, Texas.

El AMERICAN GI Forum de Corpus Christi

Requiere su presencia para que venga a oir los datos acerca de esta **CRUEL HUMILLACION** a uno de nuestros **HEROES** Soldado de esta última gran GUERRA. Todos los **VETERANOS** y sus familias y público en general deben asistir sin FALTA o sin EXCUSAS.

Cuando una casa Funeraria se Niega a Honrar a los RESTOS de un Ciudadano Americano solamente porque es de origen mejicano entonces es TIEMPO que no unicamente el American GI Forum sino todo el pueblo se levante a protestar esta injusticia.

Se le Ruega Respetuosamente a las MADRES de Soldados Muertos en la GUERRA se sirvan ASISTIR.

Hoy esta Noche, Martes 11 de Enero de 1949

Estara presente la Sra. Beatriz Longoria Viuda de el Valiente Soldado Felix Longoria.

American GI Forum
Dr. Hector P. Garcia, Pres.

Figure 6.2. Gran Junta de Protesta (Big Protest Meeting) flyer sent to GI Forum members in Corpus Christi, urging them to come to a meeting on January II, 1949, to protest the treatment of Pvt. Félix Longoria, who was killed in the Philippines during World War II. The funeral director in his hometown of Three Rivers, Texas, refused the use of the chapel for funeral services because of Pvt. Longoria's Mexican ancestry. Dr. Héctor P. García Papers. Courtesy of Special Collections and Archives, Mary and Jeff Bell Library, Texas A&M University, Corpus Christi, Texas.

Figure 6.3. The group of servicemen who formed the first American GI Forum organization at Rose Hill Cemetery in 1949 in Corpus Christi, Texas. The veterans of the GI Forum took part in all returning veterans' funerals. Dr. Héctor P. García Papers. Courtesy of Special Collections and Archives, Mary and Jeff Bell Library, Texas A&M University, Corpus Christi, Texas.

a Navy veteran of World War II, joined the cso and recruited other Mexican Americans, including Dolores Huerta, Antonio Orendain, and Gil Padilla, all of whom became cso organizers. Eventually, Chávez became the executive director of the cso in California. In the early 1960s, using his experience with this organization, Chávez built a farmworkers association that later became the United Farm Workers Union, a major component of the Chicano civil rights movement in the 1960s.

Outside of California, in New Mexico, Arizona, and West Texas, returned Mexican American GIs were also largely responsible for the creation of the Asociación Nacional México-Americana (ANMA), a labor-based political organization originating from the International Union of Mine, Mill and Smelter Workers headquarters in Denver, Colorado.[11] In 1948, they called for a conference of progressive organizations, including supporters of Henry Wallace's presidential campaign. Their call was to form "a permanent national organization to defend the rights of the Mexican American people."[12] In its newsletters and subsequent conferences, ANMA called for militant response to racial and cultural discrimination as well as opposition to deportations of undocumented immigrants. Eventually, ANMA established more than thirty-five local organizations

Figure 6.4. A young Bert Corona (left) with, from left to right, David Morales, Charlie Peña, unidentified, and Chive Carrasco, all members of the Mexican American Movement, a youth organization in 1939. Corona would become a major community organizer after World War II and was cofounder of California's Mexican American Political Association (MAPA). Courtesy of the California Ethnic Multicultural Archives, Department of Special Collections, Donald C. Davidson Library, University of California, Santa Barbara, California.

throughout Arizona, Colorado, and California and claimed a membership of fifty thousand. ANMA, more than any other organization formed in the postwar period, prefigured the radical demands of the Chicano movement in the 1960s by advocating an international alliance with progressives in Mexico, a strong position on civil and women's rights, and a rebirth of cultural pride in being of Mexican origin.[13] Eventually, harassment by the FBI and cold war fears killed off ANMA, but its brief life was a stepping stone to the militancy of the 1960s.

Another California-based organization built by World War II veterans was the Mexican American Political Association (MAPA). According to Bert Corona, a labor activist who was one of its founders, MAPA grew out of the frustrations born of the electoral defeats of Mexican American candidates. MAPA was a nonpartisan political association that was based on the premise that increased political representation and voice for Mexican Americans would influence legislation and policy in the arena of civil rights.[14] The organization included activists from labor unions, former organizers of El Congreso, and workers from the Community Service Organization. Together they sought to increase Mexican American voter registration and consciousness. In the presidential election of 1960, MAPA threw its energies into the Viva Kennedy Clubs and registered more than 130,000 new voters.[15] Some claimed that this margin was responsible for John F. Kennedy's presidential victory in 1960.

Through the efforts of these organizations and many others, the desegregation of public facilities such as public swimming pools, movie theaters, and the like proceeded slowly, region by region, town by town. In small towns and barrios throughout the Southwest, local organizations sprang up, and lawsuits were threatened, filed, and won. In 1946, in Bell Town, a barrio near Riverside, California, Mexican American parents formed a Bell Town Improvement League and petitioned the local school board to do away with discrimination in the schools. After countless meetings with local school officials, they won. That same year, forty-five hundred residents of Chavez Ravine, a barrio in Los Angeles, formed an organization to demand that the city provide bus service to their neighborhood.[16] These kinds of unheralded actions took place throughout the Southwest during the late 1940s and into the 1950s, led by men and women who remembered their sacrifices for democracy and who now expected more of America.

After World War II, many Mexican American organizations dedicated themselves to working for equal rights: the American Council for Spanish-Speaking People, the Alianza Hispano-Americana, the Mexican Civic Committee, unions like the International Union of Mine, Mill and Smelter Workers, and countless local clubs and parents organizations dedicated to challenging the unequal treatment of Mexican Americans. For leadership and support, they drew on the adult experience of those who had fought and lived through World War II. As has been noted, their involvement in civic change was a continuation of efforts that had begun during the 1930s and continued even during the war years. But what was new, after 1945, was a recently solidified confidence in their right to equal treatment, especially since Mexican Americans had sacrificed for their country. Anglo-Americans who were elected as government officials to school boards, city councils, and state legislatures were beginning to realize that the evil they had fought against with words and bullets was also present in the United States. Racism's ugly face was now much less overt or popular. Mexican Americans attended colleges and universities and purchased new homes in integrated neighborhoods using the GI Bill, to which all veterans were entitled. Many returned to jobs they had held before the war and began families. Only a small number were able to devote their lives to organizing for civil rights, but this small group ultimately had an impact on the larger society.

Building a Legacy of Civil Rights

World War II was an important catalyst intensifying impulses that had long been developing within the Mexican barrios of the Southwest. Recent scholarship has uncovered the many ways that Mexican Americans defended, advanced, and organized for their civil rights in the barrios, *colonias*, and fields of the Southwest prior to the 1940s. Mario García's landmark 1989 study of Mexican Americans provides a detailed analysis of the men and women who organized LULAC, El Congreso, and labor unions like the International Union of Mine, Mill and Smelter Workers.[17] George J. Sanchez' 1993 study of Los Angeles during the 1930s showed how the young people within the Mexican American movement organized to achieve the American dream through education, which they saw as one of their civil rights as Americans.[18] Most recently, Zaragosa Vargas convincingly argued in his 2005 book that labor unions and associations articulated some of the first demands for civil rights, starting in the 1920s. The wretched discriminatory condition of workers led to the fight for the right to decent housing, jobs, equal pay, education, sanitation, and health. The struggle for economic civil rights was expressed through countless strikes, conflicts with the police, deaths, slowdowns, formal complaints, and lawsuits. Progressive members within the CIO especially were active during World War II in trying to eliminate discrimination in jobs and employment as well as in mobilizing workers to vote.[19]

Before 1941, there was a strong heritage of struggle for civil rights by Mexican Americans. The effect of World War II was to mobilize Mexican Americans on a national scale under the campaign to save democracy and eliminate totalitarianism. The net result was that it added a new dynamic to the building of Mexican American identity and intensified a process that had been ongoing through much of the twentieth century.[20] The emergence of the term "Mexican American" in official discourse signaled a heightened expectation of inclusion in the American project, and this, in turn, would lead to more coordinated actions to achieve civil rights in the postwar era.

Mexican Americans, along with the larger society, were not dramatically altered with respect to their attitudes toward civil rights. During the immediate postwar years, many of the lawsuits against school districts and the successful protests against discrimination had only local impact. Segregation and discrimination continued in many places, especially in Texas, until the more militant civil rights movements of the 1960s began to significantly alter the government's responsiveness regarding civil rights for African and Mexican Americans. More importantly, it would take a national campaign against racial discrimination, led by African American leaders like Martin Luther King Jr., Medgar Evers, and Malcolm X, along with many bloody urban riots, to awaken many Americans to the evils of racism. By then, the Mexican American generation was ready to assume leadership in advocacy of national remedies. Their vision of America was one conditioned by their experiences during World War II, and as such, it was one shared by others in power. In the 1950s, their effectiveness in helping to change America's response to Mexicans and Mexican Americans was limited by political factors beyond their control, including the cold war and a pervasive conservatism. The Chicano generation in the 1960s, following a different vision of what America should become, began to challenge the Mexican American leadership. Their struggle also had its limits and contradictions, but the successes that took place, at the national level especially, were built upon the efforts of those who had come of age during World War II, the men and women who were laying the foundation for a new ethnic awareness of Mexican Americans and their civil rights.

APPENDIX A

"The Minority Citizen"

RUTH TUCK

During World War II, Ruth Tuck conducted ethnographic interviews with Mexican Americans in the town of Descanso (probably San Bernardino or Pomona), California, and published her work in 1946.[1] She took her title, *Not with the Fist*, from Charles Horton Cooley's belief that discrimination was often not intended to be malicious but was done with the "elbows," not with the fist. Indeed, the general theme of the book was to downplay the overt acts of racism toward Mexican Americans. Ignacio López, a civil rights activist and publisher of *El Espectador*, wrote in the foreword to the book that "the author could have been harsher with the dominant community," but that Tuck had, nevertheless, managed to give "a rounded exposition of the way millions of our little Americans like and move and have their being. She has "got underneath."[2]

In the selection here, Tuck describes the kind of discrimination Mexican Americans encountered in Southern California during the war and discusses the civil rights actions they took as a community. This was one of the first major community studies devoted to describing the complex and nuanced realities of barrio life.

CHAPTER IX

THE MINORITY CITIZEN

"Discrimination"

FOR TWO years or more, the Spanish-language paper in the *colonia* has carried on a campaign against the refusal of certain rights and privileges to Americans of Mexican extraction. "Discrimination," in this sense, has no exact equivalent in Spanish; it has to be translated *"abusos contra los derechos civiles"* [1] or *"prejudicios raciales en contra de los Mexicanos,"* [2] both of which phrases more exactly describe the situation than "discrimination." For, according to dominant Descanso, discrimination is just a little social quirk or idiosyncrasy, an expression of personal taste which could not possibly have legal implications. From this premise, Descanso proceeds to argue that moves to curtail discriminatory practices constitute infringements of personal liberty. The personal liberty of the dominant group is meant, of course, for the personal liberties of other groups are not a factor, from this point of view. Descanso tries to place a dislike for seeing little Americans of Mexican descent in a public swimming pool in the same class as a dislike of seeing onions on the dinner table. It has not only so rationalized its breaches of civil trust for itself. It has, in the past, succeeded in convincing many a Mexican-American that fighting for equal privileges constituted a social error, a simple case of bad manners—pushing yourself in where you weren't wanted.

There are few legal bars, as such, against the Mexican or American of Mexican descent. He is counted on the white side of miscegenation statutes, as a rule. No Jim-Crowism is part of

[1] *abusos contra los derechos civiles:* abuses of civil rights.
[2] *prejudicios raciales en contra de los Mexicanos:* racial prejudices against Mexicans.

197

NOT WITH THE FIST

his life, even in the sovereign State of Texas. School segregation
is put upon a basis other than the ethnic, officially. Courts have
held that the non-Caucasian clauses of restrictive residence
covenants do not include persons of Mexican ancestry. If he is
a citizen, he is not barred from the polls. These are advantages
which the dominant community is quick to point out, particularly when it is trying to drive a wedge between the Mexican-
American minority and other minorities less favored. In some
ways, this position is an asset, but in other respects it is a liability. It makes the job of fighting the extra-legal discrimination
all the more difficult. Rather than having the job of battering
down a wall, the Mexican-American finds himself entangled in
a spider web, whose outlines are difficult to see but whose clinging, silken strands hold tight.

For many years, the immigrant and his sons made no effort to
free themselves. They burned with resentment over a thousand
slights, but they did so in private, or among others of their kind.
"Docility" was the most admired characteristic of the Mexican
immigrant, by the dominant group, who often added "cowardly"
to the description. The immigrant was not a coward, but he was
bewildered, leaderless, and desperately in search of security.
"Don't go where you're not wanted," "Keep your mouth closed
and you won't give yourself away," and "Don't get *la raza* in
trouble" were some of the admonitions he gave himself and his
children. Violations of civil rights were likely to be greeted in
the *colonia* with an apathetic, saddened shrug and the comment,
"Yes, that is how they treat us Mexicans." The man who submerged himself in *Mexicanismo* was a more admired figure than
the man who stood up for his rights and so "got us all into
trouble." Perhaps this passivity is the mark of any minority which
is just emerging from severe exploitation, but the immigrant and
his sons seemed to remain in this stage a long time.

In the end, it was the war which really awoke Descanso's
colonia, as it did many another Mexican colony in the Southwest. In a world in which the heroic sacrifice of Americans of
Mexican descent at Bataan and Corregidor could be followed, in
eighteen months, by riots against Americans of Mexican descent
in Los Angeles, passive accommodation lost much of its value. It

THE MINORITY CITIZEN

has become trite to make this observation, but there is force and clarity in the triteness. The immigrant mother in the *colonia,* who had lost a son in battle, felt quite simply that his little brothers should be able to attend a public plunge or an unsegregated school.

The incident in the *colonia* which fired it to social action made such a direct connection between sacrifice in war and civil rights. The son of one of the prominent men in the *colonia* was killed in flight training and the body was shipped home for military burial. Wishing the best last resting-place possible, the father bought a lot in a near-by "memorial park." The man in charge thought him an Italian, it was later explained. When the father returned with the mother and her relatives to view the lot, his money was returned and the purchase refused with the explanation, "Oh, we didn't know you were Mexican. We don't bury Mexicans here." The military funeral was eventually held elsewhere. Now, this sort of thing had been happening for years. It still happens, and the bodies concerned are often in uniform, to be interred with American flags. But the fact that it took place in such a dramatic fashion, involving such a shock to a grief-stricken mother, striking such an exemplary, *gente decente* family, aroused the whole *colonia.* The story is still told by indignant women in the *colonia,* written in letters to relatives in Mexico, and recounted on visits there. Every *nacional* (imported contract worker) eventually hears it. As a nullifier of "good-will" policies, it and stories like it are potent forces.

Indignation coalesced in the formation of the Defense Committee and the successful fight to open the public plunge to the public, regardless of national or ethnic origins. The plan for the committee originally embraced a series of such court cases, based on concrete situations, and touching one after another of the spheres in which Mexican-Americans encountered discrimination. The *colonia* had its steam up. Instead, however, of finding another concrete case like that of the public plunge, it ran into a network of half-defined, nebulous situations. All of them involved discriminatory practices, but none of them provided the explicit detail needed for legal action. In some cases, the city,

NOT WITH THE FIST

having no mind to be caught flat-footed again, had hastily put in a little legal window-dressing.

The display of "white trade only" signs and the refusal of service to persons of Mexican descent was to have been a target for the committee. The city council quickly made the display of such signs illegal, but scarcely a month passes when some Mexican-Americans are not refused service in a bar or café. Techniques for doing so are facilitated by the plethora of customers in these establishments. The tables are all filled, and none ever seem to empty for Mexican-Americans—those people who were let in ahead had "reservations." Or the ethnically undesired customer is seated, but got no service—for as long a period as two hours. Or it just happens to be "club night" in a certain establishment, and the management is very sorry that it cannot serve those without a card. Or, if the case is finally brought to court, the judge may blandly rule that no "demand" for service was made, regardless of the evidence presented. The *colonia* leaders have learned that the best place to press a case is the federal court, if jurisdiction can be obtained, and that the most experienced and expensive legal talent is none too good.

Segregated schooling was also on the agenda of the Defense Committee. The school board quickly forestalled possible action by doing away with segregation in the *barrio pequeño*. About the school situation in the West End, the board wrings its hands, protesting, "But, you see, no amount of re-districting will improve this. It's just an unfortunate situation our predecessors wished on us. Anyway, it's the fault of the Mexicans. They all like to live in the same place." Any admission by *colonia* leadership that the situation is difficult and that the concentration of Mexican population does not improve it, is seized upon by administrators as proof that the *colonia* approves segregation—hence nothing should ever be done about it.

Contrary to the wishful thinking of Descanso, all Mexican-Americans do not like to live "in the same place," particularly if that place represents the most inadequate, ramshackle, crowded housing in the city. Volumes have been written about the poor housing of the Mexican-American throughout the Southwest; Descanso is no exception to the general picture. A quick look at

200

THE MINORITY CITIZEN

the County Housing Authority's map is all that is necessary to confirm this fact. Two dark-brown sections, labeled "sub-standard," stand out—they are the *colonia* and the *barrio pequeño*. They represent *the* sub-standard housing for the city. They also represent the areas of greatest population density.

The history of any family who had an income beyond a subsistence level usually contains an incident somewhat like the following: "When my father got to be assistant foreman, he decided to look for a better house. He answered the ads in the paper, but the people just said flatly they wouldn't rent to Mexicans. Then he decided he'd buy, but it was the same thing there. The house we wanted wasn't much, and it was only about four blocks the other side of the tracks. The sale was all ready to go through, when the owner backed out. The neighbors had been raising hell about selling to Mexicans. So finally my father just bought another shack, next door to the one we already had, to have room for his family. It's the one where my married brother lives now." A college student said, "The sociology courses can't teach me anything about 'invasion.' One of the first things I remember is the time we tried to rent a house just north of here. We'd been there for two weeks when the agent came around to say that we'd have to move at the end of the month—the neighbors had protested to the owner. That evening, some teachers—Anglo-Americans who were friends of my father's—came down to talk about the 'Mexican problem.' The real Mexican problem, the one that had mother in tears, they couldn't do anything about."

The housing bars against the Mexican-American have been exactly this sort—invisible ones. While there are restrictive covenants in many a deed in the north of town, they are thought of as applying to Negroes or Orientals. Actually, about fifty families of Mexican extraction live outside the *colonia,* and thirty-five of them have moved across the tracks in the last two years. Some families, of "high type" pseudo-Mexican or "Spanish" origin, have always lived outside the *colonia;* this group usually includes the consular officials and their families. Once a Mexican-American family is settled in a neighborhood, there is little friction. Sometimes there is active good will and friendliness, if the neighbors happen to be Catholic also. The friction arises when another

201

NOT WITH THE FIST

family of Mexican extraction tries to move into the same general neighborhood. "We don't want any more Mexicans on this street," is the slogan, applicable no matter how "high type" and "Spanish" the invaders may be. If a number of families of Mexican extraction begin to move into a neighborhood, it may suddenly develop that there are no houses for sale for miles around. Owners have just changed their minds about selling, say the agents, and what can one do? Thus, without recourse to anything so crude as a restrictive covenant, a quota system is actually set up for movement away from the *colonia*.

The less desirable the Anglo-American neighborhood the smaller the quota is. The professional man of good income may encounter little difficulty in moving near the country club, but the workingman who wants to move five or six blocks east of the *colonia* is likely to find no takers for his down payment. This has the effect of bottling up those families who are most in need of improved housing. The result is to multiply shack upon shack on the crowded streets and narrow lots west of the tracks.

Descanso has, in the past, turned a deaf ear to any sweeping proposals for slum-clearance and decent low-cost housing. Nice, civic-minded ladies have actually talked in favor of retention of the slum areas. "You know, I'd hate to see Barbarita Street [a crowded alley known in social-work circles as 'Delinquency Row'] go. It's just like a bit of old Mexico, with the cactus fences and tiny houses covered with roses. When I have visitors I always take them down to see it." The number of Mexican-American families buying in the north and east of Descanso, however, has recently given such civic-planners pause. "With money in their pockets," says Descanso, "they'll all be trying to move into our part of town. It may be that better housing, privately financed if possible, in that end of town, would keep them where they belong." There is even talk of making everything terribly "old Spanish" and picturesque, with rows of oleanders and mission arches; and the Confederation of Mexican Societies, with its plans for a *Casa de la Colonia*, is helping segregation along. "See," say the civic planners, "even those prominent Mexicans would rather stay in the West End. They're happier among their own kind."

It is true that about 60 per cent of the *colonia* either owns its

THE MINORITY CITIZEN

homes or is buying them; this is as true in the meanest streets as in those where housing is not sub-standard. Most of the purchases have involved hard work, sacrifice, and considerable planning. A man like Juan Pérez may not have received much for his money, by the time interest charges are counted in, but to him it means a degree of security. He will not be willing to give it up unless he is sure that he will get at least as much security in return. Neither will he be happy in a barracks-like apartment structure, no matter how scientifically planned. He likes to have a small yard, a few fruit trees and flowers, and some chickens. "It's obvious," said a housing authority on a tour of the *colonia*, "that the pattern for Mexican-American rehousing should be the cottage community type—with fences for every front yard!" Give Juan Pérez a chance at such a home, even outside the *colonia*, on some rental or purchase basis which will guarantee him tenure, and he would jump at the chance. He gets a hungry gleam in his eye when he sees pictures of the bright, clean homes of Swedish workers' villages, and he would not be at all reluctant to see his children farther away from the *cantinas* and drunks of Monticello Avenue.

Certainly some of the elderly, to whom ownership of anything—even a board-and-batten with the battens off and the roof leaking—represents a miracle, would be difficult to move. Much of their stubbornness is fear of falling into the hands of another *explotador*. The *padre*, too, would probably represent an obstacle. Sincerely anxious as he is for better living conditions for his parishioners, he is not eager to see them dispersed. The colony scoffers say, "If the flock ever scattered, he'd never collect it again." His plans for a parochial school in the *colonia* depend upon new generations of Mexican-Americans being born there. To date, he has seemed to incline strongly toward privately erected family units, no slum clearance, and oleanders.

The second generation, however, has little nostalgia for the *colonia*. "Sure, maybe it's picturesque," said a high-school boy, "to Anglo slumming parties who can live anywhere they want to. Maybe they'd feel differently if they tried it here for a while. I don't want to lose touch with my family, but, if I make any wages at all, I'm sure going to get out of this sink-hole." "No

NOT WITH THE FIST

kids of mine are going to be brought up there, if I can help it,"
is another very general comment. Only one thing, apparently,
will hold the second generation in the *colonia*. "Maybe I should
get out, for my children's sake," said a young father, "but I'm
afraid of losing touch with my people, while they still need help.
It's a question many of us face—whether it's better to move across
town and show, by example, what can be done, or to stay here,
in the middle of things, and help more of our people move
eventually."

In housing, as in other matters, there are no obvious barriers,
legally labeled as such, before the Mexican-American. But the
invisible barrier can be just as impenetrable and far more tan-
talizing. Its operation is often more effective than if it had been
embodied in law, because it is difficult to isolate and fight. To
a group as distinguished by sensitive pride as the Mexican-
American, such techniques are cruelly effective. An honest insistence on a basic right can be made to look like a mere social
faux pas, "pushing in where you aren't wanted." To a few elite,
the hope is always held out that, if they are sufficiently "high
type" and willing to cut themselves off from the rest, the invisible
barrier can be broken. The dominant community can always
pretend that its right hand does not know what its left hand is
doing. "Why, we haven't any discrimination—we have a Mexican
in the Elks."

As a last resort, the Mexican-American can always be encouraged to ponder how much better off he is than the Negro or the
Oriental. This tactic has the added advanatge, from the point of
view of the dominant group, of setting one minority against
another. If it can divide minority action on such an issue, for
example, as a permanent Fair Employment Practice Committee,
it can say, "The very people who would profit from this are
squabbling among themselves. If they will cut one another's
throats for advantage, what can you expect the poor employer
to do?" On questions of educational facilities, access to public
facilities, relief budgets, and even unionization, the same dividing tactic is used time and time again. One minority group is
offered a little *atole con el dedo,* and off it trots, wagging its tail.
The Mexican-American group has certainly fallen for this bait

204

THE MINORITY CITIZEN

repeatedly, to the ill-disguised amusement of those who proffered it.

Many of the problems of the Mexican-American are different than those of the Negro or the Oriental. He has an advantage in that the caste is not closed, completely, at the top for him. With this advantage, the Mexican-American could easily constitute the spearhead for advance in all minority gains. He has a freedom of action and movement often denied to other minority members; he can attempt things impossible for them. But the gains he would make for all minorities would be gains for him, too. Desperately as the Mexican-American has pretended—particularly under snobbish, self-seeking leadership—that he is better off than *los tintos*,[3] he knows that the difference is one of degree rather than of kind. Whatever the ethnic niceties of the situation may be, that is the way the sociological cards fell, from 1910 on.

The same sensitive pride which makes the Mexican-American wince unduly under slights also makes him too anxious to please—to be judged favorably by the dominant group. When *la plebe* says, of its prejudices toward *los tintos* and others, that "they are things we learned from you people," it is not far from the truth. Los Conejos offered little scope for race prejudice. Members of the *gente decente* felt themselves, in general, superior to the few Negroes or Chinese they encountered; but the preoccupation with race, the allergy to a darker skin, the thousands of status-weighted allusions to it, was something they had to learn here. In states like Texas, it was in the very air they breathed. There was no surer way to please an Anglo than to slight a Negro, and much of the early accommodating leadership among Mexican immigrants made ample use of this technique.

The *colonia*, apparently, has a divided mind on the subject. Among its top leadership, there are at least two individuals who openly proclaim and practice minority solidarity. A third recognizes the necessity of working with Negro groups, particularly in politics, but adds a few private reservations about "knowing them socially." The others, pushed in some cases by *gente decente* families, would like to cling to the advantage of being "better than *los tintos*," even in public action. The second generation,

[3] *los tintos:* slang for colored, usually applied to Negroes.

NOT WITH THE FIST

even among its leaders, is uncertain in regard to public action with Negro groups—for the most part, it is uninformed regarding their objectives. Friendships and alliances in school activities, among them playground fights, occur between Mexican-American and Negro youth, but they are seldom sustained after school hours. There is little contact of an intimate social sort between the *colonia* families and the Negroes who have moved in at its east edge, save among very young children. (In the *barrio pequeño*, however, where families of the two groups have lived side by side for several years, there are not only friendships among children but visiting and sociability among families of the two groups.) However, for all the distance between the two groups in the *colonia*, there is instant, quick sympathy for the Negro who is obviously exploited or mistreated by dominant groups.

In regard to the Orientals, there is still remoteness, but of a slightly different sort. To *la plebe,* the Oriental businessman—market owner, nurseryman, "herb doctor," or vegetable whole-saler—represented an economically advantaged person, sometimes a potential employer. He was not, as the Negro often was, a competitor in the same labor market. He could be admired for his acumen and success; to do him credit, he apparently did not take undue advantage of his position. There was genuine sympathy in the *colonia,* for the exiled Japanese-Americans, several of whom lived and had businesses within the *colonia.* Even the Mexican-Americans who occupy Nisei-owned property have no theoretical objections to their return, although, should return coincide with a housing shortage, there might be friction. Nor do families who have lost sons in the Pacific area confuse the issue of the Japanese enemy with that of the loyal resident or citizen of the United States—a rather remarkable achievement, considering the radio and press campaign to which they have been exposed. With regard to the Japanese-Americans, there seemed to be cognizance by *la plebe* that mistreatment of this minority threatened other minorities. However, aside from re-spect for the Oriental's financial success and sympathy for his minority status, there is little closeness between the two groups in the sense of friendship or intermarriage. Both disapprove

206

THE MINORITY CITIZEN

such closer connections, although they are able to live side by side in harmony.

In speaking of people and their groupings, one must be very careful—as Descanso is not—to distinguish between (1) the tendency of persons of like interests, background, and taste to cluster together and (2) the refusal of basic rights, such as access to education, public facilities, or employment, by one group to another. It is the latter which is "discrimination." That it may have originally grown out of the former does not justify its existence, as Descanso appears to think. No one should know better than Descanso that "natural" tendencies, uncurbed, fast develop into vices! It is something the *colonia* could consider before, out of a desire to curry favor, it copies the vices.

On Being a Citizen

Seventy-eight per cent of the individuals in the *colonia* are American citizens, but most of them have attained citizenship through birth. Out of 277 immigrant individuals interviewed, only one was a naturalized citizen and only three others had taken out first papers. Yet every one of these persons intended to stay in the United States permanently and considered it his country. Not one had the slightest desire or intention of returning to Mexico. Still, few in this group had any definite plans for becoming naturalized citizens of the United States. One gathered that naturalization would be deferred and postponed until death overtook the immigrant group, still aliens in a country in which they had lived most of their lives.

To the Native Son or vociferous professional patriot in Descanso, such a situation can mean only one thing: if such a resident is not actually disloyal, he is certainly indifferent to the institutions of his adopted country and ungrateful for the benefits he has received. Curiously enough, a like charge is not made against the comparatively large numbers of Canadians and Englishmen who have shown a similar reluctance to naturalize themselves. "Well, you know, they're so much like us, anyway," says Descanso deprecatingly, "that you could hardly consider them foreigners." The word alien is seldom applied to an English-

207

NOT WITH THE FIST

man, even when he indisputably is one and intends to remain so.

Concerning the reluctance of Juan Pérez and his countrymen to becoming citizens, many guesses have been hazarded. A feeling of attachment to Mexico, strengthened by the physical nearness of the home country, has often been thought one of the reasons. *Mexicanismo,* it has been pointed out, does exist, but it seems to be rather a refuge and an escape from the difficulties of integration with American life than nationalism as such. The fact that naturalization confers no added status or privileges in American life is undoubtedly a factor. As long as the tenet that "once a Mexican, always a Mexican" is held by the dominant community, the position of the naturalized citizen is little different than that of his alien neighbor. In some respects, it may be worse, because the protection of the consulate is thereby withdrawn.

Behind these reasons, however, is an eminently practical one, which seems to have been generally overlooked. For the Mexican immigrant who entered the United States prior to 1924, the process of proving that he ever got here at all is complicated, expensive, and fraught with potential danger. He may very likely succeed in proving only that he was an illegal entrant and find himself holding, instead of first papers, a one-way deportee's ticket to the border. Such was the general chaos of entry, spurred by the labor demands in the United States, and such has been the zeal of immigration officers in pouncing on technicalities, that no immigrant, no matter how valid his intentions were, is at all sure that he is now in the United States legally. It is a recurring nightmare for him, making a crisis of applications for public assistance and certain types of employment, as well as for citizenship. Even if he decides to steel himself to the possibility of deportation, the process of proving continuous residence in the United States since entry and/or the legal nature of any subsequent return and re-entry, no matter how brief, is a herculean undertaking. For persons who have been excessively migrant, or for those who were brought to the United States at an early age by their parents, proof may be simply impossible. At best, it is likely to involve fees for expert assistance running as high as fifty to a hundred dollars.

208

THE MINORITY CITIZEN

Anyone who has tried to assist a Mexican immigrant—as compared to earlier European immigrants whose records of entry were in good order—in the preliminaries to citizenship is well aware of the difficulties involved. It is no accident that the bulk of naturalized citizens in the *colonia* are those who entered after 1924, when regulations for entry were enforced and some sort of orderly accounting maintained. A large number of quasi-immigrants who remain unnaturalized, even though they have spent their lives in the United States and speak perfectly acceptable English, quite frankly admit that they remain aliens because they have neither the finances nor the courage to tackle the job of proving that they got here legally. Even the older immigrant, after he has given all the customary reasons about having a "hard head" for the learning of English, is likely to settle on the difficulty of proving entry as a main deterrent. "Look at that Pedro Saenz. He was going to be a citizen. And where is he now? Back in Juárez, with his wife and children starving here."

In view of the fact that slipshod entry was largely the result of American zeal for cheap labor, it might seem as though some of the unholy punctiliousness after the act might be relaxed. A reasonable construing of facts of entry prior to 1924, combined with some conveniently located and resourcefully taught adult education classes, might result in a veritable rush of Mexican applicants for citizenship. As it is now, even the enticements of old age assistance, so desperately needed by the elderly laborer, are insufficient to entice him into the perilous and costly business of applying for citizenship.

For the person of Mexican extraction who is a citizen, either through birth or naturalization, it might be well to inquire what extra privileges he receives and in what fashion he discharges particular responsibilities or duties. He need not imagine that, by becoming a citizen or being born one, he will escape any of the limitations of the semi-caste. There is a street in Descanso on which three families live side by side. The head of one family is a naturalized citizen, who arrived here eighteen years ago; the head of the second is an alien who came to the United States in 1905; the head of the third is the descendant of people who came to Descanso Valley in 1843. All of them, with their families,

NOT WITH THE FIST

live in poor housing; earn approximately $150 a month as un-skilled laborers; send their children to "Mexican" schools; and encounter the same sort of discriminatory practices. To dominant Descanso, all are "Mexicans"—none are "Americans."

There is a large potential voting population in the *colonia*, and it is getting larger every year. The *colonia's* vote could easily swing the ward of which it is a part, because, although the ward is large, population density at its upper end is slight. Any group which composes 12 per cent of the population is a force on the ballot, if it is active. If the *colonia* is not aware of this, there is certainly awareness elsewhere. The Mexican-American vote is watched carefully, by men with political "know." Those who would like to maintain the status quo draw a long breath when it shows its customary apathy.

Politics in the *colonia* is incredibly lily-white and naive, com-pared to that in the rest of the city. What activity exists is con-ducted just the way the civics books say it should be, with the result that it is often as far removed from reality as the civics books. In many ways, this high-principled behavior is an asset. An honest vote, if it could be registered in quantity at the polls, would advance the *colonia* much farther than attempting to play fancy games with the old hands on the other side of town. To date, the Mexican-American vote in Descanso is not "sold," nor can it be "delivered." The cynics and the disappointed among the Anglo-Americans say that is because it just cannot be aroused. But whenever it shows any activity at all, there is considerable excitement on the other side of town; and the activity is likely to be interpreted as being more significant than it really is.

The *colonia* leadership is aware that voting power is potential strength, but it has not yet learned the techniques, nor is it will-ing to do the hard foot-work necessary to turn it out, precinct by precinct. A special ward election produced the Liga Cívica, an attempt in this direction, but too hastily organized to count for much in the election it was supposed to influence. Most of the persons thus registered voted in the national primaries, though. Registration of additional voters proceeded sporadically through-out the spring and early summer, with the result that the na-tional election produced what county officials considered a record

THE MINORITY CITIZEN

Mexican-American vote of 73.90 per cent in this ward, not too far below the city average of 79.75. It is, however, a general and dangerous tendency of masses everywhere in the United States to display political activity only once every four years. The Mexican-American will have to learn, along with many other groups, that it is unceasing vigilance at the polls—all the way from Congressional primaries down to school board and water district elections—which counts.

Jury duty presents a startlingly biased picture in Descanso. No Mexican-Americans serve on juries, nor are they apparently wanted—although several Negroes do serve. The story is an interesting one. In Descanso, for county jury duty, the judges draw up lists of prospective jurors, to whom the clerk then sends questionnaires. On the basis of the returned questionnaires—and by judgments which include such items as "neatness of handwriting"—lists of jurors are formed. These lists are constantly revised, and one of the bases for removal of a juror's name is his continued unacceptability to lawyers trying cases before the Superior Court. "In a big county like this, we can't keep calling people in, at five cents a mile, if the lawyers won't take them when they get here."

In 1942, after prodding from some quarter or other, it was decided to include Mexican-American names for the first time on the judges' lists. Ten names were obtained, some of them, apparently, from the police. The incident of "the nicest little Mexican housewife, who wrote such a good hand, but was found to have been a shoplifter" may have been a by-product of the method of selection. Several others were eliminated because they were found "not mentally alert" or "just too ignorant." Inasmuch as the *colonia* contains several persons with college degrees and a hundred or so, all perfectly bilingual, with high-school diplomas, it rather appeared as though the original selection had been faulty. However, the real slaughter apparently came through the attorneys. "The attorneys just would not permit them to serve," said a minor court official. "We had a lot of criminal cases involving Mexicans that year, and attorneys just would not have Mexicans on the jury for these cases." That was the end of

NOT WITH THE FIST

Mexican-American jury service; there are no Hispanic names on the jury lists today.

However, Negro jurors serve in comparatively large numbers, and attorneys like to have them on juries for criminal cases involving Negroes. This may be the hand of the National Association for the Advancement of Colored People—or it may be something quite different. "You see," explained an attorney, "the Negroes who serve are all old-timers here in town. We know them and they know us. They're all good, conscientious people. We don't call any of these excitable new Negroes." At one time, jury lists contained as many as fifteen Negro names for 500 white names, a figure which made the unofficial quota of one-half of one per cent of the Negro population look rather badly ciphered. Inasmuch as registered voters may apply for jury duty and the inclination of the judges, who have to maintain reasonable rotation of names, is to consider those applications, the *colonia* has a job before it. There are plenty of mentally alert and well-educated merchants who could afford to let the relatives run the *tienda* for a day and numerous respectable housewives, innocent of the slightest thought of shoplifting, who would make intelligent jurors. Jury duty may be a bore and an inconvenience, but it is a "must" for a minority.

The Police and the Press

With this brief glimpse of the exit end of the judicial hopper, it might be well to turn to its intake department, that of law enforcement. The Mexican immigrant in the United States has been accused of having an unusually high rate of crime and delinquency; and the doings of some of his children, tagged as "zoot suiters" or "*pachucos*," have furnished copy for sensational journalistic imaginations to an extent not even exceeded by Hollywood. To Descanso's press, any scared fifteen-year-old who falls into the hands of the police on Monticello Avenue is a "zoot suiter," complete with knife, bicycle chain "knuckles," and a criminally mature philosophy. Furthermore, he is a *Mexican* "zoot suiter," a *Mexican* "gang member," or a *Mexican* delinquent, regardless of the fact that he was born in the United States.

THE MINORITY CITIZEN

The press, in Descanso and elsewhere, has succeeded in building up a body of highly spiced misinformation in the public mind, whereby a Mexican colony is peopled entirely by vicious youth with criminal tendencies. The presence of a few Mike Maldonados and Jimmy Garcías idling on a street corner is sufficient to send a thrill of eager horror up the spines of a slumming party. "See—*pachucos!*"

As has been pointed out, the number of Mexican-American youth who have any degree of criminal maturity is small. Still, the number of arrests of juveniles of Mexican extraction is large, compared to the proportion of the population their group represents. The *colonia* and the *barrio pequeño*, with 12 per cent of the population of Descanso, furnish 28 per cent of juvenile arrests. It must be remembered that bad housing and slum conditions, whatever the population concerned, are conceded to account for a 15 per cent rise in delinquency rates. Not only are these two areas *the* slums of Descanso, but they have been notably lacking, to date, in public recreation facilities. It is certain, furthermore, that the prejudices, conscious or unconscious, of law enforcement officers provide further impetus to frequent arrest. The average Descanso police officer is not an unkindly man —the flagrant abuses of justice and decency toward minorities which are routine in some cities occur here only sporadically. Police officers simply share the run-of-the-mill biases of the dominant group; they are in a position to act on them oftener. Untrained in the philosophy of juvenile work in general, they certainly have no special equipment for the delicate business of handling second-generation youth. To such an officer, the youthful population of the West End is likely to appear as "jail bait."

If the arrest pattern of juveniles points to one moral, it is that the young Mexican-American leaves himself statistically unprotected by his habit of idling on street corners. The places at which arrests most commonly occur and the times at which they are made point up the picture vividly. Mike Maldonado and his pals are gathered at the corner of Sixth and Monticello, with no more criminal intent than that of "watching what is going on." If they are noisy, when the police car comes around at 9:30 P.M., they are "disturbing the peace." If they move a hundred feet in

213

NOT WITH THE FIST

one direction or another, they are "loitering in the vicinity of a pool hall." If they have succeeded in getting some liquor from one of the disreputable *cantinas*, they may be "drunk and disorderly," by the time of the next appearance of the police car. At a later hour, a few may have committed "malicious mischief," out of idleness and curiosity. If they drift over to a municipal dance, their very appearance in a body may lead to further disturbance of the peace. The tragedy of juvenile misbehavior everywhere is its essential unplanned, undeliberated nature. Even serious offenses have their genesis in aimless drifting; the criminal action is so spontaneous that it surprises even the doer. "We was just standing around and we saw this car with the keys in it," has been the inception of many a juvenile case of grand theft, among all groups. The boy of Descanso's *colonia,* in following the village pattern of recreation set by his elders—that of idling and conversing on the streets—puts himself in further jeopardy.

The average boy who gets arrested in the *colonia* is not a recidivist. Few boys are arrested twice within a year's time, but new little fish swim into the net all the time. Their home addresses correspond, with terrifying exactitude, to those areas designated by housing authorities as most sub-standard. Their offenses run much higher during the winter months, when these homes seem more crowded and unattractive. Not all such boys, by any means, come from the disorganized fringe of the *colonia,* but most of them come from homes where the parents know little of American life. It might be added that, say what you will for the cloistering of girls, it has a positive effect on delinquency statistics. Practically *no* Mexican-American girl is ever arrested by the police. The old tradition of male freedom at adolescence, however, is certainly a contributing factor to the difficulties of the *colonia's* boys.

Rarely is a Mexican woman in difficulties with the law, either, and still more rarely does she slip into prostitution. Adult males, however, contribute more extensively to arrest records than do their sons. The offense which leads to their involvement with the law is always the same one, repeated with monotonous regularity over acres of police blotters. It is drunkenness, as a rule uncomplicated by any other charge. The offenders are, largely, the

THE MINORITY CITIZEN

laborers of middle age and over. They stagger coming out of a *cantina*, they go to sleep in parks, or they relieve the demands of nature at a picket fence. They are arrested, they pay fines of ten or fifteen dollars apiece, and they start the whole cycle over again the next week or month. They represent, with amazing fidelity, those families in the lower disorganized fringe of the *colonia*.

The *colonia* is not proud of these befuddled oldsters, but it has a certain sympathy for them. "Those police cars are like *zopilotes*.[4] They circle these streets. It doesn't make any difference how quiet a man is. If he is alone on the streets at night, he is stopped. If he has had a drink or two, he is drunk." One old man proudly described a certain function he performs for his neighbors. "I have lived here forty years and the police know me for a good man. Anyway, it now upsets my stomach to drink. But I go with my friends and when we come home, I keep the edge of the sidewalk. The police car stops and I say, 'Good evening, Mister Policeman, it is just me, Tomás Valdes, and these boys here are my nephews.' They make a joke and go away. But it is very dangerous to be on the streets at night if you do not know the police." The police frankly admit that they arrest any Mexican, particularly a laborer, who seems to have been drinking, while they would exercise greater leniency toward other groups in other places; they feel that the person of Mexican extraction has a greater propensity for "getting into trouble" after having a few drinks. They also admit that this vigilance has no appreciable effect in reducing adult arrests for drunkenness—nor to their recollection, did prohibition. Total adult fines, from this district, average as much as $500 to $700 monthly, particularly during the winter months. Like the young, the adult male seems to be more law-abiding during the summer. One repeated offender of middle age, asked why he never got in jail during the summer, replied, "It's warm at home in summer, but, when it rains, the *cantina* is more comfortable."

The question of what to do with the old, ill-adjusted, discouraged laborer who has no place to go except a *cantina* is not a simple one. Perhaps he is as difficult of rehabilitation socially as

4 *zopilotes:* buzzards.

NOT WITH THE FIST

he is vocationally. But the question of what to do with a fifteen-year-old who has no place to go except the streets is comparatively easy. Descanso has proved, in a small way, that solution is possible; unfortunately, it has shown little interest in following the matter up. During the summer of 1943, delinquency was appreciably lowered by a night-park program of ball games held on a vacant lot one block north of "Delinquency Corner." During the summer of 1944, the same program reduced delinquency to zero for six weeks and to a previously unknown low for the remainder of vacation. Winter recreation admittedly involves more resource, equipment, and personnel, but that is scarcely an excuse for its non-existence. The very fact that the *colonia* has no entrenched gang organizations, little recidivism, and juvenile delinquency chiefly of a casual and accidental type argues that recreational therapy would work well. If decent housing were added to the cure, recovery might very well be complete.

"The same old stuff," says Descanso when it hears about recreation and housing as solutions of juvenile problems. The trouble is not that they are the "same old stuff," but that they have never been adequately tried. If a quarter of the energy Descanso has expended, in the last three years, in solemn conclaves on "the delinquency problem" had been turned to getting decent recreation on the West Side, it would now have less to talk about. If a sixteenth of the energy expended in shuddering over headlines about "zoot suiters" and mongering rumors about girl *pachucas* with knives secreted in their pompadours had been so turned, it might have nothing at all to talk about. The inescapable conclusion is that Descanso prefers to keep delinquency as a conversation piece.

In that decision, it gets considerable assistance from its press. The Descanso *Reporter* is not a yellow sheet, by any means; nor does it entirely reflect the entrenched reaction of a great deal of the national press.[5] It usually curbs sensationalism and scandal sharply in its pages. Sporadically, it espouses a liberal point of view, much in the manner of a swimmer putting a toe in a cold

[5] A prize-winning *Atlantic Monthly* article provides an excellent discussion of the press in the United States. Robert Lasch, "For a Free Press," *Atlantic Monthly*, CLXXIV (July, 1944), 39-44.

THE MINORITY CITIZEN

plunge. Most of the time, however, it attempts to keep in exact step with the prejudices and biases of the communities it serves—or, more exactly, with the points of view held by the powerful groups in those communities. This, its editors sincerely believe, is "reflecting public opinion." On the question of the Mexican-American minority, it has not been guiltless of helping to form those biases and prejudices.

A specific incident will serve as an example. At one of the municipal dances, a group of sailors made passes, verbally and otherwise, at some Mexican-American girls. Their boy friends protested—the sailors persisted, saying, "Do you want to make something of it?" In the fight that ensued, a fifteen-year-old Mexican-American boy slashed a sailor's wrist with a penknife. No one in the excited crowd gave first aid, and the sailor lost considerable blood. The next afternoon—a Sunday—a crowd of servicemen gathered in the park near the municipal auditorium, and there was talk, apparently, of a "march on Monticello Avenue." The military authorities, grown wise in such matters, promptly canceled leaves for a ten-day period. There—except for the trial of the boy who, outnumbered by older and heavier opponents, had unwisely used a knife—the matter might have rested, as the sailor recovered very promptly.

The *Reporter*, however, ran headlines in its city section, and followed them by some very imaginative misstatements. Not a word was said about the provocation given the Mexican-Americans. Phrases like "undeclared war between servicemen and zoot-suited Mexican youths," "a gang of twenty-five Mexican *pachucos* attacked four service men," "the zoot suiters fled in the darkness at the approach of officers," and "military authorities ordered a ten-day state of emergency" worked the city up to the boiling point. Rumors of all varieties circulated over every bar and soda fountain. The sailor had died, and the Mexican community had begged the *Reporter* to suppress the news for fear of reprisals. Nine *pachuca* girls with knives in their hair had been arrested and had confessed to a pact to seduce and murder sailors. A Mexican-American youth had been discovered hanged. Armed *pachucos* from other communities were planning a "march on Descanso."

217

NOT WITH THE FIST

As if to nullify the prompt quieting action taken by military authorities, the *Reporter* published a long interview with a man who described himself as head of the Fathers of Fighting Sons. "It is not right that our sons are denied the right to freely walk the streets of the country while criminals and lawless elements are permitted to roam at large at all hours," said this dignitary, who was privately characterized by his familiars as a "Texas crackpot." The police, meanwhile, were arresting Mexican-American youths for questioning. The paper published the names and addresses of all of them and made no retractions when it was clear they had nothing to do with the knifing. Ironically enough, the boys and girls who had been the focus of the disturbance were in no sense *pachucos*. They came from good homes, on the upper levels of the *colonia,* and had good school and employment records. The fifteen-year-old who wielded the knife had not come with them. He had inserted himself, gratuitiously and certainly unwanted, into the fracas, apparently to show off. Nothing about the whole incident connoted gang organization or "criminal and lawless elements."

The matter of securing a fair hearing for the boys who had done no knifing, but had merely defended girls of their group, proved to be a complicated matter. At the first hearing, the presiding judge acted as though he had been doing too much newspaper reading. It took the expenditure of considerable money, the hiring of an attorney outside the area, and another hearing to bring out the real facts of the case. Those facts received no newspaper headlines, needless to say, nor even any mention. Dominant Descanso is still convinced that twenty-five "Mexican *pachucos*" wantonly attacked some heroic men in uniform. When it goes to Monticello Avenue to eat "Spanish food," it imagines every shadowy street peopled with lurking, stealthy criminal figures, armed with "razor-sharp four-inch blades" (the *Reporter's* journalese for "pocketknife").

Why a respectable, civic-minded man like the editor of the *Reporter,* which normally forswears the sensationalism of metropolitan journals, lent himself to a display of this sort is difficult to imagine. There is complete evidence by now—of which he must have been aware—that, if you want a riot, this is the way

THE MINORITY CITIZEN

to produce it. Descanso certainly displayed riot psychology for three or four days. The *colonia* says, "Oh, he just wanted to sell some more newspapers," or, more perceptively, "Maybe he got mad at something and he felt like taking it out on the Mexicans." Anyone who believes in the essentially dualistic nature of man would have been fascinated, during those three days in Descanso, in watching normally kind, friendly faces display sadism, fear, and spite. It was impossible to believe that these average citizens, too, did not have something they wished to "take out" on a scapegoat—perhaps their own frustrations, insecurities, and self-mistrust.

The damage worked by one of these incidents lasts a long time. The public mind seems to have a genius for retaining dramatic untruths. It desperately wants to blame somebody or something else for situations which arise from its own shortcomings. The editor of the *Reporter* has annulled much of his courageous stand on slum-clearance and improvement of conditions in the West End. "Why give those people anything?" say the shrill voices of Descanso's citizenry. "They're criminals and foreigners and generally low!" As if finally aware of this, the *Reporter's* editorial page, some months later, carried eight paragraphs headed "True Americans." After listing the names of boys of Mexican ancestry who had died in battle, the editorial made a plea for "plans for the postwar era" which would take into account "the part these young Americans of Mexican ancestry are to play in our tomorrow." The editorial might have added: "These young men are exactly like those other youngsters—no better, no worse—whom we were mistakenly calling criminals three months ago. Two of those youngsters are now in the service. Let us hope that, when they are in battle for us, they will remember us with a charity which we do not deserve."

Armed Service

That its young men of Mexican extraction are coming back from the wars with a "new concept of life"—to quote the editorial—Descanso has no doubt. It is a little nervous about the situation. In public offices and places of influence, one hears con-

NOT WITH THE FIST

stantly repeated the idea that "these things will really be problems when all the Mexican boys who've seen service get home."
Will these boys be docile track laborers and orange pickers? Will
they want to live in a shack in the *colonia?* Can they be refused
service at bars and cafés? Will they be satisfied to "stay in their
own part of town"? Will they insist on "social equality," with
its connotation of friendship and intermarriage? Will "once a
Mexican, always a Mexican" still hold true?

Descanso is inclined to think it will not, but of how such a
change will come about it has no idea. "Gradually," it says, or
"by education." It shows, by every action, that it hopes the day
of reckoning will be far in the future. It maintains, meanwhile,
the old barriers against the mothers, fathers, sisters, wives, and
little brothers of Mexican-American veterans. Does it imagine
that it can "do something" for these veterans which will not include their families, their communities, and the very climate of
opinion of Descanso itself? Does it fancy that "doing something,"
in the honest sense of granting full integration with American
life, will not involve reconstruction of its whole status-system,
with the corollary cheap labor complex? If the expressions of
its leading citizens are any criteria, this is exactly what it does
fancy. It wants to make a gesture and still preserve the status
quo. Like an unwilling horse, it feels itself dragged, by national
and international events, toward a goal it sniffs suspiciously.

There is scarcely a home in the *colonia* which did not have
a son in service; many had three or more. The big families the
social workers used to frown on have their uses in time of war.
By and large, the experiences of the *colonia's* youth in the services have been satisfying ones. Unlike Negro youth, they have
not found, in uniform, a denial of the democracy for which they
are asked to fight.[6] Few are commissioned officers, but many have
had the satisfaction of working up to the top of non-commis-
sioned ranks. They have made close friends among Anglo-Americans. They have, in some cases, married into Anglo-American

[6] Earl Brown and George C. Leighton, *The Negro and the War,* Public Af-
fairs Pamphlet No. 71 (New York: Public Affairs Committee, Inc., 1944).
Gunnar Myrdal, *An American Dilemma,* Harper, 1944, Vol. I, pp. 419-423;
Vol. II, pp. 1308-1309.

THE MINORITY CITIZEN

families from other parts of the country and have found that the
social prejudices of Descanso did not exist. They have found that
they can do things well, that they can command and take responsibility. Even the misfits and comparative failures feel that they
have been judged, not as "Mexicans," but as individual men, by
the same standards as other men. The successful have had the
heady experience of accomplishment free of the tag "pretty good
for a Mexican." They are, as they say, "all steamed up."

A pharmacist's mate said: "The years on the ship are the best
ones I ever spent. When you learn to get on with a thousand
men and do your work and hold your own without ever hearing
'Mexican,' you get on to a lot of things. In a way, I wish I could
stay with the Navy. I hope they don't discharge me right now
on account of this leg. If I came back to the colony now, I think
I'd blow up after a few months. Two weeks is bad enough. It's
like breathing good, clean air—salt air, maybe—and then getting
back to a swamp. I'd like to finish the war. Then there'll be a
lot of us back together." A former corporal in the ground forces
said: "I've had a swell time and I've been treated swell. The rest
of the United States isn't like Descanso, I've found out. I'd like to
live in the East—I've got a girl there. But you couldn't move my
mother, and I've got to help her until the kids are grown. My
girl says she wouldn't mind living in the *colonia,* but she's just
dumb. She thinks it's romantic or something. I'd sure hate to
risk it." A discharged private in the infantry said: "I'm glad I'm
going to have one of those little buttons to wear in my coat. And
a flock of foliage to put on my uniform for Armistice Day pa-
rades. I'm going into politics. There's seven or eight of us, all
from Southern California, who've talked it over. Things are going to happen in these colonies, and we're going to see that they
do."

It is true that great potential leadership developed among
Mexican-American youth in the armed forces. If it keeps its
drive, many barriers may go down before it. Its effect on the
youngsters still in school is already great. The caustic comments
of the returned veteran on *Mexicanismo* make it seem what it
really is—a ridiculous, antiquated day-dream. Accommodating
leadership is just a way of getting yourself fooled, to the veteran.

221

NOT WITH THE FIST

Being a *pachuco* is just being a little punk. Getting an education is all-important. "Why, if I'd had a decent education, I bet I'd have been a captain." And as for the other side of town—but here the fresh voice of confidence and direction wavers.

The alert and mature veteran realizes that, in spite of all he can do and say, dominant Descanso *is* dominant. When he walks down Monticello Avenue, he feels the pressure of all the old childhood patterns of restriction, defeat, and helplessness. He feels, as one young ex-sergeant said, "as if something was being taken away, like I wasn't myself the way I am in camp." If there is a severe depression, followed by a fascism which takes it out on minority groups, where would the veteran who has returned to the *colonia* be? He is already handicapped, en masse, by insufficient education. Would he be one of the discouraged, broken cynics, like many a veteran of the first World War—at home only in a bar? Would he be a contributor to a crime wave like that which followed the last war? Or would he be like the youthful European veteran of 1918, rioting in the streets? The steam is up. The veteran knows the channels into which he would like to have it go: a good job, a happy family life, and full status in American life for his group. Where it actually goes is something dominant Descanso and the nation of which it is a part will determine. By the portents now observable, the veteran is not going to be put off with *atole con el dedo;* but sometimes he mistrusts, not only life and the times, but the power of his own newly acquired manhood to hold out against pressure.

Statement of Carlos E. Castañeda before the U.S. Senate Regarding the Need for a Fair Employment Practices Commission, March 12, 1945

During World War II, Carlos E. Castañeda served as the assistant director and then director of the regional office of the Fair Employment Practices Committee, spending a good deal of his time traveling throughout the Southwest gathering information about the discrimination that Mexican Americans experienced in the workplace. Even though he was frustrated by the inability of the FEPC to change patterns of prejudice, he, along with many other Mexican American leaders, supported a continuation of the committee's work after the war. Castañeda read this statement before the Senate subcommittee considering a bill to prohibit employment discrimination based on race, creed, color, national origin, or ancestry.[1] It summarizes the extent of the problem as he encountered it during the war. Unfortunately, the bill did not pass the Senate, and federal legislation outlawing employment discrimination would not be passed for another twenty years.

FAIR EMPLOYMENT PRACTICES ACT HEARINGS

before a
SUBCOMMITTEE OF THE COMMITTEE ON
EDUCATION AND LABOR, UNITED STATES SENATE.
Seventy-Ninth Congress
First Session on S. 101

A BILL TO PROHIBIT DISCRIMINATION IN EMPLOYMENT
BECAUSE OF RACE, CREED, COLOR, NATIONAL ORIGIN,
OR ANCESTRY
AND S. 459

A BILL TO ESTABLISH A FAIR EMPLOYMENT PRACTICE
COMMISSION AND TO AID IN ELIMINATING DISCRIMI-
NATION IN EMPLOYMENT BECAUSE OF RACE, CREED,
OR COLOR
March 12, 13, AND 14, 1945

STATEMENT OF DR. CARLOS E. CASTAÑEDA, SPECIAL
ASSISTANT ON LATIN-AMERICAN PROBLEMS TO THE
CHAIRMAN OF THE PRESIDENT'S COMMITTEE ON FAIR
EMPLOYMENT PRACTICE, BEFORE THE SENATE COM-
MITTEE ON LABOR AND EDUCATION IN THE HEARINGS
HELD SEPTEMBER 8, 1944, ON S BILL 2048, TO PROHIBIT
DISCRIMINATION BECAUSE OF RACE, CREED, COLOR,
NATIONAL ORIGIN OR ANCESTRY.

For more than twenty years I have been interested in the
problems arising from the various forms of discrimination against
the Spanish-speaking people of the Southwest. I have been an
active member of the League of United Latin-American Citizens,
Loyal Latin-American Citizens, the Catholic Association for International Peace on its Committee on Inter-American Relations,
The Southwestern Committee on Latin-American Culture, The
Inter-American Bibliographical and Library Association, and other
national and international associations interested in the promotion of better relations and understanding between Anglos and
Latin-Americans.

92

I was appointed Senior Fair Practice Examiner in Region X, comprising the states of Texas, New Mexico and Louisiana, on August 23, 1943, and was made Acting Regional Director in charge of the Dallas Office until December 17, 1943, when I was made Special Assistant to the Chairman on Latin-American problems, in which capacity I have served the Committee since that time.

Our Spanish-speaking population in the Southwest, made up almost entirely of American citizens of Mexican extraction and Mexican nationals are ill-dressed, ill-fed, ill-cared for medically, and ill-educated, all because of the low economic standard to which they have been relegated as the result of the general policy of restricting their employment and utilization to the lowest paid, least desirable, and most exacting jobs from the physical standpoint. Not only have they been restricted to the lowest bracket jobs, but even in these jobs they have been paid wages below the minimum of sound and tested going rates in all the various industries in which they have been employed.

In the investigation of complaints filed with the President's Committee on Fair Employment Practice involving discrimination against Spanish-speaking Latin-American citizens of Mexican extraction and Mexican nationals, I have visited the states of Arizona, California, Colorado, New Mexico, and Texas and I have had an opportunity to study conditions at first hand. I have gathered statistics that reveal the magnitude of the problem insofar as it affects what is the largest underprivileged minority group in the Southwest.

In the State of Arizona, according to the 1940 census, there is a total population of 449,261, of which about 30% are persons of Mexican extraction. Of the 160,000 Spanish-speaking persons of Mexican extraction, only 24,902 are foreign-born Mexican nationals. The mining industry in Arizona normally employs between 15,000 and 16,000 men. The percentage of Mexicans, that is American citizens of Mexican extraction in the main, is over 50% on an average and in many mining centers it runs as high as 80%. In round figures there are between 8,000 and 10,000 persons of Mexican extraction employed in the mining industry in Arizona. Their employment is restricted, however, very largely 'o common labor and semi-skilled jobs and even the urgent need óf Manpower as the result of the war has not broken down the prejudice which bars large numbers of skilled laborers from promotion in order that they might be utilized at their highest skill and thus contribute more fully and more efficiently to the total war effort.

The total population of California, according to the 1940 census, is 6,907,387. The number of persons of Mexican extraction according to the same census is 457,900, of which 134,312 are foreign-born, or Mexican nationals. In the Los Angeles area with a population of 1,673,000, the persons of Mexican descent number about 315,000, or approximately 20%. As late as the summer of 1942, more than six months after Pearl Harbor, only 5,000 persons of Mexican extraction were employed in basic industries. This figure was ascertained in a survey conducted by the CIO in November, 1942, among whose membership there are over 10,000 Mexican-Americans.

Equally revealing as regards the failure to utilize more fully the Mexican labor supply along the West Coast of California are the figures given in a study made by the War Manpower Commission as late as April 13, 1943. Out of the 315,000 persons of Mexican extraction, only 10,000 were being employed in the Southern California shipyards, 2,000 in the San Diego aircraft industry, and 7,500 in the Los Angeles aircraft industry, making a total of 19,500 employed in essential war industries in the area included between Los Angeles and San Diego. Much better utilization was being made of Mexican labor in the San Francisco area where, with a total population of some 30,000 persons of Mexican extraction, 8,000 were engaged in basic war industries. In percentage, 22% of the Mexican-Americans were being employed in San Francisco, while only 6% had found employment in basic war industries in the Los Angeles and San Diego area.

The failure to utilize the available Mexican labor supply in California, traceable in a good measure to prejudice, was not limited to essential and war industries. In an institute sponsored by the Los Angeles City and County Schools and the Southern California Council of Inter-American Affairs to discuss the problem of "What is the Vocational Future of Mexican-Americans", held on February 19, 1944, Mr. Sid Panush, Personnel Examiner for the Los Angeles County Civil Service Commission, stated that out of 16,000 employees, about 400 were of Mexican extraction; that is, a 2½% of the total amount. Mr. John F. Fisher, Director for the Los Angeles Civil Service Commission explained, at the same time, that out of the 16,500 civil service employees in the city government about 450 were of Mexican extraction, which makes the percentage the same as that in the County.

The population of Colorado, according to the 1940 census, is 1,123,296. The number of foreign-born Mexicans is given as 6,360. In the southern part of Colorado, where the larger portion of the Mexican-Americans reside, many of them descendants of the first settlers in the area, there are approximately some 50,000 Spanish-speaking Latin-American citizens of Mexican extraction. In Denver, in Pueblo, and in Trinidad itself these Mexican-Americans are restricted in their employment to common labor jobs in the main. The number of Mexican-Americans employed in the steel industry, in Civil Service jobs, in military installations and in other war and essential industries, is less than 6% of the available Mexican labor supply. Mexican-Americans have been refused employment in clerical and office positions, and they have been denied promotion and upgrading in accord with both seniority and ability in private industry and by military installations in the area.

In the State of New Mexico, with a population of 531,818, there are 8,875 foreign-born Mexicans according to the 1940 census. The number of Mexican-Americans is about 40% of the total population. In the southwestern corner of the state there is a large mining area between Santa Rita and Silver City. Investigation of complaints by Mexican-American citizens in this area has shown that from 40 to 60% of the men employed by the mining companies are of Mexican extraction; that they are barred from promotion into certain departments and that they are refused upgrading into skilled jobs because of their national origin.

Texas, with a population of 6,414,824, has approximately 1,000,000 Mexican-Americans. According to the 1940 census there were 159,266 foreign-born Mexican nationals in the state, or about 1/6 of the total number of Spanish-speaking persons of Mexican descent were Mexican nationals. Less than 5% of the total number of persons of Mexican extraction in Texas are employed at the present time in war and essential industries. Such industries as have given employment to Mexican labor have restricted them to common or unskilled labor jobs largely, regardless of their ability, training, or qualifications. In the oil, aircraft and mining industries, in the numerous military installations, in the munitions factories and shipyards, and in the public utility corporations, such as gas, light, and transportation companies, their employment has been limited and their opportunities for advancement restricted.

The prevalent idea or belief among employers for the various industries, personnel managers, officials of military installations, and various government agencies in the Southwest is that the Mexican-American is incapable of doing other than manual, physical labor; that he is unfit for the type of skilled labor required by industry and the crafts. Back of this belief is prejudice.

Mr. A. O. Anderson, Personnel Department, Lockheed Aircraft Corporation, has stated that in the company's two Los Angeles plants, 10 to 15% of the employees are Mexican-Americans;

95

that 80% of these are women; that they work principally in detailed assembly, general assembly and riveting. He added:

"Mexican-American women workers have shown that they are capable of adapting themselves to difficult job conditions more readily than others; that this is, they are less bothered by physical discomfort, fumes, and varying temperatures.

"We have many Mexican-Americans who now perform some of the more complicated assembly jobs and others who assumed supervisorial responsibilities."

This statement, repeated by all those who have had the courage to give the Mexican-American an opportunity to work at other than manual jobs, shows that the Mexican-American can be integrated into American industry and that the failure of the Mexican-American to enter the ranks of industry has been largely due to prejudice. This fact is borne out of Mr. Floyd L. Wohlwend, Member WMC Management-Labor Committee and Personnel Officer in the California Shipbuilding Corporation, one of the largest employers in the Southwest, who stated:

"Generally speaking our Mexican workers for the most part have come to us in recent months . . . They just lately began to filter in and our majority of Mexican employees have come in the last 18 months . . . The Mexican-Americans are not only capable, but the variety of jobs at which they can be utilized is limitless if employers, managers, and general management simply will make a point of using them . . . Production records indicate that they have an equal aptitude with other groups or other individuals . . . They are definitely on a par . . . there is no difference."

That the Mexican-American, if given an opportunity, is capable of performing any job in industry was affirmed by Mr. Robert Metzner, President, Pacific Sound Equipment Company, who stated that his company had begun to employ Mexican-Americans in 1942 as the result of the increasing shortage of labor in the Los Angeles area. He declared that:

"As the result of training, Mexican-Americans qualified for skilled jobs, inspectors, both Class A and Class B, radio repairmen, machinists, Turret lathe operators, spot welders and leadmen."

When the Mexican-American asks for equal economic opportunities he is not asking for a favor or privilege. Dr. C. D. Trillingham, Superintendent of the Los Angeles Schools, stated their case well when he said during the Institute at Los Angeles on February 19, 1944:

"We are not being asked to grant something to the Mexican-American out of our benevolence if you please, but to grant them that to which they are entitled along with us, certain inalienable rights as human beings . . ."

The belief held by some that certain racial or national groups have different mechanical aptitudes, a conviction that is at the bottom of the prejudice held against Mexican-Americans, is completely unfounded in fact. Mr. Richard Ibañez, Member of the City Council of Upland, California, who is also a member of the Board of Governors of the California Housing Association, was merely repeating what is well known by students of anthropology, when he said:

"Any one who has taken an anthropology course knows that the Gods gave their skills equally to those of dark skin and light skin."

The urgent need of manpower, in view of the increasing shortage of labor, forced industry to give the Mexican-American an opportunity, but not without the greatest reluctance and misgivings. Wherever he has been given an opportunity he has shown the ability to learn and produce with the same efficiency as members of any other group. To what extent has the President's Committee on Fair Employment Practice enabled war and essential industries to utilize more extensively this neglected pool of labor and given an opportunity to the ready and willing Mexican-American to contribute more fully to the war effort is shown by the following statistics on cases involving Mexican-Americans handled by the President's Committee on Fair Employment Practice during its first year of operation.

In Region X, comprising the States of New Mexico, Texas and Louisiana, 124 complaints were filed and docketed. These included complaints against oil companies, shipyards, public utility companies, Government agencies, military installations, mining companies, and chemical plants. These different agencies and industries had either refused employment to qualified workers, or denied them proper classification and adequate upgrading in accord with their seniority, experience and ability, or paid them a differential wage scale because of their national origin. Of the 124 complaints, without having to recur to a public hearing, through interviews and conferences with employers, 68 were settled; that is, 54.9%. The settlement of these complaints resulted not only in the correction of the individual complaint but in bringing about a relaxation of general discriminatory policies which resulted in the fuller utilization of available Mexican labor by the industries and agencies involved. The 124 complaints filed, represent about 37% of all the cases docketed in Region X involving other minority groups.

In region XII, comprising the states of California, Nevada, and Arizona, out of 279 cases filed and docketed, involving discrimination, 63, or 22.6% were complaints by Mexican nationals and Mexican-Americans. Some of these have been settled, but the majority are still being processed.

Bill S 2048, being considered by your Committee to prohibit discrimination in employment based on race, creed, color, national origin or ancestry will enable three million Mexican-American citizens throughout this country, from California to New York and from Illinois to Texas, to secure equal economic opportunities in employment in the post-war era. The President's Committee on Fair Employment Practice is a war agency, designed to secure equal participation in the total war effort by all Americans regardless of race, creed, color or national origin. During its short period of operation it has done m u c h to integrate Mexican-Americans in war and essential industries and in Government employ. Mexican-Americans have generously responded to their responsibility in the present world struggle for the victory of the democracies. They have unstintingly made the last sacrifice on a world-wide battle front in order that all peoples may enjoy the blessings of freedom and peace. Equal economic opportunities, the right to work and earn a decent living on a par with all other persons regardless of race, creed, color, national origin or ancestry, is a basic principle of American democracy which will be safeguarded by the establishment of such an agency as Bill S 2048 proposes.

Executive Order 8802 Establishing the Fair Employment Practices Committee, June 25, 1941

Early in 1941, A. Philip Randolph, president of the National Association for the Advancement of Colored People (NAACP), along with other African American leaders, threatened to lead a march on Washington of 250,000 African Americans to protest job discrimination. As a result of this pressure, President Franklin D. Roosevelt issued this executive order establishing the President's Committee on Fair Employment Practices which declared that "there shall be no discrimination in the employment of workers in defense industries or government because of race, creed, color, or national origin."[1] The FEPC was not legislation passed by Congress, but it relied on that body for funding. Its enforcement powers were limited, and compliance depended on the goodwill of the employers. Due to political considerations, the executive order did not address the issue of segregation. Conservative and southern opposition to establishing a permanent FEPC after the war resulted in the failure of bills put forward for that purpose in 1948 and again in 1950.

Executive Order 8802 was the first commitment by the federal government to oppose racial discrimination in the workplace. Despite its many limitations, the FEPC mobilized African American and Mexican American leaders to seek federal assistance in fighting racism.

EXECUTIVE ORDER 8801

[Exemption of Archie W. Davis from compulsory retirement for age]

EXECUTIVE ORDER 8802

REAFFIRMING POLICY OF FULL PARTICIPATION IN THE DEFENSE PROGRAM BY ALL PERSONS, REGARDLESS OF RACE, CREED, COLOR, OR NATIONAL ORIGIN, AND DIRECTING CERTAIN ACTION IN FURTHERANCE OF SAID POLICY

WHEREAS it is the policy of the United States to encourage full participation in the national defense program by all citizens of the United States, regardless of race, creed, color, or national origin, in the firm belief that the democratic way of life within the Nation can be defended successfully only with the help and support of all groups within its borders; and

WHEREAS there is evidence that available and needed workers have been barred from employment in industries engaged in defense production solely because of considerations of race, creed, color, or national origin, to the detriment of workers' morale and of national unity:

NOW, THEREFORE, by virtue of the authority vested in me by the Constitution and the statutes, and as a prerequisite to the successful conduct of our national defense production effort, I do hereby reaffirm the policy of the United States that there shall be no discrimination in the employment of workers in defense industries or government because of race, creed, color, or national origin, and I do hereby declare that it is the duty of employers and of labor organizations, in furtherance of said policy and of this order, to provide for the full and equitable participation of all workers in defense industries, without discrimination because of race, creed, color, or national origin;

And it is hereby ordered as follows:

1. All departments and agencies of the Government of the United States concerned with vocational and training programs for defense production shall take special measures appropriate to assure that such programs are adminis-

tered without discrimination because of race, creed, color, or national origin;

2. All contracting agencies of the Government of the United States shall include in all defense contracts hereafter negotiated by them a provision obligating the contractor not to discriminate against any worker because of race, creed, color, or national origin;

3. There is established in the Office of Production Management a Committee on Fair Employment Practice, which shall consist of a chairman and four other members to be appointed by the President. The Chairman and members of the Committee shall serve as such without compensation but shall be entitled to actual and necessary transportation, subsistence and other expenses incidental to performance of their duties. The Committee shall receive and investigate complaints of discrimination in violation of the provisions of this order and shall take appropriate steps to redress grievances which it finds to be valid. The Committee shall also recommend to the several departments and agencies of the Government of the United States and to the President all measures which may be deemed by it necessary or proper to effectuate the provisions of this order.

FRANKLIN D ROOSEVELT

THE WHITE HOUSE,

June 25, 1941.

EXECUTIVE ORDER 8803

AMENDING SCHEDULE A OF THE CIVIL SERVICE RULES

By virtue of the authority vested in me by Paragraph Eighth of Subdivision Second of Section 2 of the Civil Service Act (22 Stat. 403, 404), it is hereby ordered as follows:

SECTION 1. Paragraph 7, Subdivision I of Schedule A of the Civil Service Rules is hereby amended to read as follows:

7. Any person employed in a foreign country, or in the Virgin Islands, or in Puerto Rico when public exigency warrants, or in any island possession of the United States in the Pacific Ocean (except the Hawaiian Islands), or in the

APPENDIX D

The "Caucasian Race—Equal Privileges" Texas House Concurrent Resolution, 1943

In 1943, the Texas Legislature passed a Concurrent Resolution affirming that Latin Americans were allies in the war against Nazism and that there would be no discrimination against any member of the "Caucasian Race."[1] This cleverly worded resolution stated that discrimination against Latin Americans was against the Good Neighbor policy of the state. Not having the effect of law, unclear as to who the members of the "Caucasian Race" were, and citing something as vague as "the Good Neighbor policy," this resolution was nevertheless hailed as a milestone. It would lead to the establishment of the Good Neighbor Commission and consequent programs to promote cultural understanding. All this was largely ceremonial and designed to get Mexico to allow braceros to work in Texas.

GENERAL AND SPECIAL LAWS

OF

THE STATE OF TEXAS

Passed By The

REGULAR SESSION

of the

FORTY-EIGHTH LEGISLATURE

Convened at the

City of Austin, January 12, 1943

and

Adjourned May 11, 1943

Published under the Authority of The State of Texas

Selling Price $3.35

Sidney Latham..................Secretary of State

Claude Isbell...........Assistant Secretary of State

CAUCASIAN RACE—EQUAL PRIVILEGES

H. C. R. No. 105

WHEREAS, All nations of the North American and South American continents are banded together in an effort to stamp out Naziism and preserve democracy; and

WHEREAS, Our neighbors to the South are cooperating and aiding us in every way possible; and

WHEREAS, The citizens of the great State of Texas are interested in doing all that is humanly possible to aid and assist the national policy of hemispherical solidarity; therefore, be it

RESOLVED by the House of Representatives of the State of Texas, the Senate concurring, That the Forty-eighth Legislature of the State of Texas go on record as declaring the following to be the public policy of this State:

1. All persons of the Caucasian Race within the jurisdiction of this State are entitled to the full and equal accommodations, advantages, facilities, and privileges of all public places of business or amusement, subject only to the conditions and limitations established by law, and rules and regulations applicable alike to all persons of the Caucasian Race.

2. Whoever denies to any person the full advantages, facilities, and privileges enumerated in the preceding paragraph or who aids or incites such denial or whoever makes any discrimination, distinction, or restriction except for good cause applicable alike to all persons of the Caucasian Race, respecting accommodations, advantages, facilities, and privileges of all public places of business, or whoever aids or incites such discrimination, distinction, or restriction shall be considered as violating the good neighbor policy of our State.

Adopted by the House, April 15, 1943; adopted by the Senate, May 5, 1943, by a viva voce vote.

Approved May 6, 1943.

Filed with the Secretary of State, May 7, 1943.

1119

APPENDIX E

"Latin-American Juvenile Delinquency in Los Angeles: Bomb or Bubble!"

MANUEL RUIZ

In Los Angeles during World War II, Manuel Ruiz Jr., a young lawyer, was president of the Coordinating Council for Latin-American Youth, an organization dedicated to fighting discrimination against Mexican American youth as well as proposing solutions to problems arising from segregation, poverty, and prejudice. Ruiz spoke out against derogatory stereotyping of Mexican American teenagers as "pachucos" and defended the twenty-two young Mexican Americans who were caught up in the sensational Sleepy Lagoon case in 1942 (see Chapter 3 in this book).

This article, published in December 1942, six months before the outbreak of the Zoot-Suit Riots, seems prophetic in predicting trouble if changes were not made.[1] Among the recommendations Ruiz makes are the employment of Spanish-speaking police, teachers, and public officials; creating more job-training programs; easing restrictions on employment of foreign nationals; and educating the Anglo population about the war contributions of Mexican Americans. These suggestions went unheeded and later became part of the agenda of activists during the Chicano movement in the 1960s.

LATIN-AMERICAN JUVENILE DELINQUENCY IN LOS ANGELES

BOMB OR BUBBLE!

by

Manuel Ruiz

It all started when the law enforcement authorities
decided to crack down. There had been some hesitation to
do so, in fact some of the leaders of the Latin-American
community in Los Angeles had indirectly been sounded out
by the expedient of being let in on the "problem." Those
in authority, too, realized that there were international
aspects involved, which could easily result in delicate
complications. It was too late to deal with the causes
for delinquency in those areas where the Latin-American
preponderated. While preventive measures would solve
the problem as to the next crop of youngsters coming up,
something had to be done NOW, concerning those juveniles
who were giving vent to their exhuberance on the community
at large.

The police question of how to crack down was not a
simple one. The orthodox course of rounding up the leaders,
and making summary examples of them, was out. Already too
much time had been lost in looking for the leaders. Inspec-
tor Lester of the Los Angeles Police Department, Juvenile
Detail, admitted that the department had been unable to find
leaders. The only alternative left then, was simply to
make mass arrests, and leave it up to the courts to separate
the chaff from the wheat. Once this course was decided on
it was rapidly carried into execution.

-1-

When groups of twenty and thirty arrestees began to
appear on the police blotters, the element which makes for
news and sensationalism was seized upon by the press. Instead
of arresting two or three trouble makers for disturbing the
peace, at some dance, the authorities arrested, on one occasion,
as high as seventy-two; the charge was unlawful assembly. Whenever a group of young boys, even on slight pretext, could be
rounded up, they were arrested. If circumstances did not permit this direct action, the group, which might consist of
anywhere from four to ten boys, was made to disperse.

Naturally, the wholesale arrest procedure gave a distorted picture. Although the rate of juvenile delinquency
convictions did not rise over any other similar period of time
among youngsters of Mexican extraction, this significant factor was lost, as the press continued to lay emphasis on group
apprehensions. The part of the public that informs itself by
news-headlines, received a picture of roving gangs of blood-
thirsty, marihuana-crazed young men, committing arson, rape,
and robbery.

Then something happened. The stage was set for international intrigue. Three prominent officials in Los Angeles
County were directly misquoted to the effect that these boy
gangs were inspired by Nazi and Fascist agents. The mis-
quotations prompted by communistic sources laid the trouble
at the feet of Mexican Sinarquists. Rome, Tokyo and Berlin
countered to the effect that the boys were not henchmen, but
simply victims of Anglo-American persecution, that while the
United States extended the good neighbor smile and glad-hand
to Latin-America, that its racial bigotry was patent in that

-2-

thousands of boys of Latin-American extraction were without
cause being thrown into jail and persecuted; and that the
nations to the South had better guard themselves in the future.
From a distorted local problem the matter had now become a
distorted international problem.

Knowing that wherever there was smoke, there must of
necessity be a fire, the United States Department of Information sent Mr. Allan Cranston, assistant to Mr. Elmer Davis,
to look for its existence and, by applying the correct remédy,
extinguish it. The Los Angeles County Grand Jury had already
gathered facts indicating the dangerous flame had been nurtured many years by an apathetic community. Karl Holton,
Los Angeles County chief probation officer, and Judge Robert
Scott, presiding judge of the Juvenile Court in Los Angeles,
had constantly called attention to it, but the facilities they
had had to work with had been limited, and public support had
altogether never been forthcoming.

But the flame had burned brightly. There it was! The
community had blinded itself to the fact that there was in our
midst a large group of children of immigrant parents. Somehow
or another, the people had not considered this problem as one
of recent immigration. Many had gotten sidetracked on arbitrary
racial theories imported from the deep south, which had made
matters worse. Our Atlantic seaboard cities, accustomed to
handle recent arrivals and their children for more than a
hundred years, recognized symptoms and causes and by experi-
mentation learned curative technique. Los Angeles had had only
one brief experience some twenty years ago, and that with a
Russian community of recent immigrants. By recognizing that

-3-

problem as one of immigration, it had been attacked as such
at the core and dissipated.

Because of our failure to diagnose the problem, owing
to the general idea that immigrants solely come from Europe,
certain erroneous conceptions resulted. Thus, the statement
of one high public school official, "why these people are
not recent arrivals, they were here before the Americans came,
their capacity is limited, they slow up other school children,
and therefore should be segregated." Another important person
has said, "they are lazy, have no ambition and won't take advantage of opportunities offered them."

The population of Los Angeles County of Mexican and
Latin-American extraction is just as new to our United States
as the family of an immigrant Dutchman in New York. To say
that they are old timers here simply because they speak Spanish,
and that their capacity is limited by reason of non-adjustment
to our institutions, would be in keeping with the expectation
that a recent arrival from Old Amsterdam to New York should
immediately fit in with the American pattern simply because
New York, once called New Amsterdam, was the original seat of
Dutch migration to this country. The large influx of Mexicans
to this community did not start until around the year 1910,
and thereafter continued to around 1925. That goes for the
entire state of California, as well.

Effective parental cooperation of these minors has not
been organized chiefly because of the existence of a law in
this State to the effect that no foreign language may be used
in the public school system as a means to teach any curricular
subject, whether it be Americanization, hygiene or anything
else. Spanish may be taught, but the Spanish language cannot

-4-

be used to teach. For years, this language barrier has been
criticized by those who know that parental education of
newly-arrived immigrants is important, but nothing has been
done about it. Those in public office who are advocating the
importation into the United States of Mexican workers, as a
temporary help to economic manpower dislocation, would do
well to advocate legislation to hasten processes of assimilation. At cross purposes with this law of superimposing
English has been the reluctance upon the part of parent
immigrants to give up their mother tongue, Spanish, by
reason of their proximity to the Mexican border and a feeling
that soon they would return to Mexico. A similar feeling
exists among old American residents of Mexico. Of course,
they rarely have returned but we have needlessly passed up
the chance of harnessing this vital force of affirmative active parental cooperation through education by the only
obvious avenue of approach, the Spanish language.

As for the children, first generation Americans, the
approach to their parents in Spanish will not deter the latter
in our program of Americanization. The apparent retention
upon the part of many youngsters of a thick Spanish accent,
interpreted by some as a lack of interest in American institutions, is simply the result of their residing in communities
where all of the oldsters speak Spanish in the home. This
situation exists almost 100% in some localities where we
find the younger people actually learning English with a
Spanish accent. This bilingual problem does not exist, however,
where the youngster of Mexican extraction has gone to school
in an Anglo-American neighborhood.

-5-

Coming from poor families from the old country, the youngsters have gone into manual and vocational occupations, to more quickly and directly help the family larder. Those who have managed to get along farther in skilled occupations, wherein they compete with Anglo-Americans, have been called uncomplimentary words and refused jobs. Economic discrimination has existed. Younger brothers, noting the said experience suffered by their older, more ambitious brothers, have naturally not wanted to repeat what to them has been a mistake and are listless to pep talks about the advantages of training, thus resulting in an opinion on the part of some people, that many of these people lack ambition and won't take advantage of opportunities in education offered them.

This brief article, however, cannot linger with causative details. To succinctly put the matter, the problem has by Federal impetus finally been placed in its true perspective. As a direct result of this impetus, a citizens committee for Latin-American youth has been organized in the City and County of Los Angeles. From a study of facts this committee has suggested a specific program by way of requesting and recommending definite steps to be taken. Thus, some of the measures advocated as sound, for the betterment of the total population, are couched in the following language:

(1) We request the Mayor of Los Angeles and the Los Angeles County Board of Supervisors to work together where possible and individually where necessary to achieve the following objectives:

(a) Increased training school facilities for war work in Spanish-speaking neighborhoods.

-6-

(b) Special transportation facilities for
Spanish-speaking people to existing training
schools until better located schools are established.

(c) Additional Spanish-speaking personnel
in present and future training schools.

(d) Night use of indoor school facilities
for recreational purposes in Spanish-speaking
communities.

(e) Use of these recreational facilities
on week-ends.

(f) Additional athletic equipment, lockers,
and other facilities for recreation centers.

(g) Additional Spanish-speaking supervisors
for recreation projects.

(h) Spanish-speaking attorneys as public
defenders in local courts.

(i) Enforcement of anti-discrimination ordinances governing public places, and the erection
of suitable signs indicating equal access without
discrimination for all persons.

(j) Establishment of more forestry camps for
juveniles between the ages of 13 and 15 on probation.

(k) Release of boys on probation to enrollment
in vocational National Youth Administration and similar training programs.

(l) Use of Spanish-speaking law enforcement
officers on cases involving Spanish-speaking juveniles.

(m) More Spanish-speaking law enforcement officers in Spanish-speaking communities.

-7-

(n)   Provision in the regular training curri-
cula of law enforcement officers for education in
minority groups problems as is already done in
New York, Chicago, and other major American communities.

(o)   Exeuction of police powers of law enforcement agencies equally and without undue emphasis
against persons of Mexican extraction.

(p)   A general agreement with the press to cut
to a minimum the publication of names of juvenile
delinquents.

(q)   Establishment of nurseries in Spanish-
speaking neighborhoods for mothers employed in war
work.

(r)   Establishment of special training classes
to provide Spanish-speaking personnel for jobs mentioned above in cases where competent personnel is
now unavailable.

(s)   Establishment of a procedure whereby competent Spanish-speaking personnel can be certified
for temporary civil service jobs for the duration
of the war in cases where present civil service regulations make it impossible to employ competent Spanish-
speaking personnel.

(2)   We request the State Youth Correction Authority
to use current funds for the establishment of additional
recreation facilities.

(3)   We request the president of the United States to
issue executive orders relaxing restrictions on friendly and

allied aliens who are now denied full participation in and
enjoyment of:

      (a)   Federal housing projects.

      (b)   National Youth Administration.

      (c)   Civil service.

      (d)   Restricted war contracts.

      (e)   Civilian defense.

      (f)   Privilege of enlistment in armed forces.

(4) We request the War Manpower Commission and the
President's Committee on Fair Employment Practice to increase
their efforts to open war industry jobs to workers of Mexican extraction and to provide more Spanish-speaking personnel
in local offices of the United States Employment Service and
to open a branch of the United States Employment Service in
Belvedere and other communities where need is indicated.

(5) We request the Office of War Information:

      (a) To intensify its Spanish-speaking language
information work among Spanish-speaking peoples in
this area in order to increase their understanding
of and participation in the war effort.

      (b) To assist in an information campaign
designed to inform the local English-speaking population of the part played by the local Spanish-
speaking population in the war, and

      (c) To assist in an information campaign
designed to publicize the progress of the local
program for better understanding between Americans
and between the Americas.

-9-

(6) We request the United States Treasury Department to conduct a vigorous war bond drive in the Spanish language in this area.

(7) We request the American Red Cross to establish training centers and blood donor centers in Spanish-speaking communities under the supervision of Spanish-speaking personnel.

(8) We request the United Service Organization to establish centers in Spanish-speaking communities under the supervision of Spanish-speaking personnel.

(9) We request the Coordinator of Inter-American Affairs:

    (a) To open a regional office in Los Angeles to coordinate our internal policy toward Latin Americans and our foreign policy toward Latin America, and

    (b) To publicize the progress of the local program for better understanding between Americans and between the Americas.

Excerpts from *Among the Valiant: Mexican-Americans in WW II and Korea*

RAUL MORIN

Raul Morin was born in Lockhart, Texas, and moved during the 1930s to Los Angeles, where he married and started a family. In 1941, he was drafted into the Army and fought with the 79th Infantry Regiment in Europe. After being wounded during the Battle of the Bulge, Morin was sent back to the United States to recuperate. While in the veterans hospitals, he decided to tell the untold story of the Mexican American combat soldiers, who were noticeably missing from the novels and movies that were generated after the war. Originally, he planned to produce a comic-book-style account, but found that there was just too much to say. So for the next ten years he sporadically worked on producing a book on the subject. He started with stories and information gathered from his interviews with wounded soldiers in the hospitals. He got the help of veterans organizations and their publications and contacts, and he gathered information from newspapers, clipping files, and his own personal notes taken during the war. Morin traveled throughout the Southwest to track down stories and information about the Mexican American soldiers of World War II. Finally, in 1961, the American GI Forum, a Mexican American veterans organization, voted to take on the publication of Morin's book as a special project. Advance sales paid for the first printing.

This was the first, and so far the only, book-length firsthand account of the Mexican American soldiers and their experience in World War II. It has gone through eight printings and remains the most authentic story of the valor of these GIs. The sections reproduced here tell of the fighting in the Pacific and European theaters and the soldiers' return.[1]

VI

AT ATTU

May, 1943. Much had taken place in both the Pacific and
the European Theaters of war. The Marines had captured
Guadalcanal and now were driving through the Solomons and
New Guinea. The battle of North Africa had ended with the
capture of the once mighty Africa Korps.

In the Aleutians, the United States initiated a move to drive
off the Japanese that were in Attu and Kiska, and the ensuing
events uncovered another 'first' for Mexican-American soldiers
of W.W. II. For it was here that Private Jose P. Martinez made
history, graphically told in the following documentary:

PVT. JOSE P. MARTINEZ

Awarded the Congressional Medal of Honor. (posthumously).
Private, Company K, 32d Infantry, 7th Infantry Division. On Attu, Aleutians, 26 May 1943. For conspicious
gallantry and intrepidity above and beyond the call of
duty in action with the enemy. Over a period of several
days, repeated efforts to drive the enemy from a key
defensive position high in the snow-covered precipitous
mountains between East Arm Holtz Bay and Chichagof
Harbor had failed. On 26 May, 1943, troop dispositions
were readjusted and a trial coordinate attack on this
position by a reinforced battalion was launched. Initially
successful, the attack bogged down. In the face of severe
hostile machinegun, rifle, and mortar fire, Private Martinez,
an automatic rifleman, rose to his feet and resumed his
advance. Occassionally he stopped to urge his comrades

48

AT ATTU   49

on. His example inspired others to follow. After a most difficult climb, Private Martinez eliminated resistance from part of the enemy position by BAR fire and hand grenades, thus assisting the advance of other attacking elements. This success only partially completed the action. The main Holtz-Chichagof Pass rose about 150 feet higher, flanked by steep rocky ridges and reached by a snow-filled defile. Passage was barred by enemy fire from either flank and from tiers of snow trenches in front. Despite these obstacles, and knowing of their existence, Private Martinez again led the troops on and up, personally silencing several trenches with BAR fire and ultimately reaching the pass itself. Here, just below the knifelike rim of the pass, Private Martinez encountered a final enemy-occupied trench and as he was engaged in firing into it he was mortally wounded. The pass, however, was taken, and its capture was an important preliminary to the end of organized hostile resistance on the island.[1]

The career of Jose P. Martinez in Attu assumed great importance, not only as United States History but to all Americans of Mexican descent because he was the first draftee enlisted man in the Pacific Theatre to distinguish himself in battle by winning the Congressional Medal of Honor in World War II.

The name of Martinez was first found in a news-communique out of Attu, an official War Department news release dated May 27, 1943.

"May 27, 1943. Jose P. Martinez, Ault, Colorado, 23 year old Private with an infantry regiment of the 7th (Hourglass) Division died from Japanese bullets after he had led his fellow doughboys in a successful attack on

---

[1] War Department Citation G.O. No. 71, October 27, 1943. *The Medal of Honor*, official publication, Department of the Army, U.S. Government Printing Office, Washington, D.C., 1949, p. 281.

PVT. JOSE P. MARTINEZ
Ault, Colorado
Congressional Medal of Honor
Attu, Alaska, World War II

AT ATTU   51

a vital pass in Attu, between East Arms Holtz Bay and
Chichagof Harbor. His name has been recommended for
the Congressional Medal of Honor by his officers."

Jose Martinez, one of nine children, was born in Taos, New
Mexico, on July 20, 1920. Although he has been known as the
first 'Mexican-American' soldier of W.W. II to receive the
Medal of Honor, his family originates from a long line of
American born Spanish-speaking ancestors from the state of
New Mexico who have always been regarded as 'Spanish-Ameri-
cans,' just like other Spanish-speaking citizens from the 'Land
of Enchantment.'

In 1927 his father packed and moved the family north into
the state of Colorado, where he hoped to make a better living
working in the fields. He had heard that good money could
be made by a large family such as his.

The family worked up and down the Northern Colorado
farm belt, as did many other Mexican and Spanish-American
families in those days. Finally, he decided to settle in Ault, a
small town near the Rockies. In Ault, Joe attended school with
his brothers and sisters, helped the family in farm work, and
assisted in managing the trucking business in which the elder
Martinez boy was engaged.

Joe loved the rich country where he grew up. The clean
fresh air that would sweep from the high Sierras, the cold
brisk winters, the high snow-covered peaks and the picturesque
rock formations along the countryside roads. He dreamed
of how he would someday own a farm where he would
harvest his own crops, raise his own cattle and hoge, here in
"God's Country."

When the Army began drafting men, Delfino, Joe's older
brother, was one of the first to go from Ault. Joe yearned for
the day when he too would be called. He wanted to be alongside Delfino.

The call finally came. Joe left his farm country and his

dreams behind on August 17th, 1942. Jose P. Martinez felt proud to be a member of the United States Army. From the induction center at Denver, he was sent to Camp Roberts, California, where he took his basic training. Upon completion of basic, he was sent to Camp Butner for some additional infantry training. He eventually found himself in the 7th (Hourglass) Division. He shipped out April 13th, 1943, with the 7th to Alaska via Seattle, Washington.

Within two weeks Joe's regiment boarded ship and sailed north, straight to Cold Bay on the northern tip of the Alaskan Peninsula. On May 1st, their convoy was joined by transports, cruisers, destroyers, and aircraft carriers—all headed for the Aleutian Islands then occupied by the Japanese.

The presence of an enemy force on the North American continent alarmed all of America. Army Chiefs of Staff made preparations to rid the Aleutians of Japanese and wipe out the threat to American soil.

After a heavy bombing attack, the Japanese had occupied the two small islands since early June of 1942, when they had landed a small force in Attu and Kiska. Joe's battalion was part of the task force that was sent to drive the Japanese out of the Aleutians. Headed by Major General Eugene M. Land-rum, the force included elements of the 7th Infantry Division, a battalion of the 4th Infantry and the Alaskan Scouts.

Early morning on May 11th, the task force neared the shore of Holtz Bay on Attu. Joe's mind was preoccupied with the day's task. He ate a light breakfast. After that, he wandered out on deck, scanning the high rocky mountain peaks of Attu. The snow-covered pinnacles reminded him of the high rockies back home in Colorado.

Now he wondered how he would behave in battle. Would he be afraid? He didn't feel he would be; he had trained well for this. He would be ready. H-Hour had been designated as 0700.

AT ATTU   53

On deck, the troops checked out their gear and equipment, and
listened to their last-minute instructions.[1]

The ships of the task forces pounded Holtz Bay and the hill
on the island with such a tremendous barrage that it rocked the
landing barges and deafened the roar of the engines. Joe's
battalion, under Colonel Frank L. Cullen, stormed ashore on
Holtz Bay, expecting to take the Japanese by surprise. Another
force landed at Massacre Bay with orders to drive back the
enemy, and then together, the two forces were to concentrate in
a drive to push back the enemy into Chichagof Harbor where
the Japanese had established their headquarters.

The enemy quickly rallied and put up a stubborn defense.
They poured heavy artillery from the high knoll, harassing the
landing troops below on Red Beach. Americans brought
in howitzers, and an artillery battle was waged. The American
artillery failed to dislodge the Japanese from their well entrenched positions. It became necessary to send out ground troops to
engage them in close combat.

Private Jose P. Martinez was in the platoon that was given
the order to attack on that cold foggy day of May 26, 1943.

The battalion was reinforced with troops that had landed on
Massacre Bay. The attacking force made slow progress. They
moved in closer to the enemy. The G.I.'s moved cautiously from
rock to rock while intense machine gun, rifle, and mortar fire
stymied their drive. They were pinned down and no one dared
to move out into the hail of fire the Japanese poured down. The
men sought protection from the exploding mortar shells that
were falling all around. Seeking to break out of the desperate
situation, the C.O. then asked for a rifle platoon to move up at
all costs.

Before the word reached the Sergeant down the line, a lone

---

[1] Rech, Franklin M., *Beyond The Call of Duty*, Thomas Crowell Company,
1944, p. 112.

54   AMONG THE VALIANT

figure rose from the ground and started up. It was Pvt. Jose P. Martinez.

Having been chosen to handle the BAR, (Browning Automatic Rifle) for the platoon, Martinez decided to take matters into his own hands. He felt it was his duty to do something about their situation. In the face of hostile fire, he rose to his feet and took off alone. Now and then he would wave an arm to the others to follow him. "Come on, lets go!", he would yell.

The pinned-down G.I.'s couldn't believe their eyes. Here was Marty, the quiet Mexican kid from Colorado, *who wasn't even in charge of the rifle squad,* setting the example and urging the others to follow. Inspired by his actions, they started to follow. Martinez climbed steadily up with the battalion following him. Incredible, the whole battalion was moving forward, led by a Private! On reaching the bench-like plateau, he engaged the Japanese in two foxholes. Their rifle fire was no match for Martinez' blazing BAR. He cleaned out the two nests and hurled hand grenades at the other enemy soldiers above him. The Japanese increased their machine gun and rifle fire.

Once more the attack bogged down. Withering fire from the front and from above kept the infantrymen hugging the earth. There was no movement, then a lone figure once more arose and started up the snow slope that led to the pass. Once more it was Pvt. Martinez. Now he was within closer enemy range and the bullets struck all around him. The brave Martinez was thinking of the others behind him and had no time to think of himself. Of one thing he was sure: it was either the enemy or him. . . . He was not afraid!

He was forced to move across open ground. Now he faced heavy crossfire from above and frontal fire from the foxholes. He came upon two enemy trenches. Jumping in, he quickly opened up with his Browning automatic and killed five more of the enemy. Without hesitation, the fearless G.I. from Color-

AT ATTU   55

ado then moved up to the second trench and accounted for two more Japanese. He reached the pass, still under heavy fire from the surrounding ridges. Standing on the ridge, overlooking the pass leading into the Chichagof Harbor, Martinez emptied his rifle into the positions just below and beyond the pass.

The last part of his citation reads, "... he was mortally wounded with his rifle still at his shoulder, absorbing all enemy fire and permitting all units to move up behind him and successfully take the pass."

Thus, the twenty-three year old Martinez died a glorious death and the Alaskan hills were covered with American blood. Many others fought, bled and died in the Aleutian campaign but it was a Private, a former farm laborer, Jose P. Martinez' heroic action that enabled the American forces to clear the pass of Japanese by May 30th. He earned praise, admiration and recommendation for the Congressional Medal of Honor from his fellow soldiers, commanding officers and Battalion Commander.

The glory of Joe Martinez will never be forgotten because historians and educators have seen fit to have his story told and retold in American college classrooms, and written in the junior high and high school history books all over America. Annual scholarships bear his name and a local Chapter of the Disabled American Veterans has been named in his honor in Colorado. A local Post of the American Legion now exists in Los Angeles, California, named after the Mexican-American hero.

All were proud of Joe, but Mexican-Americans were just a little more proud of him. His widely heralded achievement occurred at a time when attitudes toward Mexicans in the United States were at a low ebb because of unfortunate happenings in Los Angeles.

56   AMONG THE VALIANT

The Zoot-Suit riots[1] in the Angel city had left a very bad impression of Mexican-Americans throughout America. Frank Lares of Los Angeles, who was then stationed in Fort Greely with Battery D, 250th Coast Artillery, in Kodiak Island, Alaska, recalls that the Pachuco Riots of June, '43, were in all the headlines, even in Alaska. He remembers how uncomfortable he felt when his own fellow comrades stationed at the same camp would give him dirty looks and ask embarrassing questions, such as, "What kind of citizens are those Mexican Zoot-Zooters that would beat up on our own Navy men?"

After the news got around about Jose P. Martinez' one-man heroic drive in the Aleutians, no questions were asked about pachuco gangs. Lares felt very proud of Martinez and very proud that he was a Mexican-American.

---

[1]On June 3, 1943, the "Zoot-suit" riots flared up in the streets of Los Angeles. For weeks, a reign of terror existed. Groups of servicemen hunted down and beat up boys of Mexican descent-so called "Pachucos" who wore the then-popular Zoot-suits. They ripped off their pants or clipped their hair, in many cases while policemen stood by. The incident which started the rioting was never acknowledged by the men in uniform or the newspapers. Several sailors in a bar in the Mexican section had attempted to entice two *senoritas* from their escorts and a fight started.

From *"My L.A."* by Matt Weinstock, Current Books Inc., A. A. Wyn, New York, N.Y. p. 125.

The so-called "Zoot-Suit" riots made front line news in newspapers all over the nation.

IX

D DAY

June 6, 1944. D Day was known in history as the greatest invasion operation of W.W. II, with the largest number of ships participating (4,000), and the biggest number of assault forces (66,000 men) landing in the longest stretch of heavily-defended shoreland, the 1,000 mile Normandy coast between La Havre and Cherbourg.

Every type of modern war weapon was utilized and every branch of service put into use by the American, English, Allies, Germans and Axis Forces. Assembled here were airplanes, Navy ships, transports, assault boats, landing craft, liners, cutters, minesweepers, warships, and gliders. Block-ships were sunk to form breakwaters and huge floating harbors were towed across the channel in sections.

The Navy, Air Force, Coast Guard, Army and Airborne troops all participated with equal effectiveness. Thousands of planes maintained a protective umbrella over the landing area. Airborne troops descended behind enemy lines. Naval guns engaged shore batteries. Mine sweepers drove in through shallow water, blowing up underwater obstacles, then the landing craft began bringing in the largest mass of men and supplies ever attempted in war history.

Catarino "Cato" Cuellar, Lockart, Texas; Raul Rosales and Joe Ramirez of Houston, Texas; Frank P. Martinez and Guillermo "Memo" Terrazas of Los Angeles, California—these were among the many thousands who participated in the memorable D Day landing on the Normandy Beach to open up a western front on the impregnable 'Hitler fortress.'

Both Cuellar and Ramirez were line sergeants in the 2nd
Division. Ramirez was reported missing. Cuellar and Terrazas
were both badly wounded, but returned later to the front lines.
They saw a lot of their buddies killed right next to them
trying to make the beach. They'll forever remember the ghastly
horrors on the beach that day. They vividly recall how the
drivers of the LST's could not get close enough to the beaches
because of the heavy fire from the Jerry 88's. They still hear
the rattle of the machine guns that raked the shore line downing
many of their comrades, who drowned in the deep waters
laden down with the heavy gear they carried. Their memory
is still saddened by the many dead bodies of American GI's
they saw floating in the waters, remembering the many who
never got ashore, and the many who died as they set foot on
French soil.

Manuel Nuñez, Manny Bernal, 82nd Airborne, "Chuy"
Galvan and Mundo Lozano with the 101st 'Screaming Eagles'
all from Los Angeles but unknown to each other, were with the
many advance troops that parachuted down behind the German
lines—the first American combatmen to do ground fighting on
French soil.

At 0100 of D Day, the Allied Airborne Paratroopers in the
dark of night plunged into space from transport planes and
gliders to prepare the way for assault troops that would be
landing all over the Normandy coast. They worked behind the
lines disrupting communications and supply lines, clearing
main causeways and fighting from the very moment they
landed. Many of them were shot down by the alerted enemy
as they descended. Despite the strange country and the necessity
of fighting in the dark, the American Airborne Infantrymen
contributed invaluable assistance to the Allied assault troops
that landed later that day.

To counteract the long anticipated move, the Germans had
built solid defensive positions with concrete-built pillboxes and

96 AMONG THE VALIANT

dug deep ditches to stop the men and armoured vehicles. They moved in railroad guns and built concrete machine gun emplacements on the hilltops; they had crossfire covering the entire beach line. Off the shore, they had floating mines and landing obstacles; along the shore they had buried land mines by the thousands in the sand. Behind their lines they had great concentration of land troops ready to give battle to the landing forces and well-planned synchronized reserves that would move additional Divisions to the front on a moment's notice.

German ack-ack installations filled the sky with flak. The Stukas and Messerschmitts of the Luftwaffe, went out to give battle to the invading airmen. Their manpower far out-numbered ours, and they had the advantage of the higher terrain. It was hard for our combat troops to move uphill, heavily-laden as they were with combat equipment and through waist-deep waters facing the murderous enemy fire. Many lives and vital supplies were lost in the landing.

Back home, the whole Nation awaited anxiously for news of how the invasion had fared. Prayers were offered for the many troops participating. We paid a dear price for this maneuver, but the invasion was a success. The Germans were pushed back, and the war picture took on a new aspect. Everyone in America and throughout the world now felt that it would not be long before Hitler would be defeated.

The 2nd 'Indian Head' Division, which landed on D Day plus one, had many Mexican-Americans from south Texas. The division called Fort Sam Houston their home. Other GI's who participated with the 2nd Division were S/Sgt. Agustin Lucio, San Marcos, Texas, of Co. L, 23rd Regt., and Pedro Rubio, Austin, Texas, who operated on a wounded comrade under heavy enemy fire, removing a bullet from his thigh with a pocket kife. Vincent Gonzales, Rio Hondo, Texas, received the Silver Star for crawling under a sheet of heavy machine gun fire from the high bluffs of Omaha Beach to give first aid to

STAFF SERGEANT AGUSTIN LUCIO
San Marcos, Texas
Silver Star, Bronze Star, Purple Heart and the French Croix de Guerre
European Theatre World War II

two wounded comrades. All of them were wounded in action and sent to ship hospitals. Lucio and Rubio returned to their outfit after being released from the hospital. Gen. Norman D. Cota headed the 29th Division at Omaha Beach.

Once ashore, the ground troops began making headway. They hurled the Nazi defenders out of their positions, blasted them right in their foxholes and pillboxes with flame throwers, automatic weapons, mortars and grenades.

June 11, 1944. The dogged infantrymen with the 1st, 2nd, 4th, 9th and 29th Divisions drove an even seven-mile wedge into the Cherbourg peninsula. By then, additional Infantry Divisions had landed in France to give aid to the fighting Allied forces. Among them were the 79th, direct from England, a division with many Mexican-Americans, many of whom I got to know personally later on. A big tank battle was waged between American and German armored units led by General Von Runsted. Five thousand German prisoners were taken by American forces in this 15-mile Normandy strip.

On June 18th, the 79th moved into the outskirts of the French port of Cherbourg. First Lt. Agustin Barron, El Paso, with the 313th Regiment, Rudy Mesa and Joe Montano, Los Angeles, with the 314th Regiment, were with the foot soldiers of the 79th who relieved the regiments of the 90th Division in the shattered French port, which had been completely destroyed by the war. Meeting stiff opposition that led to bitter hand-to-hand fighting, the Yanks finally took Cherbourg and trapped 30,000 German 'supermen.'

After his return from a base hospital for treatment of wounds received in the D Day landing, Memo Terrazas also joined the 79th and was assigned to the 315th Regiment. He saw heavy action with the 79th at Saint-Lo, Fougeres, Le Mans, and later when the 79th crossed the Seine River. After the crossing of the Seine River, Terrazas was wounded for the second time. He received serious wounds of the head and arms. His

side and leg were shattered by artillery blasts. His critical
condition required immediate evacuation from the front lines.
He was first sent to England, then finally to the U.S. by plane.
He remembers 'coming to' in a mental ward of some Army
hospital in the States with impaired speech and complete loss
of memory.

LAST DAYS AT HOME

June 6th, 1944. D Day in Europe . . . and we were still in
dirty old Camp Roberts. Weren't we ever going into the damn
war? Some of the younger GI's really felt that way, but not
us old family men. With us, the feeling— and wishful thinking
—was that somehow the war would be over before we would
be sent overseas. If only we were as free as the single men in
camp, we would not have to worry about leaving a family
behind. It was not easy to tear away from your loved ones.

Basic training had been a vigorous routine. By the end of the
17 weeks, most of us were rounding into shape. Everyone
looked 'sharper,' and the drinking bouts we staged by the PX
kept getting rougher and rougher. They all ended up in the
same way .. . GI's fighting and slugging each other. Everyone was itching to get into the big scrap.

Despite all the talk about what a lousy camp Roberts was,
we were beginning to enjoy it there. Things were changing.
The non-coms, who at first delighted themselves in browbeating
us, started treating us like decent human beings, except for
a few duty-bound morons who were always bucking for an
extra stripe. Most sergeants and corporals still acted the hard-
boiled-type, all we did about it was just look at each other.
They would over-do it more when they were within earshot
of company officers. A few of us would be invited to the
'private' gambling games in Cadre Sgt. Harris' quarters, where
most of the non-coms would take off their stripes to become
'regular guys.'

Mexican-Americans in Roberts still ganged around together, and in addition, we had picked up a lot of *'gabacho'* (Anglo) buddies. For instance there was Tony Despagne, born and raised in Texas, who could understand *chicano* talk better than English, and who was familiar with all our customs; Leonard Muschinsky, a young Polish kid from Brenham, Texas, of all places; and Robert Smargeanian, an Armenian, who got indoctrinated with *pachuco-ism* in East Los Angeles. They, and many others got a bang out of hanging around with the Mexican-American *plebe*. They even learned to eat the 'hot stuff' the fellows used to bring in from town to spice the tasteless (to us) G.I. chow.

Because most of the trainees at Roberts were from the Middlewest and Northern part of the United States, it was not surprising to find many who had never associated or had ever seen a Mexican before. We were amused with the description they gave and the concept they had of a Mexican back in their hometowns. Walt Musick, from South Dakota, was being very frank when he told us, ("The only Mexicans we ever saw back home were those that worked in the Railroad and lived in section houses. I always heard that they were not to be trusted, and if you turned your back to them, they would knife you in the back. But these fellows I have known here in Roberts are just like other Americans."

Even the trainees who hailed from Texas were a friendly lot. Back in the old CCC days, every time a Texan and a Mexican crossed paths there was sure to be a brawl. There never was any trace of racial strife in Camp Roberts.

The most appreciated fact about Camp Roberts was that it was close to Los Angeles. Everyone who got a weekend pass made a bee-line to the "City of Angels." Every Saturday afternoon we had to fight for space in cars belonging to some of the comrades who lived in Los Angeles. On week-ends, there was always a steady stream of cars tearing into Los Angeles both on the coast and the inland routes. One chap whose father owned a mortuary drove a hearse into camp and always had a fullhouse going into town.

After the hectic week-ends in Los Angeles, the gang would always gather around to tell of the good times they had in the City and about the many popular night-clubs they had taken in. To hear them say it, everyone of them was a playboy and a great lover. They bragged about the many *'lindas'* and 'shack-up jobs' they had in town.

When at last our company, the 76th, completed the 17-week training cycle, all kinds of 'latrine rumors' began to circulate. Some said we were going to the Pacific, others said that we were going to Europe, and another said—this one we liked— that we were staying in the States and would be given a job to train other Army recruits. Everyone smiled when they heard that one.

Late in July, 1944, our moving-out orders came through. These included a ten-day furlough and specific orders to report to Fort Meade, Maryland, on the East Coast.

My first five days were spent in Los Angeles at home with the wife and three children. I found the great city going full blast with war activity. The whole town was overcrowded with defense workers, *braceros*[1], sailors, marines and soldiers on pass or AWOL.

Out on North Main Street, Provost Sgt. Pete Despart, Chief Little Wolf and Jerry Gioviano were kept busy making room for more G.I.'s in their hotel (the Army stockade) due to the many AWOL's the MP's kept rounding up.

My five days at home went by too soon. It wasn't easy to leave, this time it was different. There were so many things to worry about . . . the wife, the children, Olivia aged 4, David aged 3, Eddie aged 2, they would have to carry on in case I

[1]Contract laborers from Mexico.

didn't return ... Most of our ugly thoughts were put off. We pretended that it was just another short trip, that I would be back in a few days.

There were church services, short visits to near relatives and friends, many goodbyes ... and off we were.

My next stop was San Antonio, Texas, where I spent the next few days with my mother and sister. San Antonio was about the busiest Army town I had ever seen. There were many Army camps, airfields, and training centers, and towering above all, the gigantic Fort Sam Houston, the U.S. 4th Corp Area Army Headquarters. With so many soldiers around, civilians were a rare sight.

Most surprising to me was the sudden disappearance of all the old *palomilla* I used to know there. They had all gone into the service, many of them had been among the early volunteers. Hardly any of them had been 'deferred' or found 'unfit for Army duty' like where I came from. Even those with three or four dependents were taken in the early part of the draft. No one was classified 'exempt' because of vital defense occupation here.

In such places as Lockhart, San Marcos and Austin, where I spent my early youth, I learned that friends and relatives with whom I had grown up were long since in the service. Many of them had already seen plenty of combat duty overseas. Some had been wounded and were being treated in Army hospitals far away from the combat zones.

At last my short furlough came to an end. Once again it was hard to say goodbye. My mother and sisters were very serious about my going away, but I managed to ease their minds, assuring them that the war was about over and that we would probably be used as occupational troops.

As I boarded the train that was to take me to Washington, D.C., I ran into some of the fellows who were also on their way to Fort Meade. At the S.P. station in San Antonio I met

Joe Ramirez, a short stocky youngster, and Tony Rodriguez, in his late forties, married and father of six. From near-by Austin, there was Gregorio 'Pancho' Ramirez, that very good singer and guitar player who had delighted us in our training days, also Jose T. Ramirez and Jose Nerios, both mature family men and farmers from south Texas. We all had been at Camp Roberts and now had the same destination. When we boarded the train, we found more of the Camp Robert's bunch. Young, recently married, Mike Tapia from Ontario, California; Juan Arlee, an oldster from Pasadena, and Bobby Nunez, Gilbert Villegas, Jimmy Desma, all from Los Angeles. The five of them, all teen-agers, were full of fun and took soldiering, the war, and the going away trip very lightly. From Denver there was Jess Martinez, a quiet married man about 30; Joe Arvisu and Lupe Gonzales from south Arizona, also Carlos Amor and Manuel Davila, two quiet men from the border who hardly spoke in English.

We represented the average Mexican-American replacement group that were being sent out to the war front in those days.

We had all trained together with the 76th Infantry Regiment at Roberts, and now were all going overseas as replacements together, some to never return, and others to just barely make it back . . .

SGT. JOSE M. LOPEZ

Awarded The Congressional Medal of Honor

Krinkelt, Belgium, December 17th, 1944. On his own initiative, he carried his heavy machine gun from Company K's right flank to its left, in order to protect that flank which was in danger of being overrun by advancing enemy infantry supported by tanks.

Occupying a shallow hole offering no protection above his waist, he cut down a group of ten Germans. Ignoring enemy fire from an advancing tank, he held his position and cut down 25 more enemy infantry attempting to turn his flank. Glancing to his right he saw a large number of infantry swarming in from the front. Although dazed and shaken from enemy artillery fire which had crashed into the ground only a few yards away, he realized that his position soon would be outflanked. Again, alone, he carried his machine gun to a position to the right rear of the sector; enemy tanks and infantry were forcing a withdrawal. Blown over backwards by the concussion of enemy fire, he immediately reset his gun and continued his fire. Single-handed, he held off the German horde until he was satisfied his company had effected its retirement.

Again he loaded his gun on his back and in a hail of small arms fire he ran to a point where a few of his comrades were attempting to set up another defense against the onrushing enemy. He fired from this position until his

THE ETO CAMPAIGN   167

ammunition was exhausted. Still carrying his gun, he fell back with his small group to Krinkelt.

Sergeant Lopez' gallantry and intrepidity on a seemingly suicidal mission in which he killed at least 100 of the enemy, was almost solely responsible for allowing Company K to avoid being enveloped, to withdraw successfully, and to give other forces coming in support time to build a line which repelled the enemy drive.[1]

Jose M. Lopez, of Brownsville, Texas, was the 4th American of Mexican descent to be awarded the Congressional Medal of Honor. The short, stocky, Mexican-American was a machine gunner with K Company of the 23rd Regiment, 2nd Division. He has the distinction of having killed more enemy soldiers than any other American in the ETO or Pacific Theaters in World War II.

Not even Sgt. York of World War I fame comes close to the number of enemy killed or personally destroyed. Lopez is credited with having killed over 100 German soldiers in the Krinkelt Wald, near Belgium on December 17, 1944.

Next to Lopez was S/Sgt. John C. Sjorgen of Rockyford, Michigan, who personally killed 43 Japanese near San Jose Hacienda, Negros, while serving with the 40th Division in the Philippines on May 23, 1945. Then stands Sgt. Veto R. Bertoldo of Decatur, Illinois, who destroyed 40 Germans in Hatten, France, with the 42nd Division on January 9-10, 1945.

All Mexican-Americans are very proud of Jose M. Lopez. Not only because he won the Congressional Medal but because of the way he accomplished this unprecedented task.

Lopez first landed in France with the 2nd Division on D-Day plus-one at St. Laurent-sur-Mer in Normandy. He was in the thick of hedgerow fighting around Saint-Lo and in the breakthrough out of Normandy. In Brest, he fought against the

---

[1]War Department Citation, G.O. No. 47, June 18, 1945.

SERGEANT JOSE M. LOPEZ
Brownsville, Texas
Congressional Medal of Honor
European Theater World War II

tough 3rd Parachute German Division where the 2nd battled for 39 days before they took the ravished city. On July 29th, he received the Purple Heart for being wounded in action.

While fighting near the Siegfreid Line around St. Vith, Lopez was awarded the Bronze Star Medal for conspicuous gallantry against the enemy.

On December 17, 1944, the second day of the German breakthrough, near the town of Rockeroth, Lopez and other men of K and L companies from the 23rd Regiment were ordered to protect an exposed left flank as the German infantry came on with two light tanks. Lopez set up his machine gun to protect the withdrawal of the other troops and began firing.

The Germans wasted no time in returning Lopez' fire, riddling the area with burp guns, rifle, and tank fire. A Tiger tank appeared at the road junction and fired point-blank at Lopez' exposed position. The long barrel of the 88 seemed to reach halfway to his foxhole, but Lopez continued to fire.[1]

The woods echoed with the rapid staccato of the hot lead he was pouring, and smoke erupted from his water-cooled barrel that was now burning up. Over the noise of Lopez' machine gun, Captain Walsh shouted to his men to withdraw, but Lopez ignored him and continued to fire. He cut down a group of the Jerries that were advancing toward him—backed up by a Tiger tank. Ignoring the tank fire, he held his position.

To the rear of the sector, enemy tanks and infantry were forcing a withdrawal . . . now he was almost alone facing the enemy. Rifle and tank fire kept hitting all around him. Then came hand grenades . . . One of the grenades landed right in his foxhole.

The action is described by his comrades as follows:

"Twice, when the Germans were overrunning his position,

---

[1]MacDonald, Charles Brown, *Company Commander,* Infantry Journal Press, Washington, D.C., 1947, p. 187.

he picked up his machine gun and withdrew to set it up and continue the "fight," Private First Class Leo J. Albert, 419 River Street, Paterson, New Jersey, reported. "The Germans were supported by tanks. Twice, fire from the gun of the first tank plowed up the ground close to his position, but he continued firing his machine."

Lieutenant Paul E. Burkhardt, of Fairground Road, Xenia, Ohio, said the engagement lasted from 11:30 a.m. until 6:00 p.m. "After beating off an attack from the flank, killing at least 35 Germans, Sergeant Lopez was forced to withdraw with his machine gun after tank fire had twice struck his position," reported the Lieutenant.

"Alone in holding up the advance, he was the target of every German weapon, but disregarding the intense fire, he again set up his weapon and continued firing. Another tank approached to within 50 yards and its 88mm was swung around, turned directly on him . . . but he kept his fire on the advancing enemy.

"A shell from the 88 struck his position and he was blown backward away from his gun, still he staggered back to it, reset it, and continued firing.

"All during this time ammunition bearers were forced to toss boxes of ammunition to him because of the tremendous volume of enemy fire being poured into his position. When his re-formed and reinforced company returned to the attack, they drove the enemy from the area."

Born in Mission, Texas, on June 1, 1912, Lopez, his wife Emilia, and his six-year-old stepson, Juan P. Lopez, lived in Brownsville. He entered the Army from his home there on April 8, 1942. It is a shame that very few Americans have heard of the record Lopez holds, and the daring exploits that won him the Congressional Medal of Honor. Yet others who did less have been glorified more. Even though he has been given little recognition here, Lopez feels very satisfied

THE ETO CAMPAIGN   171

because the people of Mexico have all heard of his courageous achievement and is well known to them. They remember him when he was guest of President Aleman in Mexico City in 1948, where he was feted and awarded the Aztec Eagle, the highest honor medal of the Southern Republic, and he later toured that country as a guest.

XVII

PRIVATE CITIZENS, FIRST-CLASS

It felt very good to have come back from the wars. Things were happening to us that had never happened before. This was a new America for us . . . we felt like shouting . . . *Hey! We did it! The Allies won the war and the Americans played a prominent part in it. Americans! . . that meant us!* As returning veterans, we were being welcomed enthusiastically everywhere. We were openly admired, loved and respected. It was a wonderful feeling, we were overwhelmed.

Most returning American war veterans found very few changes in their hometowns. Overjoyed with excitement incident to being home again, they gave no thought nor noticed many changes in the American way of life. Furthermore, most of them did not want it to be any different from that of the day they had left. This was home . . . they preferred it this way—this was the way the remembered it in their dreams during the long days overseas.

For the returning Mexican-American veteran, things *were* different and furthermore he did not want to find things the way he had left them. Not that he had not dreamed of coming home to his loved ones, but there were a few things he did not care for when he got back.

For too long we had been like outsiders. It had never made very much difference to us and we hardly noticed it until we got back from overseas. How could we have played such a prominent part as Americans over there and now have to go back living as outsiders as before? We began to ask ourselves, how come? How long had we been missing out on benefits

277

derived as an American citizen? Oldtimers had told us and we had read in books how the early settlers had invaded our towns and had shoved us into the 'other side of the tracks'. But we ourselves had never made much attempt to move out of there. The towns had grown up, population had increased, State, County, City and community government had been set up and we had been left out of it. We never had any voice. Here now was the opportunity to do something about it.

Soon now, we left the other side of the tracks and began to move into town. We moved to better neighborhoods and, thanks to the GI Bill, we continued our education. We were able to buy new homes. We began to go into business for ourselves, obtain better positions of employment and some even managed to get chosen, appointed or elected to public office.

We acquired new ways in everyday doings. New thoughts and dreams entered our minds. We embarked on many unheard-of—for us—projects and developed many ideas and new perspectives. In the old days, our lives were governed mostly by patterns set by our elders. We had accepted without question edicts, taboos, restrictions, traditions and customs that our ancestors had brought over from the old country. Many such were long since outdated in Mexico proper. After having been to many other parts of the world, meeting other people from different parts of the country, we cast aside these old beliefs and we began anew in America.

Many were the things we could enjoy now, that had not been easy to acquire before. One was Priority. Never had we been given preference over anyone in the purchase of goods, automobiles, new homes, homesteading, leases or rentals and employment in civil service. Now, as veterans, we had priority over non-veterans in all these shortages and it was something new to us.

Loans and Credit. Limited credit was about all we could get before. Prior to the war Bank Loans were hard to get.

PRIVATE CITIZENS, FIRST-CLASS 279

Nowdays we are just as eligible as any other citizen and bankers no longer consider racial background as a yardstick on ability to pay. If you are a veteran, you are eligible for a loan.

Our purchasing power increased greatly. With better jobs, Government allotments and compensation pay, we could well afford luxuries we never before could buy, such as good clothes, expensive furniture and late-model autos. Many alert businessmen and store owners began to scheme ways to snare our dollars. They hired Spanish-speaking clerks and salesmen, and solicited our trade through well-conducted advertising campaigns in Spanish newspapers and Spanish radio programs.

We entered the business field. The grand old American system of free enterprise had never meant much for us. Not because anyone would keep us from going into business for ourselves, but mostly because there would not be very many customers for us. Now we have added grocery markets, service stations, *tortillerias,* insurance and real estate offices, accounting, hardware, and drug stores in addition to the Mexican restaurant, the small *cantina* and corner grocery store we had in the old days. Then there are the many service fields we entered which were not too common before WW II; television and radio repair, auto mechanics, upholstery, painting, plumbing, trucking, carpentry and electrical work, dry cleaning, barbering, cabinet-making and printing—all were included. Many veterans who were employed in these trades before going into the service are now owners of small business establishments, or are employers with several employees in the same trade.

We also have now many veterans who have taken advantage of the educational opportunities offered by our government, engaged in professional occupations. Today, many of our people have entered the medical, legal and educational professions, and others have earned high degrees in all kinds of specialized fields. Many men and women have achieved high success in the entertainment and sports fields. The art, music and theatre circles, bi-lingual radio broadcasting programs, advertising and sports—other than boxing—have been invaded by our veterans and their contemporaries all over the Southwest where Spanish-speaking Americans abound.

We developed intense pride in America. Our standard of living has improved 100 percent. As veterans, we have become serious-thinking Americans. We have enlarged our circle of friends to include not only Mexican-Americans like ourselves, but Americans of many other nationalities.

In organization we have also made great strides. After World War II a wave of social development unfolded. The Mexican-American became more aware of the growing need for self-improvement. He has become better informed on the changing complexities of the State and Nation. Responsibility and participation has developed a greater Race and ethnic-consciousness. All post-war organizations that have emerged propose improvement, envolement and unification of the Mexican-American. Among the standouts are, (CSO) Community Services Organization, The American GI Forum, a veterans family organization with a program geared to improving the status of the Mexican American in the United States: and in politics, it is (MAPA) Mexican-American Political Association, also known as (PASO), Political Association of Spanish-speaking Organizations.

World War II and the Korean Conflict were without a doubt the prime factors in having our economical, educational and social status raised far above that which we had prior to World War II. It definitely made a great change in the lives of all Mexican-Americans in the United States of America.

—END—

APPENDIX G

Affidavits of Mexican Americans Regarding Discrimination in Texas during World War II

COLLECTED BY ALONSO S. PERALES

Alonso S. Perales, a lawyer from South Texas, served as a diplomat to several South American countries and was a cofounder of the League of United Latin American Citizens (LULAC) in 1929. He was a highly respected civil rights leader of the Mexican American community. During the 1930s, he published a two-volume collection of essays and speeches exposing the discrimination in Texas.[1] As president of LULAC, he pushed for civil rights for Mexican Americans and, in 1943, helped introduce a bill to the Texas legislature outlawing racial discrimination. As part of LULAC's effort to present evidence of racial discrimination to the legislature as well as to the FEPC, Perales gathered affidavits from Mexican Americans and Mexicans who had experienced segregation and exclusion. Some of these were published in the San Antonio newspaper *La Prensa* to mobilize the Mexican American community. Other affidavits involving Mexican citizens were passed on to the Mexican consulate for diplomatic action.

This sample of some of the testimonies Perales gathered gives a vivid firsthand account of the kind of racial prejudice Mexican Americans experienced during the war.[2]

On November 7, 1945, about 3:45 P. M. I went to the_____
Barber Shop in South San Antonio, Texas, and asked one of
the barbers there to cut my hair. He told me that he could not
give me a hair cut, and I asked him why. He replied: "Because
you are a Mexican". I said: "OK", and I walked out.

Further affiant sayeth not.   Albert Gomez

Sworn to and subscribed before me, this 8th day of November,
A. D. 1945.

Alonso S. Perales.

Notary Public in and for Bexar County, Texas.

THE STATE OF TEXAS, COUNTY OF BEXAR

My name is Jose Herrera. I live in Adkins, Bexar County, Texas. I am 24 years of age. I served 14 months in the United States
Army in World War No. 2. I was born and reared in Texas.

On October 27, 1945, about 3:00 P. M., I went into a beer
parlor called "4-Points", on the Seguin Highway, about 15 miles
from San Antonio, Texas, but in Bexar County. As soon as I went
in the owner of the beer parlor told me that Mexicans were not
allowed there. I asked him for his name and he said: "I will not
give it to you and you get out immediately." Whereupon I got out.

My information is to the effect that the owner of said beer
parlor is German. I do not know his name.

There is a sign affixed to the glass part of the door reading:
"No Mexicans Allowed".

Further affiant sayeth not.   Jose Herrera

Sworn to and subscribed before me, this 27th day of October,
A. D. 1945.

Alonso S. Perales.

Notary Public in and for Bexar County, Texas.

THE STATE OF TEXAS, COUNTY OF BEXAR

Before me, the undersigned authority in and for said County,
State of Texas, this day personally came and appeared Gabriel
Gonzalez and wife, Refugia Rodriguez de Gonzalez, and Agustin
Gonzalez and wife, Berta Barrientes de Gonzalez, to me well
known, and who, after being by me duly sworn, did depose and say:

Our names are as above stated. We live in Hondo, Texas.

On October 14, 1945, about 7:30 P. M., we went into the
PARK THEATER in Hondo, Texas, and sat down. Then one of
the ushers came and told us to move away from there to a section
intended for Mexicans, which is on the extreme right side of the
theater and right in front of the screen. He stated that the seats
we were occupying were for white people only. We told him that
we did not want to move from there because we had paid our
money for these seats just the same as other people, and besides
that we had sat there on previous occasions and no one had objected.

170

He said that we would have to move, otherwise he would call the Sheriff. We told him to go ahead and call the Sheriff. He did, and Sheriff Jack Fossman, Sheriff of Medina County, came in accompanied by Deputy Sheriff Reinhard Weber, and told us to move or else leave the theater and have our money refunded. Mrs. Refugio Rodriguez de Gonzalez told Sheriff Fossman that in San Antonio, Texas, there were large and beautiful theaters and they did not segregate the Mexican people there, and Sheriff Fossman replied that it did not make any difference, that that was San Antonio and this was Hondo. Whereupon we left the theater. We did not ask for a refund of our money for the reason that our feelings were deeply hurt and we did not care to talk to him or see them any longer.

We were all born and reared in Texas and are long time residents of Hondo, Texas.

Further affiants sayeth not. Agustin Gonzalez, Berta B. Gonzalez, Gabriel Gonzalez, Refugia R. de Gonzalez.

Sworn to and subscribed before me, this 15th day of October, A. D. 1945.

Alonso S. Perales.
Notary Public in and for Bexar County, Texas.

THE STATE OF TEXAS, COUNTY OF BEXAR

My name is David Ponce Rodriguez. I am 29 years of age and reside 733 E. Magnolia St., in San Antonio, Texas, I am a native born citizen of the United States of America. I served in the United States Army four years and eight months, 30 months of which was overseas service.

On October 10th 1945, about 4:00 P. M., I went into an Anglo-American barber shop in San Marcos, Texas, for the purpose of having my shoes shined by a colored boy that has a shoe shine stand in the barber shop. An Anglo-American barber told me that the colored boy could not shine my shoes there because that place was for white people only. I told him that I was going to complain to the Sheriff of Hays County and he said: "Go ahead". I went and talked to the Sheriff, but he said he could not do anything about it. Then I went and talked with the Military Police in San Marcos and they said they could not do anything about it for the reason that I was now a civilian and was wearing civilian clothes.

I received an honorable discharge from the United States Army on October 6, 1945, after participating in several battles in the European Theater.

Further affiant sayeth not.   David P. Rodriguez

Sworn to and subscribed before me, this the 11th day of October, A. D. 1945.

Alonso S. Perales
Notary Public in and for Bexar County, Texas

THE STATE OF TEXAS, COUNTY OF BEXAR

My name is Longino Mendez Reyes. I am 41 years of age and reside in Hondo, Texas. I am employed at the Air Field Navigation School at Hondo, Texas.

On October 3, 1945, my wife, Mrs. Paula P. de Reyes, and I went to the _____ operated by Mr. Garrison, in Hondo, Texas, intending to order some root beer. As soon as we went in a lady asked Mr. Garrison whether it would be all right to serve us and Mr. Garrison then came and told us that he could not serve us because it was against the rules of the house. Whereupon we left the place.

I served in the United States Army one year and three months during World War No. 2, and received an honorable discharge.

Further affiant sayeth not.　　　　*Longino M. Reyes*

Sworn to and subscribed before me, this the 6th day of October, A. D. 1945.

Alonso S. Perales
Notary Public in and for Bexar County, Texas

THE STATE OF TEXAS, COUNTY OF BEXAR

My name is Pedro Muzquiz. I am 37 years of age, a citizen of the United States and a resident of Moore, Texas. I am a merchant.

The evening of September 18, 1945, Mr. Henry Crane, Mr. Theodore Juarchek and I went into the MONTE CARLO INN, in Devine, Texas, and we ordered three beers. A man named Davidson, who I understand is the owner of the establishment, brought a beer for Mr. Crane and one for Mr. Juarchek, but he did not bring one for me. When Mr. Juarchek asked him for the third beer (the one for me) he replied that he did not have any more beer. We noticed, however, that he continued to serve beer to the other customers there. I asked Davidson if the reason he did not serve me beer was that I was a Mexican, he replied that he did not have any more beer. Then Mr. Crane and Mr. Juarchek interceded in my behalf and tried to persuade him to sell me a beer, but he refused. Mr. Crane even told Davidson that he should treat me right because I was a good citizen and had a brother in the United States Army overseas. We got disgusted and left the place. Later Mr. Crane went into the place again and asked for a beer for himself and Davidson served it to him. Davidson then told Mr. Crane that he did not serve beer to Mexicans in this establishment.

Further affiant sayeth not.　　　　*Pedro Muzquiz*

Sworn to and subscribed before me, this the 19th day of September, A. D. 1945.

Alonso S. Perales
Notary Public in and for Bexar County, Texas

EX-SOLDIER STILL UNCONSCIOUS WEEK AFTER
ASSAULT; NONE OF ASSAILANTS APPREHENDED.
By GRADY HILL

Pvt. Ben Garcia Aguirre- now just a 20-year-old ex-GI Joe of Latin-American extraction following an honorable discharge from the Army remained unconscious in a basement room in a local hospital late last night.

And a number of Anglo-American youths- Aguirre's two companions asserted that the number was "about 15"- remained at large- a full week after police, answering a call, found Aguirre, beaten unconscious, in the street at 1021 S. Chadbourne St. He could not tell them who his assailants were.

Both eyes blackened and bloody, and with a cut inches long X-ed above his left ear, little 115-pound Ben Aguirre still could not talk last night.

His lips moved without speaking, as his eyes opened without seeing.

His quiet-spoken father, Manuel J. Aguirre of 5 W. Ave. L, said, not with bitterness: "No, I don't know who beat my boy. It is bad".

And in broken sentences: "Ben had a medical discharge. He never was under the care of a doctor before, but he was not a strong boy. He never drinks. He never had a fight before in his life, that I know of. He was a good boy".

And Pete Gonzalez, 16, who was fleeter of foot than Aguirre and escaped the gang which downed his slighter companion, talked a bit, too. However, he indicated that he didn't want to. He had previous experiences with groups of "white boys" who came over into South Angelo.

He agreed last night that "both sides had better stop having these fights". And he insisted that "You won't find us starting any trouble- and we sure didn't start it last Saturday night".

Rudolph Salazar, 19, the third Latin-American in the group attacked, was not interviewed last night. He had got away last Saturday night without injury when the three were first accosted on W. Washington Drive.

Gonzalez said that he "hit at" some five or six Anglo-American boys who seized him on Washington Drive, and broke away. "They tried to hold me, and when I broke away they threw rocks at me," he said. "Ben and I were going down Chadbourne, trying to get away, when they drove up in a pick-up and piled out.

"I broke away from them again and ran down Highland and then down Irving. I didn't know about Ben until the next morning. I thought he had got away, too," the youth declared.

173

Gonzalez said that they first noticed the other group at a service station south of the railroad tracks, as he, Aguirre and Salazar were returning from a Latin-American resort across town in Sharp End where "some television thing with recordings" was being exhibited.

"There are three Mexicans!" the trio heard the larger group shout. But they weren't accosted until they got to Washington Drive.

Chief of Police Clarence Lowe reported Friday that he hadn't been informed of the gang attack until the preceding day. It was confirmed last night that two policemen, answering a station call, had waited beside Aguirre until an ambulance arrived.

The two, J. E. Fread and Bill Owens, turned in a report to Walter Green, then desk sergeant. Last night, Desk Sergeant Frank Wood said the yellow sheet report was on file at the police station.

HE DIDN'T KNOW HOW IT HAD MISSED BEING BROUGHT TO LOWE'S ATTENTION.

It was learned, too, that Dr. J. S. Hixson, president of the Shannon Memorial Hospital, had seen that the casualty report was given to the police.

Giving information last night to others on which afforded possible leads to two of the assailants Gonzalez explained that he didn't discuss those factors with the police "because they didn't ask me just about that".

Chief of Police Lowe, who had joined Sheriff J. F. Bryson Friday in an ultimatum to the teenage gangs to "break it up," reiterated early Saturday his determination to bring a halt to the interracial "gang fights."

He recalled a previous fight in which the Latin-Americans failed to identify several teenage suspects.

Lowe could not be reached Saturday afternoon or early Saturday night for further comment.

Meanwhile, the father of the injured boy said that he had not had time to think about his hospital bill. He had been at the bedside steadily all week.

No organizations had offered to help.

"No, nobody. But of course they couldn't have known about this until yesterday," he sought to explain.

San Angelo, Texas, Sept. 9, 1945.

622 Arbor Pl.
San Antonio, Texas.
Aug. 23, 1945.

Mr. A. Perales,
Gunter Bldg.,
San Antonio, Texas.

Dear Sir:

I hope that the facts in this letter will interest you as much they do me.

The main reason of this letter is to tell you about an incident which happened during a trip I made to Temple, Texas, about two weeks ago.

We happened to stop at Lockhart, Texas to drink some coffee my wife her two sisters and brother. I was really enjoying my coffee when suddendly one of the girls waitress said "do not speak Spanish in this place or I'll be fired".

Tell me are we losing our freedom of speech here in U. S. A.?

Another thing they told us is that we weren't allowed to eat there.

Right now I am wondering how many of us (Mexicans) have gone to this "cheap cafe" as I would say it, and not be served.

Won't you please do something about this or it will go on and on forever.

As a matter of fact, the name of the cafe is "West Side Cafe" on Main Avenue.

I am just a poor decent man, but I still don't like the way they treated us on such small town, I am a veteran of War II, and I should like to see all of us treated like human beings.

I hope to see you personally sometime.

Yours truly,
Mr. Jose G. Cruz.

THE STATE OF TEXAS, COUNTY OF BEXAR

My name is Jose Z. Herrera. I live at Jourdanton, Atascosa County, Texas, where I have resided with my parents for the past eight (8) years. My occupation is farming, and I entered the service of the United States on November 30th 1942, serving up to the present date in Co. L. 333, Infantry Division 84, as Private First Class.

On or about May 5th, 1945, I went to the CITY BARBER SHOP, owned and operated by one KING HAYES, in the town of POTEET, Atascosa County, Texas, seeking to have my hair cut, and Mr. Hayes refused to serve me, and stated to me that he could not give me the service that I wanted, and that I should go to the barber shop called "the Mexican Barber Shop" and when I

175

told him that I had the right to demand service and went and sat on the barber chair, then he went out and talked to Deputy Sheriff Tom Lott, and the Deputy Sheriff sent a boy by the name of Eduardo Treviño to tell me to get out of the shop if I did not want to have any trouble.

Further deponent sayeth not.   Jose Z. Herrera

SWORN AND SUBSCRIBED before me on this the 21st day of May, A. D. 1945.

Jacob I. Rodriguez
Notary Public, Bexar County, Texas

THE STATE OF TEXAS, COUNTY OF BEXAR

My name is Adolfo Salomon. I reside at 1811 Colima St., in San Antonio, Texas. On Sunday, April 15, 1945, my daughters went to the bus station at Seguin, Texas, about 11:00 P. M., to board a bus for San Antonio, Texas. While they were waiting in the white people's waiting room, the ticket clerk told a porter to tell my daughters to go into the waiting room designated for "Colored People". My daughters refused to go into the Colored People's Waiting Room, and then later an officer came and told them to go into the said Colored People's Waiting Room. It was cold and raining outside, so my daughters decided to go into said room, but they did so under protest and because the officer compelled them to do so. The names of my daughters are: Miss Victoria Salomon and Mrs. Juanita Salomon. With them were the following other ladies: Mrs. Margarita Sifuentes, Mrs. Maria Ochoa, Mrs. Lupe Guillen and Miss Rosa Guillen.

The husbands of the following four ladies are in the United States Army: Margarita Sifuentes, Juanita Salomon, Maria Ochoa and Lupe Guillen. The husbands of Margarita Sifuentes and Maria Ochoa are serving overseas.

Further affiant sayeth not.   Adolfo Salomon

Sworn to and subscribed before me, this the 19th day of April, A. D. 1945.

Alonso S. Perales
Notary Public in and for Bexar County, Texas

THE STATE OF TEXAS, COUNTY OF BEXAR

My name is Ofelia B. Martinez. I reside at 114 Rosita Place, in San Antonio, Texas. My husband's name is Fred Martinez. On April 17, 1945, my husband and I make a $500.00 initial payment upon a house that we intended to buy at 1243 Highland Blvd., in San Antonio, Texas. Mr. J. W. Carraway was going to sell it to us for $8000.00 cash. We wanted this home for us and for our daughter, Mrs. Alfonso Cadena, whose husband, Pvt. Alfonso Cadena, is *serving in the United States Army overseas. They have one 5 year old daughter.*

On April 19, 1945, Mr. and Mrs. J. W. Carraway told us that they were very sorry, but that they could not sell us the property for the reason that they had received several telephone calls warning them not to sell the property to Spanish people. The telephone calls came to them from Anglo-American neighbors of theirs, they said. Mr. and Mrs. Carraway returned the $500.00 to us.

My husband and I and my daughter and her husband are all native born American citizens.

Further affiant sayeth not.   Ophelia B. Martinez

Sworn to and subscribed before me, this the 19th day of April, A. D. 1945.

Alonso S. Perales
Notary Public in and for Bexar County, Texas

(Translation of Telegram received from Dr. Enrique Gonzalez Martinez, President of the Mexican Committee against Racism, of Mexico City).

Mexico City,
March 26, 1945.

ALONSO S. PERALES
SUITE 714 GUNTER BLDG.
SAN ANTONIO, TEXAS.

The reproachable discriminatory act perpetrated in a restaurant in Pecos, Texas, against Senator Eugenio Prado, President of the Permanent Commission of the Congress of Mexico and persons accompanying him is additional proof that only through sanctions imposed upon those who practice discrimination against Mexicans will it be possible to end a situation which offends all Mexicans and which hinders President Roosevelt's Good Neighbor Policy stop We have sent telegrams to Governor Stevenson and Senators Fred Mauritz and Franklin Spears protesting against discriminatory act Stop We are sure that we can count upon good friends of Mexico like you to bring about approval of Spears Bill now under consideration in Texas Senate which will end once for all acts of this nature. Stop. Kindest regards.

ENRIQUE GONZALEZ MARTINEZ
PRESIDENT MEXICAN COMMITTEE
AGAINST RACISM

THE STATE OF TEXAS, COUNTY OF BEXAR

My name is Abel F. Gonzalez. I am a Private First Class in the United States Army. My Army Serial Number is 18105383. I have just returned from the Aleutian Islands where I had been stationed since April 15, 1943. I am now on a furlough. I was born and reared in Gonzalez, Gonzalez County, Texas. I am 21 years of age.

177

On Thursday, March 15, 1945, about 9:30 A. M., I went into the Smith & Bowen Barber Shop, in Gonzalez, Texas, to have my shoes shined. A negro who shines shoes there told me that he was sorry, but that he could not shine my shoes.

Other American soldiers of Mexican descent have likewise been refused service at said shoe shine stand and the negro shoe shine man has told them that he himself has no objection, but that his Anglo-American boss told him he must not shine the shoes of Mexicans in his barber shop.

There is not a single Anglo-American Barber Shop in Gonzalez, Texas, that will cut the hair of American soldiers of Mexican descent.

Further affiant sayeth not.   Abel F. Gonzalez

Subscribed and sworn to before me this the 16th day of March, A. D. 1945.

Alonso S. Perales
Notary Public in and for Bexar County, Texas

THE STATE OF TEXAS, COUNTY OF BEXAR

Our names are Emilio Uriegas and Sixto Obregon. We are 19 years of age and we were born and reared in Texas. We live at 814 S. Brazos Street and 517 South Leona Street, respectively, in San Antonio, Texas.

On Friday, March 2nd 1945, about 2:00 P. M., we went into the West Side Cafe, in Lockhart, Texas, and we were about to sit down at a table when a waitress came and told us that she was very sorry, but that she could not serve us because the West Side Cafe was for white people only. One of the boys who was with us asked her what we were, and she then turned around and left. We left the place. When we went to the said Cafe we were accompanied by John Estrada, Eusebio Chavez and Ramon Uriegas, all of San Antonio, Texas.

Further affiants sayeth not.   Emilio Uriegas - Sixto Obregon.

Subscribed and sworn to before me this the 5th day of March, A. D., 1945.

Alonso S. Perales
Notary Public in and for Bexar County, Texas

THE STATE OF TEXAS, COUNTY OF BEXAR

My name is Reginaldo Romo. I am 39 years of age and reside at Uvalde, Texas. I am a native born citizen of the United States and have lived in Uvalde fourteen years.

On Wednesday, February 21st 1945, Messrs. Julian Quiroga, Apolonio Canales and I were in a saloon, in Uvalde, Texas, drinking and shooting dice. The saloon was closed, but we were inside drinking and shooting dice, as aforesaid. Just then a peace *officer August Zimmerman, who we understand is employed by the City of Uvalde, came in and came to where I was and struck me in the head with his gun.* He did not utter a word when he came in, but came straight to where I was and struck me in the head with his gun. After he struck me, he told me to stay away from him or else he would kill me.

I know for a fact that he has beaten up in like manner the following man: Jose Arredondo. He not only struck him in the head with his gun, but shot at him twice. Another man who has been beaten up by the said August Zimmerman.

Further affiant sayeth not.   Reginaldo Romo

Sworn to and subscribed before me, this the 23rd day of February, A. D. 1945.

Alonso S. Perales
Notary Public in and for Bexar County, Texas

THE STATE OF TEXAS, COUNTY OF BEXAR

My name is Felipe Rodriguez. I am 43 years of age and married, and reside at 121 Duval Street, in San Antonio, Texas.

On February 19, 1945, about 4:45 P. M., my wife, Mrs. Maria G. de Rodriguez, and I went into a small cafe situated on the corner of Travis Street and Avenue E, in San Antonio, Texas, and as we went in a lady who appeared to be the Manager of the place, asked us what we wanted, and I told her that we wanted some soft drinks. She then said: You go into the kitchen and I will serve you. My wife and I went out of the place, rather than suffer the humiliation of being served in the kitchen. We were neatly dressed.

Further affiant sayeth not.   Felipe Rodriguez

Sworn to and subscribed before me, this the 20th day of February, A. D. 1945.

Alonso S. Perales,
Notary Public in and for Bexar County, Texas.

THE STATE OF TEXAS, COUNTY OF BEXAR

Our names are Ernestina Villarreal and Josefina Garcia. We reside at 307 Hawthorne Street and 300 Howthorne Street, respectively. We are native born citizens of the United States of America. We are both married.

On the 1st day of February, 1945, we went to a restaurant known as _____, situated on the corner of East Commerce and Blum Streets. We sat at a table. Then an Anglo-American or German-American man came to where we were and said: "We cannot serve you at this table." I, Ernestina Villarreal, asked him why, and he replied: "The service is for whites only". Then I asked him what he thought we were, and he said: "I am

179

sorry; we cannot serve you." I told him: *"We are just as much Americans as you are"*, and he again said: *"I am sorry"*. Then we left the place.

I, Ernestina Villarreal, wish to add that my husband, Mr. Cosme Villarreal, has been serving in the United States Navy for two and one-half years.

Further affiants sayeth not. Ernestina Villarreal - Josefina Garcia.

Sworn to and subscribed before me, this the 2nd day of February, A. D. 1945.

Alonso S. Perales,
Notary Public in and for Bexar County, Texas.

THE STATE OF TEXAS, COUNTY OF BEXAR

My name is Rosendo Salinas. I am 39 years of age and married. I reside at Robstown, Texas, where I am in business. I was born in Seguin, Texas, and am an American citizen.

On November 14, 1944, Mr. Alfonso Gutierrez, Mr. Alfredo Gutierrez and Mr. Jose Gonzalez were denied service at the Liddel Cafe, in O'Donnell, Texas. They were told: *"We don't serve Mexicans"*. Alfonso and Alfredo Gutierrez are brothers and reside in Kerrville, Texas. Jose Gonzalez lives in Melvin, Texas. I saw all these men go into the Liddel Cafe and I noticed that they came right out a minute or so after they had gone in. I asked them what had happened and they told me that they had been denied service because they were Mexicans..

The Roy Cafe, at Lamesa, Texas, has a sign on a screen door reading: *"No Mexicans"*. I saw this sign on November 7, 1944.

The Owl Cafe has no sign on the door, but Mexicans are denied service just the same. This Cafe is at Lamesa also.

At the QUICK LUNCH in Big Spring, Texas, there is a sign on one of the screen windows which reads: *"Mexicans served on the window only"*. I saw this sign on November 14, 1944.

TING'S CAFE, at Big Spring has a sign on the door reading: *"No Mexicans"*. I saw this sign on November 14, 1944.

In Lubbock, Texas, the WHITE HOUSE CAFE has a sign on the door reading: *"We reserve the right to sell to whites only"*. I saw this sign on November 10, 1944.

While in O'Donnell I took a shirt to a laundry to have it laundered and an Anglo-American lady told me that they did not do any work for Mexicans.

Further affiant sayeth not.   Rosendo Salinas

Sworn to and subscribed before me, this the 21st day of November, A. D. 1944.

Alonso S. Perales,
Notary Public in and for Bexar County, Texas

180

STATEMENT OF MISS AURORA ALCORTA
Route 1, Box 194
Von Ormy, Texas

My name is Aurora Alcorta. I am 16 years of age and single. I reside at Von Ormy, Texas, and attend the Poteet High School. I am in the 10th grade. My father's name is Guadalupe Alcorta and my mother is Mrs. Angelita Alcorta.

On Oct. 5, 1944, about 8:00 A. M., affiant and the girls named below were riding on the bus on the way to school: Misses Olivia Hernandez, Sylvia Hernandez, Frances Lopez, Asela Aguilar, Maria Lopez, Virginia Lopez, Cristina Alcorta, Virginia Alcorta, and Mr. Manuel Lopez. I was seated with Mr. Manuel Lopez. An Anglo-American boy named Harold was pushing another Anglo-American boy over me or against me. I then told him please do not push the boy against me, and he said: "A darn Mexican like you is not going to make me stop it." He thereupon struck me on my right eye with his closed fist. Then I said to him: "OK, white trash".

After the incident with me, the said Harold boy picked up a fight with Frances Lopez. Then the bus driver stopped the bus and then stopped the fight. As soon as the bus stopped the fight ceased. When we got to Poteet I went and complained to Miss E. O. Mangum. She said she could not do anything to Harold because we Mexicans were to blame. Then Mr. Brown, School Superintendent, called us into the Mathematic Room and asked how the fight had started. Then he started reprimanding us, but he reprimanded me the most. He said that I was very lowdown because I had used bad language on the bus.

The following day, in the morning, when we boarded the bus on the way to school the bus driver, Mr. Cowley, said that the "whites" were to ride on one side of the bus and "Mexicans" on the other. The next day Frances Lopez, Aurora Alcorta, Asela Aguilar and Virginia Alcorta, went and spoke with Superintendent Brown and told him about the segregation on the bus. He asked us: "Do you girls really mind where you sit". Virginia Alcorta said to him: "We do not mind where we sit, but we do not want to be treated that way". Then he said: "Well, girls, we'll arrange that." That was the day we complained and the bus driver is still segregating us. Every time he sees an Anglo-American sitting with a Mexican he tells the whites: "I don't want to tell the whites again where to sit."

The afternoon of the 16th Manuel Lopez sat with two Anglo-Americans on our side of the bus. Then the bus driver got up and said: "Hey, Manuel, there is a seat for you back there, (meaning the rear of our side of the bus), whereupon Manuel got up and went to sit in the rear of the bus as requested.

181

Further affiant sayeth not.   *Aurora Alcorta*
Sworn to and subscribed before me, this the 17th day of
October, A. D. 1944.

Alonso S. Perales,
Notary Public in and for Bexar County, Texas.

We, the undersigned, were riding on the same bus and witnessed what happened. What Miss Aurora Alcorta says is true.

Olivia Hernandez   *Virginia Alcorta*
Christine Alcorta   *Sylvia M. Hernandez*

THE STATE OF TEXAS, COUNTY OF BEXAR

My name is Oscar Molina. I am 47 years of age. I reside at 309 San Luis Street, in San Antonio, Texas. I am employed by the Ferd Staffel Co., 321 E. Commerce St., in San Antonio, Texas.

On Saturday, September 2, 1944, about 12:30 P. M., I went to the Spanish Village Restaurant, situated at 237 Blum Street, in San Antonio, Texas. I was accompanied by Mrs. Francisca Arriaga and Miss Alicia Yzaguirre, both of whom are also employed by the Ferd Staffel Co. I had been to said restaurant about three times previous to this one and I had always been served. To-day, however, after we had been served, one of the waitresses, who happened to be a Mexican girl, came and told us that the owner of the Spanish Village Restaurant did not want her to serve us Mexicans and that she was going to be reprimanded for having served us. Before she told us this the waitress had told us that we would have to leave the table ten minutes before one o'clock, as that table had been reserved. Then she returned and said: "I am very sorry to have to tell you that the lady owner of this restaurant does not want us to serve persons of Mexican descent, and she is going to reprimand me for having done so." Whereupon we left the place.

I should add that all three of us were well dressed and we deported ourselves with propriety. Mrs. Arriaga and I are Mexican citizens and Miss Izaguirre is an American citizen.

Further affiant sayeth not   *Oscar Molina*
Sworn to and subscribed before me, this the 2nd day of
September, A. D. 1944.

Alonso S. Perales,
Notary Public in and for Bexar County, Texas.

THE STATE OF TEXAS, COUNTY OF BEXAR

My name is Ben Martinez. I am a Corporal in the United States Army. My Organization is Company I, 162nd Infantry, 41st Division. I am a legal resident of Rotan, Fisher County, Texas, where I was born and reared. I am now on a furlough after having served in Southwest Pacific for a period of two years. Altogether I have been in the United States Army two and one-half years. I am 25 years of age.

I have three other brothers in the United States Army. Their names are : Emilio Martinez, Jose Martinez, Alejandro Martinez.

On July 3rd 1944, I went to the City Barber Shop, at Rotan, Texas, and sat down on the Barber's Chair to get a hair cut. The Barber told me: "We don't cut you people's hair", meaning that he did not cut the hair of Mexicans. I am an American citizen of Mexican descent and I was wearing the United States Army uniform at the time.

My brother, Alejandro Martinez, was likewise refused service in the same Barber Shop last year, and he, too, was wearing the United States uniform at the time.

Further affiant sayeth not. Ben Martinez

Sworn to and subscribed before me, this the 26th day of July, A. D. 1944.

Alonso S. Perales,
Notary Public in and for Bexar County, Texas.

THE STATE OF TEXAS, COUNTY OF BEXAR

My name is Emeterio Pastrán. I am a legal resident of San Antonio, Bexar County, Texas, but am temporarily residing at Eagle Pass, Texas, where I am employed by the United States Government at Eagle Pass Army Air Field.

On Sunday, June 11, 1944, about 10:15 P. M., Mr. Bruno Salazar, of Eagle Pass, Texas, went into the "Dinette Cafe", at Uvalde, Texas, for the purpose of dining there, and as soon as we went in a lady, who appeared to be the owner or manager, told us that we would have to go somewhere else. When we first went into the Cafe a waitress saw us and went and told the other lady, who, as I said, appeared to be the owner or manager, and the latter came and told us to go somewhere else. She appeared to be in an angry mood as she advanced toward us.

An Anglo-American man who was travelling with us in Mr. Martin Delgado's car, on our way to the Eagle Pass Army Air Field, went into said Cafe at the same time we did, and he was served, but we were not.

Further affiant sayeth not. Emeterio Pastrán.

Sworn to and subscribed before me, this the 28th day of June, A. D. 1944.

Alonso S. Perales,
Notary Public in and for Bexar County, Texas.

THE STATE OF TEXAS, COUNTY OF BEXAR

Our names are Enrique Flores and Hilda Gonzalez de Flores. We reside in Port Lavaca, Texas. We own and operate a restau-

rant there. We were born and reared in Texas, and we are American citizens. We have about fifteen nephews in the United States Army, most of whom are serving overseas.

On Sunday, April 2, 1944, about noon, we stopped at the WHITE SPOT CAFE, at Nixon, Texas, on our way to San Antonio, Texas, and as soon as we went into the Cafe a waitress told us to go out and around into the kitchen if we wanted service, as we could not be served in the front part of the Cafe. There were five of us in the party and we were all clean and well dressed. The names of the other three members of our party are: Mrs. Juanita Dominguez, 33 years of age, who is our sister; Miss Juanita Garcia, 17 years of age; and our son Manuel Flores, who is 12 years of age.

There are several public places of business in Port Lavaca, Bay City, New Gulf and Palacios where persons of Mexican descent are not served.

In Port Lavaca our school children are segregated up to and including the fourth grade. The school bus driver separates the Mexican children from the Anglo-American children on the buses.

Further deponents sayeth not. Henry Flores - Gilda G. Flores
Sworn to and subscribed before me this 3rd day of April, A. D. 1944.

Alonso S. Perales,

Notary Public in and for Bexar County, Texas.

THE STATE OF TEXAS, COUNTY OF BEXAR

Our names are Jose Alvarez Fuentes, Joe D. Salas and Paul R. Ramos. We are members of the Armed Forces of the United States as above indicated. We are permanent residents of the City of San Antonio, Texas, but are temporarily residing elsewhere. We are now on furlough. On Tuesday, March 7, 1944, about 2:30 P.M., when we were on our way home the bus stopped at Fredericksburg, Texas. We were hungry and, therefore, we went into the "Downtown Cafe", at 323 East Main Street, Fredericksburg, to order something to eat. We sat on stools at the counter. There were two waitresses in the restaurant, but neither one waited on us. One of them went and told the Manager or Proprietor that we were there. He came to where we were and Seaman Jose Alvarez told him that we wanted a barbecue sandwich. The Manager said: "I am sorry, but I cannot serve you in front; you will have to go out and around to the rear." Seaman Alvarez Fuentes asked him why and he said: "Those are the orders." Whereupon we left the place. Seaman Juan Garcia, United States Navy, was also with us at the time. He lives

*in San Antonio, Texas, and he too was on his way home on a
furlough.*

Further deponents sayeth not.

Jose Alvarez Fuentes

Joe D. Salas

Paul R. Ramos

*Subscribed and sworn to before me this 11th day of March,
A. D. 1944.*

Alonso S. Perales,

Notary Public in and for Bexar County, Texas.

THE STATE OF TEXAS, COUNTY OF BEXAR

*My name is Leonardo Rodriguez. I was born in Hoye, Texas,
and am now residing in Boerne, Kendall County, Texas. I am 21
years of age and single, I attended the public schools at Boerne
for about eight years. I finished the seventh grade.*

*On Sunday, March 5, 1944, about 8:00 P. M., I went to the
CASCADE THEATER in Boerne. Mexicans are segregated from
the Anglo-Americans downstairs. There is a special section downstairs where Mexicans may sit. That section was occupied. Therefore, I went upstairs. There were no seats available upstairs either
and for this reason I remained standing. I had been standing there
for about ten minutes when Mr. Miller, the Manager of the
Cascade Theater, approached me and requested me to go downstairs. I told him that the only way we could see the show was to
remain where we were; whereupon he stated that if I did not like
his telling me to go down, that he could refund me my money. I
told him to bring me the money. Then he went and got the money
and brought it to me, but he also brought with him a stick about
two and one-half feet long, one inch thick and two inches wide.
He handed me the money and he punched my ribs with the stick
and told me to get out. I told him that it was not necessary for
him to get angry about it, and as I turned around to get out he
struck me in the head with the stick and fell me to the floor and
while I was lying down he struck me in the back with the stick.
When he struck me in the head he broke my glasses. As soon as I
got up he struck me on my left cheek with the same stick. He also
struck me on my right hand and in the mouth. I told him that
was no place to fight and for him to come outside. He came
outside of the theater, but he brought a pistol with him. I was un-
armed.*

185

*I reported the case to Sheriff Sidney F. Edge, of Kendall
County, but he said there was nothing he could do about it.*
Further deponent sayeth not.   Leonardo Rodriguez
*Sworn to and subscribed before me this 7th day of March,
A. D. 1944.*

Alonso S. Perales,
Notary Public in and for Bexar County, Texas,
My Commission expires on May 31, 1945.

THE STATE OF TEXAS, COUNTY OF BEXAR

Our names are Beatriz Balboa de Espino and Zenobia Silva
de Aguirre, ages 33 years and 23 years, respectively, and married.
We reside at 523 Santa Clara Street, in San Antonio, Texas.

About 2:00 P. M., to-day we called at the Office of R. L. White
Co. 314 Nolan Street, San Antonio, Texas, and made application
to rent a house situated on Elm Street. We had seen a "For Rent"
sign on said house which stated that any one interested should
apply at the Office of R. L. White Co. When we told the young
lady at the office of the R. L. White Co., that we wanted to rent
the house on Elm Street she replied: "We don't rent to Spanish
people. We rent only to whites". Mrs. Beatriz Balboa de Espino
asked her: "What is the matter with Spanish people?" and she
replied: "We have our choice to rent it to whomever we want to."
Whereupon Mrs. Beatriz Balboa de Espino retorted: "But they
can go to war all right, can't they?", whereupon the young lady
said: "Well, get out, get out, I don't want to be bothered."

Speaking for herself the said Beatriz Balboa de Espino further says: I have two brothers in the United States Army; one is
stationed in England and the other is in Wisconsin.

Speaking for herself the said Zenobia Silva de Aguirre further says: My husband, Daniel Aguirre, is in the United States
Army and is stationed in India. I also have a brother-in-law (the
husband of a sister of mine) serving in the United States Army
overseas. I wanted to rent the house on Elm Street in order that
my family and myself might occupy it as a homestead.

Further deponents sayeth not.   Beatriz Balboa de Espino
Zenobia Silva de Aguirre

*Sworn to and subscribed before me this 26th day of January,
A. D. 1944.*

Alonso S. Perales,
Notary Public in and for Bexar County, Texas.

Notes

Introduction

1. Vargas, *Labor Rights*, 6.
2. M. T. Garcia, *Mexican Americans*, 20.
3. See M. T. Garcia, *Memories of Chicano History*, and Canales, *Personal Recollections*.
4. See Montejano, *Anglos and Mexicans*; Arnoldo De León, *Mexican Americans in Texas: A Brief History*, 2nd ed. (Wheeling, Ill.: Harlan Davidson, 1999); Rudolfo Acuña, *Occupied America: A History of Chicanos* (New York: Addison Wesley, 2003).
5. See especially Perales, *Are We Good Neighbors?*; see also Kibbe, *Latin Americans in Texas*, and Cletus, *Chicano Workers*.
6. Morin, *Among the Valiant* (1963).
7. Maggie Rivas-Rodriguez, ed., *Mexican Americans and World War II* (Austin: University of Texas Press, 2005).
8. See Vargas, *Labor Rights*, chap. 5. For other important studies, see Takaki, *Double Victory*, selected chapters; M. T. Garcia, "Americans All"; Campbell, "Madres y Esposas"; Marín, "Mexican Americans on the Home Front"; Santillán, "Rosita the Riveter"; Griswold del Castillo, "The Los Angeles 'Zoot Suit Riots' Revisited." For a more complete listing of the published work on this topic, see the annotated bibliography in this book.

Chapter One

1. For a detailed discussion of stereotyping of Mexican immigrants in film, see David R. Maciel and María Rosa García-Acevedo, "The Celluloid Immigrant: The Narrative Films of Mexican Immigration," in *Culture across Borders: Mexican Immigration and Popular Culture*, ed. David R. Maciel and María Herrera-Sobek (Tucson: University of Arizona Press, 1998), 147–202.
2. George Gallup, "An Analysis of American Public Opinion Regarding the

War," September 10, 1942, in President's Personal File 4721, Franklin D. Roosevelt Library (hereafter FDRL), Hyde Park, NY.

3. Ibid.

4. The character of the early Mexican immigration is discussed by Manuel P. Servín in "The Pre–World War II Mexican-American: An Interpretation," *California Historical Quarterly* 45 (1966): 325–338.

5. One account notes that a 1938 report by the National Resources Committee, a federal agency, estimated the total population at three million; Donald R. McCoy and Richard T. Ruetten, *Quest and Response: Minority Rights and the Truman Administration* (Lawrence: University Press of Kansas, 1973), 3. Nelson Rockefeller, Coordinator of Inter-American Affairs, estimated their number at about 2.5 million; Memo "Meeting in the Office of the Attorney General," April 28, 1942, Department of Justice file 146-13-5-0, in accession 53A 10, Federal Records Center, Suitland, Md. Assistant Secretary of the Interior Saul Padover estimated the number at three million; Padover, "Office of Race Relations," June 29, 1943, President's Secretary's File: Interior, FDRL.

6. George I. Sánchez, *Forgotten People: A Study of New Mexicans* (Albuquerque: University of New Mexico Press, 1940; reprinted with a new introduction by Calvin Horn, Publisher, 1967); Richard L. Nostrand, *The Hispano Homeland* (Norman: University of Oklahoma Press, 1992).

7. See especially Montejano, *Anglos and Mexicans*; Mark Reisler, *By the Sweat of Their Brow: Mexican Immigrant Labor in the United States* (Westport, Conn.: Greenwood Press, 1976); and Devra Weber, *Dark Sweat, White Gold: California Farm Workers, Cotton, and the New Deal* (Berkeley: University of California Press, 1994) for discussion of Mexican immigrant labor prior to 1940.

8. Douglas Monroy, "Like Swallows at the Old Mission: Mexicans and the Racial Politics of Growth in Los Angeles in the Interwar Period," *Western Historical Quarterly* (October 1983): 444–446.

9. Described in Servín, "Pre–World War II Mexican-American," 331, and Griffith, *American Me*, 113–114. Also see David G. Gutiérrez, *Walls and Mirrors: Mexican Americans, Mexican Immigrants and the Politics of Ethnicity* (Berkeley: University of California Press, 1995), 94.

10. For migratory character, see Monroy, "Like Swallows at the Old Mission," 435–458. The new "transnational" culture is examined in David G. Gutiérrez, "Migration, Emergent Ethnicity, and the 'Third Space': The Shifting Politics of Nationalism in Greater Mexico," *Journal of American History* 86 (September 1999): 499–501.

11. Throughout American history, except in wartime, large numbers of immigrants returned to their homelands either permanently or on extended visits. From 1931 to 1935, over a million left, thus for the first time exceeding the number who arrived by a quarter of a million. U.S. Bureau of the Census, *Statistical Abstract of the United States, 1953* (Washington, DC: U.S. Government Printing Office, 1953), 97; Weber, *Dark Sweat, White Gold.*

12. Matt S. Meier and Feliciano Rivera, *Mexican Americans/American Mexicans: From Conquistadors to Chicanos* (New York: Hill and Wang, 1993), 147–148.

13. The relationship between race and class in attitudes toward Mexican Americans is ably discussed in Tomás Almaguer, *Racial Fault Lines: The Historical*

Origins of White Supremacy in California (Berkeley: University of California Press, 1994).

14. G. J. Sanchez, *Becoming Mexican American*, 254.

15. Quoted in Gunnar Myrdal, *An American Dilemma: The Negro Problem and Modern Democracy* (New York: Harper and Brothers, 1944), 393.

16. Living conditions among the Mexicans of Southern California are described in Griffith, *American Me*, 13, 113–114, and in Carey McWilliams, *Factories in the Field: The Story of Migratory Farm Labor in California* (Boston: Little, Brown, 1939), 149, 246. The death rate from tuberculosis among Mexican Americans in 1930 was more than four times the rate among Anglos, and babies born to Latinas in Los Angeles in the 1930s were among those citizens least likely to outlive their infancy. Conditions improved considerably in the late 1930s, probably as a result of public health measures, so that by 1944 the tuberculosis death rate was eighty-four per thousand, not quite double that for Anglos, and the infant morality rate was about equal to that for Anglos. Griffith, *American Me*, 113, 132, 137.

17. Kibbe, *Latin Americans in Texas*, 85.

18. Charles Wollenberg, *"Mendez v. Westminster:* Race, Nationality, and Segregation in California Schools," *California Historical Quarterly* 53 (Winter 1974): 316–332.

19. On indifference, see Carey McWilliams, *Ill Fares the Land* (Boston: Little, Brown, 1942), 256.

20. Discussion of segregation laws in general, with occasional reference to Texas, can be found in Charles S. Mangum, *The Legal Status of the Negro* (Chapel Hill: University of North Carolina Press, 1940), 79–87. Actually, Texas was more generous in its treatment of African Americans than other southern states. Its expenditure of $63 per African American student in 1943–1944 was two-thirds of what it spent on whites. Ira De A. Reid, "Southern Ways," *Survey Graphic* (January 1947): 40.

21. San Miguel Jr., *"Let All of Them Take Heed,"* 23–65. San Miguel also provides a good survey of the status of the Mexican American community in Texas.

22. Kibbe, *Latin Americans in Texas*, 229.

23. L. Outhwaithe for Will Alexander (fepc), April 13, 1942, reporting on three weeks' travel along the Mexican border, concluded that American officials were often dilatory, negligent, discourteous, and in some cases insolent in their handling of Mexicans and other South American travelers. In "Hearings, Background Material," fldr. entry 19, Records of the Department of State, Record Group (hereafter rg) 226, National Archives (hereafter na), Washington, DC. See also San Miguel Jr., *"Let All of them Take Heed,"* 67, and Kibbe, *Latin Americans in Texas*, 229.

24. McWilliams, *Brothers Under the Skin* (Boston: Little, Brown, 1964), 124. McWilliams blames the discrimination largely on the poverty of the victims.

25. Kibbe, *Latin Americans in Texas*, 5, 208–212.

26. James A. Fisher, "The Political Development of the Black Community in California, 1850–1950," in *Neither Separate nor Equal: Race and Racism in California*, ed. Roger Olmsted and Charles Wollenberg (San Francisco: California Historical Society, 1971), 36–46.

27. According to Manuel Servín, a scholar studying the 1930s, the Hispanos

(descendants of pre-annexation Mexicans?) did not offer the Mexican immigrants and their offspring any leadership. See Servín, "Pre-World War II Mexican-American," 328. See also Moses Rischin, "Continuities and Discontinuities in Spanish-Speaking California," in *Ethnic Conflict in California History*, ed. Charles Wollenberg (Los Angeles: Tinnon-Brown, 1970), 43–59; and Leonard Broom and Eshref Shevky, "Mexicans in the United States: A Problem in Social Differentiation," *Sociology and Social Research* 36 (January–February 1952): 150–158.

28. On the consulates, see G. J. Sanchez, *Becoming Mexican American*, 133. See also Broom and Shevky, "Mexicans in the United States," 157; and Griffith, *American Me*, 187. Although Protestant churches tended to segregate (exclude) Mexican Americans, those that accepted them tended to foster assimilation and political activism among them (Griffith, *American Me*, 191–193).

29. Special Service Division, Office of Facts and Figures, to Kane, "The Spanish Americans of the Southwest and the War Effort," May 19, 1942, "owi-Misc.," entry 155, rg 229, na.

30. Through the 1920s at least, *La Opinión*, the largest Spanish-language newspaper in the country, devoted a little more than 11 percent of its editorial and news coverage to Mexicans in the United States. G. J. Sanchez, *Becoming Mexican American*, 116.

31. The pattern of low naturalization was established in the 1920s, but there was a marked upsurge in naturalization during the deportations of 1934–1936. See G. J. Sanchez, *Becoming Mexican American*, 105, 261; Gutiérrez, *Walls and Mirrors*, 123; "Aliens Rush for U.S. Citizenship: Federal Machinery Is Swamped," *New York Times*, April 22, 1939, 19.

32. G. J. Sanchez, *Becoming Mexican American*, 113.

33. Gutiérrez, "Migration," 488.

34. Carey McWilliams, quoting George Sanchez in *The Education of Carey McWilliams* (New York: Simon and Schuster, 1979), 108, calls them "the least vocal minority in the nation."

35. Meier and Rivera, *Mexican Americans*, 157–158.

36. Carey McWilliams notes that the "Mexican problem" drew considerable attention during the 1920s, with the *Readers' Guide* listing fifty-one articles on the subject. Interestingly, the succeeding decade had only nineteen. This was a time when the problems for Mexican Americans were greatest, but the problems for the Anglo majority had subsided because of repatriation. McWilliams, *North from Mexico: The Spanish-Speaking People of the United States* (New York: Greenwood Press, 1968; first published in 1948), 206. Some discussion of the civil rights aspect was available from Emory S. Bogardus, *The Mexican in the United States* (Los Angeles: University of Southern California Press, 1934), and Paul S. Taylor, *Mexican Labor in the United States* (Berkeley: University of California Press, 1929–1932), a series with various subtitles. Bogardus lists an extensive bibliography in his *Mexican in the United States*, 99–123.

37. G. I. Sánchez, *Forgotten People*.

38. Monroy ("Like Swallows at the Old Mission," 439) notes that almost 14 percent of Mexicans could claim white-collar status in the 1930s. G. J. Sanchez (*Becoming Mexican American*, 229) comments on the weakness of a middle class in Southern California in comparison to San Antonio.

39. Ralph Guzman, "The Function of Anglo-American Racism in the Political Development of Chicanos," in *Neither Separate nor Equal: Race and Racism in California,* ed. Roger Olmsted and Charles Wollenberg (Berkeley: California Historical Society, 1971), 109–112, argues that political socialization was retarded by the hostility of the host society, and that Anglo attitudes toward Mexicans were more negative than toward any European ethnic group. African Americans, although racially segregated, appear to have had more political weight in Texas than did Mexican Americans. Fifty thousand African American Texans voted in the 1940 election, and they were an important component of the political machine in San Antonio. Myrdal, *American Dilemma,* 475.

Chapter Two

1. Robert C. Jones, "Integration of the Mexican Minority in the United States into American Democracy," *Events and Trends in Race Relations: A Monthly Summary* 4 (January 1947): 177. The Selective Service Act of 1940 required aliens to register, but provided compulsory service only for those who had declared their intent to become citizens. This was amended after Pearl Harbor to include all aliens except those of neutral countries who declared their exemption. This would have covered Mexican aliens until June 1942, when Mexico declared war on the Axis. Military service accelerated the process of obtaining citizenship. See Hugh Carter and Bernice Doster, "Social Characteristics of Aliens from the Southwest Registered for Selective Service during World War II," *Naturalization Service Monthly Review* 8 (1951): 88–94.

2. Meier and Rivera, *Mexican Americans,* 159–160.

3. Gary Gerstle, "The Working Class Goes to War," *Mid-America* 75 (October 1993): 304–322.

4. Richard W. Steele, "'No Racials': Discrimination against Ethnics in American Defense Industry, 1940–42," *Labor History* 32 (Winter 1991): 66–90.

5. Justice Department Report on "Exclusion from Defense Employments [*sic*] of National and Racial Populations and the Press Reactions of the Excluded Groups," November 17, 1941, attached to L. M. C. Smith to Lowell Mellett, "Special Policies Unit" file, Lowell Mellett papers, FDRL, Hyde Park, NY.

6. Justice Department, "Exclusion from Defense Employments."

7. The Coordinator of Inter-American Affairs (CIAA) tried to get the Secretary of War to clarify rules so that Mexican aliens might be employed in defense jobs (N. Rockefeller to H. L. Stimson, April 8, 1943), and the Mexican ambassador registered the same complaint (Under Sec. State S. Welles to Sec. State, December 1, 1943); both in decimal file 014.31, "Rights of Aliens," Records of the Adjutant General's Office (RG 407), NA.

8. Justice Department, "Exclusion from Defense Employments."

9. The following discussion is based on Steele, "'No Racials,'" 66–90.

10. See correspondence of Will Alexander to John MacLean, in "Spanish" fldr., entry 25, RG 228, NA.

11. Nelson Lichtenstein, in "The Making of the Postwar Working Class: Cultural Pluralism and Social Structure in World War II," in *The Historian: A Jour-*

nal of History 51, no. 1 (November 1988), http://www.biblio.com/books/14559864
.html, 62, discusses the suppression of class-based militancy in favor of "cross-
class unity" during the war. Lichtenstein also notes that the success of the union
movement, beginning in the New Deal period, had the effect of undermining
the relative insularity of various ethnic identities and replacing it with a generic
"white ethnic" identity with racist overtones. African Americans, Mexicans, and
women were excluded from this redefined working class.

12. Gutiérrez, *Walls and Mirrors*, 95–114.

13. M. T. Garcia, *Mexican Americans*, 146–174.

14. David Saposs, himself a leftist who had been accused of Communist affiliation, informed the CIAA that the Congress was a Communist front. Saposs
to Laves, May 11, 1942, "Spanish Speaking People's Congress" fldr., entry 155,
Records of the Office of the of Inter-American Affairs, RG 229, NA. See also
Cletus, *Chicano Workers*, 8.

15. Broom and Shevky, "Mexicans in the United States," 158. G. J. Sanchez
(*Becoming Mexican American*, 249) notes as well that the membership was cut by
the draft.

16. African Americans numbered about 124,000 in all of California out of a
state population of almost seven million. Fisher, "Political Development," 36–
46. Fisher points out the long history of African American activism in the state.
The state's first African American assemblyman was elected in 1921, and African
Americans spearheaded passage of a public accommodations law in 1897 and (in-
effectual) civil rights legislation in 1919 and 1923. Arthur C. Verge, in "The Impact of the Second World War on Los Angeles," *Pacific Historical Review* (1994):
298–311, talks about wartime African American activism.

17. Corona testimony in transcript of the public hearings of the FEPC in Los
Angeles, 518–522, entry 19, "Legal Division Hearings, 1941–46," box 338, RG 228,
Records of the Committee on Fair Employment Practices, NA.

18. Cletus, *Chicano Workers*, 6.

19. Kevin Allen Leonard, "'Brothers under the Skin': African Americans,
Mexican Americans, and World War II in California," in *The Way We Really Were:
The Golden State in the Second Great War*, ed. Roger W. Lotchin (Urbana: Univer-
sity of Illinois Press, 2000), 192.

20. Robert Dallek, *Franklin D. Roosevelt and American Foreign Policy, 1932–
1945* (New York: Oxford University Press, 1979), 233.

21. Irwin F. Gellman, *Good Neighbor Diplomacy: United States Policies in Latin
America, 1933–1945* (Baltimore: Johns Hopkins University Press, 1979), 54.

22. On Manuel Ávila Camacho's and Ezequiel Padilla's friendship toward the
United States, see Jesse H. Stiller, *George S. Messersmith, Diplomat of Democracy*
(Chapel Hill: University of North Carolina Press, 1987), 175.

23. The Mexican government, in an effort to keep out poor African Americans from the United States, demanded a fee from any African American who
sought to travel in Mexico. The practice was ended in 1939. Gellman, *Good Neighbor Diplomacy*, 30.

24. This view is expressed in a front-page article covering an interview given
to the *Los Angeles Times* by Ignacio F. Herrerías, a Mexico City publisher. "We

are of mixed blood but all really proud of our ancestry . . . How come you are so indignant at Hitler's inhuman persecution of the Jews and don't eliminate racial prejudice against Mexicans?" Reported in U.S. Embassy in Mexico to State, June 24, 1942, 811.4016/465, RG 59, NA.

25. Mexican Embassy to State, March 24, 1941, 811.4016/304, RG 59, NA.

26. Ibid.

27. Mexican Embassy to State, May 6, 1941, 811.4016/288, RG 59, NA.

28. United Press story, "Discrimination Hearings Announced for July," May 11, 1942, Blocker to State, May 12, 1942, 811.4016/360, RG 59, NA.

29. Cramer to MacLean, April 25, 1942, "US Government—Mexican Workers" fldr., RG 228, NA.

30. Welles to Roosevelt, June 20, 1942, Official File (hereafter OF) 4245-G, FDRL.

31. Cramer to FDR, July 10, 1942, OF 4245-G, FDRL.

32. Quoted in Amy Kesselman, *Fleeting Opportunities: Women Shipyard Workers in Portland and Vancouver during World War II and Reconversion* (Albany: State University of New York, 1990), 110.

33. Gutiérrez, *Walls and Mirrors*, 88; Servín, "Pre-World War II Mexican-American," 331.

34. The following discussion of LULAC is based on Benjamin Márquez's *LULAC: The Evolution of a Mexican American Political Organization* (Austin: University of Texas Press, 1993), 2–53; and on M. T. Garcia, *Mexican Americans*, 29–56.

35. Bogardus (*Mexican in the United States*, 75) discusses the resentment at the "Mexican" stereotype.

36. San Miguel Jr., *"Let All of Them Take Heed,"* 64–82; M. T. Garcia, *Mexican Americans*, 48–72.

37. In 1940, the Bureau of the Census informed the State Department that it would eliminate a separate classification of "Mexicans" in the forthcoming census. Welles to E. D. Salinas, January 13, 1940, cited in Secretary of State to Director of Selective Service, August 25, 1943, 811.4016/677. In mid-1943, local draft boards in the Southwest were instructed not to use the term "Mexican" in referring to U.S. citizens of Mexican descent, but to classify them as white or Indian. However, it took some time to gain uniform compliance. Weckler to Sanchez, June 25, 1943, "Aid to Spanish-Speaking Minorities in Texas . . ." fldr., entry 155, RG 229, NA. The difficulty of achieving even minor changes in established practices was revealed by the fact that as late as 1944 officials reported that the U.S. Employment Service in Region XII consistently included "Mexicans" in its "non-white" bracket. The fact that it had such a bracket is instructive. See H. Kingman to Clarence Mitchell, February 2, 1944, "U.S. Government—Mexican Workers" fldr., RG 228, NA.

38. Márquez, *LULAC*, 10, 39.

39. M. T. Garcia, *Mexican Americans*, 27, 29, 244.

40. Idea expressed by Asst. Sec. State A. A. Berle in a memo for Sec. State, January 26, 1942, "Hull, Cordell" fldr., Berle papers, FDRL.

41. Louis T. Olom, Special Asst. to the Director of the Division of Inter-American Activities in the United States (CIAA), commenting on an Office of War

Information Report on propaganda among special populations, August 19, 1942, "Program for Cooperation with Spanish-Speaking . . ." fldr., entry 155, RG 229, NA.

42. Herbert S. Bursley, Asst. Chief of Division of American Republics (head of the Mexican Section), labeled LULAC's leaders unreliable self-seekers. "Conference in the office of Herbert S. Bursley, April 17, 1942, in "Program for Cooperation with Spanish-Speaking . . ." fldr., entry 155, RG 229, NA.

43. Case study addressed to Winters and Bursley, September 12, 1941, 811.4016/323A, RG 59, NA.

44. Welles to Blocker, November 25, 1941, 811.4016/323A, RG 59, NA.

45. Ibid.

46. Frank A. Warren, *Noble Abstractions: American Liberal Intellectuals and World War II* (Columbus: Ohio State University Press, 1999), 65.

47. Memo by William B. Cherin (Justice Department Special War Policies Unit) for David Niles, June 16, 1943, "General Politics, Letters/Documents, 1939–43," David Niles papers, Harry S. Truman Library. Cherin was urging creation of a federal agency to coordinate intelligence and remedial action. The same idea appeared in a memo by Saul K. Padover, "Office of Race Relations," June 29, 1943, which Secretary of Interior Harold L. Ickes sent to FDR, PSF-Interior, FDRL.

48. "Conference in office of Bursley," April 17, 1942, "Program for Cooperation with Spanish-speaking . . . ," in entry 155, RG 229, NA.

49. Wallace to Charles Dorocourt, June 25, 1941, in incident 49, enclosure #1 to dispatch 14144, February 27, 1942, "Transmitting Results of a Confidential Survey of the Problem of Racial Discrimination Against Mexican and Latin American Citizens in Texas and New Mexico," 811.4016/337, Records of the Department of State, RG 59, NA.

50. Warren, *Noble Abstractions*, 65.

Chapter Three

1. The exception was American Indians, a smaller, more remote minority that attracted more attention largely because of the duration of their problems and the glaring national injustice they represented. It was also important that the Indians had national spokesmen (usually white men) who kept their issues alive. Alison R. Bernstein, *American Indians and World War II: Toward a New Era in Indian Affairs* (Norman: University of Oklahoma Press, 1991), 3, 5, 10.

2. Carey McWilliams became West Coast correspondent of the *Nation* in 1945, and an editor of the journal in 1950. McWilliams, *Education of Carey McWilliams*, 134.

3. How great was the expansion of the Mexican American population is uncertain, but the number of arrests of juveniles charged with assault increased 171 percent in 1941 over the previous year, and increased again in 1942. Boys with Mexican surnames, who represented 15 percent of the school-age population, constituted 24 percent of the arrests in the city in 1942. "Findings and Recommendations of the Grand Jury of Los Angeles County for 1943, Based upon Its

Inquiry into Juvenile Crime and Delinquency in That County," July 21, 1943, attached to Bowron for State, 811.4016/695, RG 59, NA.

4. Police attitudes are discussed in Griffith, *American Me*, 202–203, 213.

5. McWilliams, *North from Mexico*, 227–238.

6. Verge ("Impact," 306–307) notes that the number of persons under age eighteen arrested in Los Angeles doubled between 1940 and 1943.

7. The stereotypical character of Mexicans, which for years had been portrayed as quaint in stories that dwelt on vestiges of a romanticized Old Mexico in California, gradually came to be defined by the equally atypical gangster. Ralph H. Turner and Samuel J. Surace, "Zoot-Suiters and Mexicans: Symbols in Crowd Behavior," *American Journal of Sociology* 62 (July 1956): 14–20. See James Gilbert, *A Cycle of Outrage: America's Reaction to the Juvenile Delinquent in the 1950s* (New York: Oxford University Press, 1986), 25–27.

8. Patricia Rae Adler, "The 1943 Zoot-Suit Riots: Brief Episode in a Long Conflict," in *An Awakened Minority: The Mexican American*, ed. Manuel P. Servín (Beverly Hills, Calif.: Glencoe Press, 1974): 142–158.

9. Recognition of the "strong feelings" in the Mexican American community in the wake of the roundups is in "Minutes of the 15th Meeting of the Interdepartmental Committee for Nationality Problems," August 12, 1942, in entry 86, RG 226, NA. Recommendations for "drastic action" can be found in Special Services Division, OWI, "Spanish Americans in the Southwest and the War Effort—Recommendations," August 18, 1942, in "Inter-Office Memos—Spanish-Speaking Minorities," entry 155, RG 229, NA. Draft letters from L.A. Grand Jury, October 8, 1942, loose in box 1082, RG 208, NA.

10. Remarks by Edward Nunn in "Papers Read to Meeting Held October 8, 1942," in "Mexicans in Los Angeles—Ethnic" fldr., entry 222, RG 208, NA.

11. Cranston for Elmer Davis, November 28, 1942, in "Subversive Activities—LA Riot Situation" fldr., entry 1, RG 208, NA.

12. Three were convicted of first-degree murder and sentenced to life in prison. The nine others were found guilty of murder in the second degree and received five years to life.

13. McWilliams to Cranston, June 1, 1943, "Alphabetic File," entry 21, RG 208, NA.

14. The fullest sources on the committee are Carey McWilliams' memoirs and the extensive reports of the FBI. The latter list thirty-three principal figures in the organization. Of these, three—Josefina Fierro de Bright, Jaime Gonzales, and Frank Corona—had Mexican surnames. All three were principally involved in labor organization, as were most of the others. Report attached to J. E. Hoover to Asst. Sec. State Berle, Sub: Spanish-Mexican Groups, Los Angeles, . . . ," March 24, 1944, in 811.4016/807, RG 59, NA.

15. Soviet intelligence's preoccupation with Hearst is suggested in Allen Weinstein and Alexander Vassiliev, *The Haunted Wood: Soviet Espionage in America—the Stalin Era* (New York: Modern Library, 2000), 31.

16. John Bright and Josephina Fierro de Bright, "Prospectus for the Office of Inter-American Affairs on the Mexican American of Southwestern US," November 10, 1942, in "Spanish-Speaking Project" fldr., entry 155, RG 229, NA. On Sinar-

quista conspiracy among Mexican Americans, see Elis Tipton to Vice President Wallace and others, October 10, 1942, "Paul Horgan" fldr., entry 155, RG 229, NA; and Telephone Rotnem to McGurk, December 15, 1942, in 811.4016/508, RG 59, NA.

17. The "Pacific First crowd" referred to those who had urged the president to concentrate American military efforts in the Pacific theater before rendering "Second Front" aid to the Soviet Union. George Morris, "'Pacific Firsters' Incite Riots," *Daily Worker,* June 12, 1943, 60. See also "Mexican 'Persecution' End Asked in West Coast Riots," *Christian Science Monitor,* June 11, 1943, 65.

18. Adler, "The 1943 Zoot-Suit Riots," 150. The Mexican/Mexican American radical tradition in the United States and the failure of the Communists to capitalize on it are discussed in Monroy, "Anarquismo y Comunismo: Mexican Radicalism and the Communist Party in Los Angeles during the 1930s," *Labor History* 24 (Winter 1983): 34–55.

19. The court rejected claims that the trial judge or proceedings were racially biased or that the judge's rulings unfairly favored the prosecution. It did find that the judge's bickering with counsel materially injured the defendants' case. *People v. Zamora,* 66 Cal. App. 2d 166 (1944).

20. McWilliams, *North from Mexico,* 231.

21. Memorandum of Conversation, subject: "Coordinator's Plans for Work with the Spanish-Speaking Minority . . . ," January 27, 1943, 811.4016/506, RG 59, NA. Attitudes of the local CIAA are discussed by Carey McWilliams in "The Zoot-Suit Riots," *New Republic,* June 21, 1943, 818–820.

22. Ruth D. Tuck, "Behind the Zoot-Suit Riots," *Survey Graphic* (August 1943): 312–316, 355. Virginia Warner, "New Group Acts Today to Aid Mexican Youth," *People's World,* November 30, 1942, clipping in FBI Zoot-Suit files, NA.

23. McWilliams, "Los Angeles' Pachuco Gangs," *New Republic,* January 18, 1943, 76–77.

24. For a firsthand account of the outbreak of violence, see "Minutes of the Citizens' Committee for Latin-American Youth," June 7, 1943, in "Latin America" fldr., entry 222, RG 208, NA.

25. "Preliminary Report by Comdr. Anderson," June 11, 1943, in file P8-5, "Zoot-Suit Collection," Records of Naval Districts and Shore Establishments, RG 181, National Archives and Records Administration, Pacific Region, Laguna Niguel, CA.

26. Harvard Sitkoff, in "The Detroit Race Riot of 1943," *Michigan History* 53 (Fall 1969): 205, notes that the federal government took only two actions in the wake of the riot—both of which involved suppression, not civil rights.

27. Karen Huck, "The Arsenal of Fire: The Reader in the Riot, 1943," *Critical Studies in Mass Communication* 10 (1993): 23–48.

28. Carey McWilliams explained the zoot suits as an attempt by Mexican American youth "to achieve the status or recognition" denied them by society; the actions of the servicemen were a "race riot"; and the indifference and hostility of the police were the latest in a "long series" of such incidents. McWilliams, "These Are Race Riots, Not Gangster Rows," PM, June 11, 1943, ACLU Archives, vol. 2512, 55.

29. Harvard Sitkoff, "Racial Militancy and Interracial Violence in the Second World War," *Journal of American History* 58 (1971): 661–681.

30. Some newspaper accounts noted that older Mexican Americans were as outraged by the behavior of the pachucos as were the sailors. Noted by the editor of *La Opinión* to Citizens' Committee for Latin-American Youth member Flores. See "Minutes of the Citizens' Committee for Latin-American Youth," June 7, 1943, in "Latin America" fldr., entry 222, RG 208, NA.

31. The origins of the outfit (among African Americans) and its meaning are discussed in Stuart Cosgrove, "The Zoot-Suit and Style Warfare," *Radical America* 18 (1984): 39–50.

32. The cartoons are reprinted in Mazón, *Zoot-Suit Riots*. Mazón contends that they encouraged Americans to be concerned about an imminent zoot-suiter takeover, and hence prepared the way for the sailors' repressive acts (ibid., 33, 36).

33. This analysis of the primacy of cultural dress in the riot is addressed in the unpublished paper "Ethnic Mexicans and the Zoot-Suit Summer of 1943: The Material Hybridity of Youth Culture on the Home Front" by Luis Alvarez, University of Texas at Austin, given at the U.S. Latinos and Latinas & World War II Conference, "Changes Seen, Changes Wrought," University of Texas at Austin Alumni Center, May 27, 2000.

34. The police reported twenty-three felonious assaults by wearers of zoot suits on uniformed servicemen in the period January 1 to June 16, 1943. See "Findings and Recommendations of the Grand Jury of Los Angeles County for 1943, Based on Its Inquiry into Juvenile Crime, . . ." [hereafter "Los Angeles Grand Jury Findings, 1943"], July 1943, found in exhibit 2.5, to dispatch 1865, file 811.4016/651, RG 59, NA.

35. Although the *New York Times* had its own correspondent in Los Angeles, his reports, and the *Times* coverage, were very much like that provided by the news services. They adopted a playful tone that ridiculed the "zoot-suiters" and implied praise for their assailants, who, they suggested, were merely seeking revenge for earlier wrongs done to them. *Times* reports referred to the "youth gangsters" identifiable by their clothing, who happened to be of Mexican descent. For the *Times* reporter, this was a juvenile delinquency problem, not a race problem; "Zoot Suiters Seized on Coast after Clashes with Service Men," *New York Times*, June 7, 1943, 15, and "Los Angeles Barred to Sailors by Navy to Stem Zoot-Suit Riots," *New York Times*, June 9, 1943, 23; Lawrence E. Davies, "Zoot Suits Become Issue on Coast," *New York Times*, June 13, 1943, IV, 10. After the riots, Davies conceded that "slum conditions, . . . with some racial discrimination . . . are blamed as contributory to a state of mind lending itself readily to crime." The *Times* thus emphasized the alleged criminality of the Mexican Americans in the riots, although conceding social origins to their criminal disposition. Lawrence E. Davies, "Zoot-Suit Riots Are Studied," *New York Times*, June 20, 1943, IV, 10.

36. J. Edgar Hoover wanted to know who the victims were. The local FBI office reported that every person arrested by police was checked for his Selective Service status and that there "has been no unusual number of these people delin-

quent in this respect." Speculation was that the high rates of tuberculosis and criminal records resulted in many Mexican Americans being rejected for military service. He pointed out that recently local draft boards had adopted a much more liberal attitude, ordering induction of larger numbers. SAC Los Angeles for Director, Re: "Mexican Youth Gangs," June 11, 1943, FBI—Zoot Suit Files, NA.

37. The L.A. grand jury found that "liquor to a large extent and marihuana to a small extent are major causes of juvenile crime." It did not address their role in the riot. "Los Angeles Grand Jury Findings, 1943."

38. "The Zoot-Suit Riots," *Shreveport Journal*, June 14, 1943, 77; "The Zoot Cesspool," *Nashville Banner*, June 12, 1943.

39. "Zoot-Suit War," *Time*, June 21, 1943, 4.

40. But even the *Time* piece appeared to be dangerous in communicating anti-Mexican sentiment to the Mexican government leaders. The day after the publication of the article, the U.S. ambassador to Mexico wrote the secretary of state informing him that the *Time* article "treats the zoot-suit disturbances in such a way as to make it appear as an anti-Mexican movement and blames the police for encouraging attacks on Mexicans and accuses the military authorities of laxity." Ambassador Messersmith ended his dispatch by suggesting that the secretary of state discuss the whole matter with the editors of *Time* magazine to suggest that they needed a change in their future coverage of such events. For a fuller treatment of the implications of this riot for Mexican and Latin American affairs, see Griswold del Castillo, "L.A. 'Zoot Suit Riots' Revisited," 367–391.

41. Blocker dispatch #1855, Sub; "Zoot Suit Disturbances at Los Angeles, California," August 3, 1943, 811.4016/665, RG 59, NA.

42. Naval intelligence provided a list of almost forty assaults on servicemen by "zoot suiters" from October 1942 through May 1943. "Counter-Intelligence Summary, Eleventh Naval District—Zoot-Suit Riots," June 1943, exhibit 3, to dispatch 1855, 811.4016/665, RG 59, NA.

43. The case is made in Bowron to P. Bonsal, and Bowron to E. Davis, June 28, 1943, both in "Subversive Activities—LA Riot Situation," entry 1, RG 208, NA; and in Bowron's remarks to Blocker recorded in Blocker's report, "Zoot Suit Disturbances at Los Angeles, California," August 3, 1943, in 811.4016/651, RG 59, NA.

44. "Los Angeles Grand Jury Findings, 1943," 7–10.

45. Meier and Rivera, *Mexican Americans*, 165, summarizes the reform efforts.

46. Memo by William B. Cherin (Justice Department Special War Policies Unit) for David Niles, June 16, 1943, "General Politics, Letters/Documents, 1939–43," David Niles papers, Harry S. Truman Library. Cherin was urging creation of a federal agency to coordinate intelligence and remedial action. The same idea appeared in a memo by Saul K. Padover, "Office of Race Relations," June 29, 1943, which Secretary of Interior Ickes sent to FDR, PSF-Interior, FDRL.

47. Memorandum, Hoover to Rockefeller, June 9, 1943, FBI "Zoot Suit" files, and "Counter-Intelligence Summary, Eleventh Naval District—Zoot-Suit Riots," June 1943, exhibit 3 to dispatch 1855, 811.4016/599, RG 59, NA.

48. Bowron made this attitude clear as well as his dislike of Alan Cranston and his suspicion of the Citizens Committee for Latin-American Youth, which Cranston had helped set up, in Bowron to Elmer Davis, June 28, 1943, "Subver-

sive Activities—LA Riot Situation" fldr, entry 1, RG 208, NA. Phillip Bonsal, of the State Department's Division of American Republics, told Welles that Los Angeles authorities were on top of the situation and that intervention might undermine popular support for what the local government decided. Bonsal to Welles, June 10, 1943, 811.4016/599, RG 59, NA.

49. U.S. and Mexican officials worked in concert to play down the episode in the Mexican press. There was one serious demonstration, but it, and the protest impulse in general, was kept under control. See correspondence between the State Department and Mexican officials, particularly "US Ambassador to Mexico to State," June 26, 1943, in 811.4016/590, RG 59, NA. See the larger discussion in Griswold del Castillo, "L.A. 'Zoot Suit Riots' Revisited," 380–391.

50. George I. Sánchez, "Pachucos in the Making," *Common Ground* 4 (Autumn 1943): 13–20.

Chapter Four

1. Acuña, *Occupied America*, 264.

2. Takaki, *Double Victory*, 60.

3. Ibid., 83.

4. Ibid., quoting Raul Morin, 88.

5. Ibid., quoting Victoria Morales, 101.

6. Emilio Zamora, "The Politics of Good Neighborliness in Texas during the Second World War," unpublished book manuscript, chap. 3, 11.

7. *El Espectador* (Los Angeles), September 11, 1942.

8. The University of Texas at Austin is attempting to collect the stories of the veterans of World War II in a project directed by Maggie Rivas-Rodriguez, UT School of Journalism. In June of 2000, they sponsored the first-ever national conference to bring together veterans and scholars to begin to assemble the national story of Mexican Americans during World War II. For additional information on this project, visit the web site http://www.utexas.edu/projects/latinoarchives/. At this site you can also read their *Narratives* publication, which contains stories of Mexican American GIs during the war.

9. See the first publication to result from this effort, Maggie Rivas-Rodríguez's *Mexican Americans and World War II* (Austin: University of Texas Press, 2005).

10. The following discussion is based on samples from the oral history archives of the Latinos and Latinas in World War II Project in Austin, Texas.

11. Ramón Saldívar, *Chicano Narrative: The Dialectics of Difference* (Madison: University of Wisconsin Press, 1990), 212.

12. *Narratives* 3, no. 2 (Spring 2002): 52.

13. Ibid.

14. Ibid., 48.

15. *Narratives* 4, no. 1 (Spring 2003): 29.

16. Ibid., 4.

17. Ibid., 44.

18. W. E. B. Du Bois coined this term to describe the African American di-

lemma: "After the Egyptian and Indian, the Greek and Roman, the Teuton and Mongolian, the Negro is a sort of seventh son, born with a veil, and gifted with second-sight in this American world,—a world which yields him no true self-consciousness, but only lets him see himself through the revelation of the other world. It is a peculiar sensation, this double-consciousness, this sense of always looking at one's self through the eyes of others, of measuring one's soul by the tape of a world that looks on in amused contempt and pity. One ever feels his two-ness,—an American, a Negro; two souls, two thoughts, two unreconciled strivings; two warring ideals in one dark body, whose dogged strength alone keeps it from being torn asunder.

"The history of the American Negro is the history of this strife,—this longing to attain self-conscious manhood, to merge his double self into a better and truer self." W. E. B. Du Bois, "Of Our Spiritual Strivings," in *The Souls of Black Folk* (Chicago: A. C. McClurg & Co.; Cambridge, Mass.: University Press John Wilson & Son, 1903), 3–4.

Du Bois saw "double-consciousness" as a pathology leading to self-hatred. The ways in which this phenomenon differed from and was manifested in the WWII Mexican American generation's experience has yet to be analyzed in any detail.

19. See especially M. T. Garcia's *Mexican Americans* and his "Americans All," which discuss the basic characteristics of the wartime Mexican American generation.

20. See G. J. Sanchez, *Becoming Mexican American*, for an analysis of this process of "becoming" prior to World War II. One woman growing up in San Bernardino recalled that her high school locker was marked with the letter "M" by school officials, while those of the Anglo teenagers had the letter "A." Josefina Sánchez to Rita Sánchez, oral interview, July 6, 2005, San Bernardino, California.

21. Interview with María Elisa Rodríguez, Austin, Texas, May 10, 1999, 3:39–3:50, 13:50–14:39, Latinos and Latinas in World War II Project Archive, University of Texas, Austin.

22. Ibid., 13:50–14:39.

23. Ibid., 29:11–29:42.

24. Interview with Andrew Aguirre, San Diego, California, November 25, 2001, 9:18–10:15, Latinos and Latinas in World War II Project Archive, University of Texas, Austin.

25. Ibid., 30:53–31:56.

26. Interview with Héctor Peña Jr., Corpus Christi, August 18, 2001, 13:29–14:38, Latinos and Latinas in World War II Project Archive, University of Texas, Austin.

27. Ibid., 14:40–15:42.

28. Santillán, "Rosita the Riveter," 138.

29. Sherna Berger Gluck, *Rosie the Riveter Revisited: Women, War, and Social Change* (Boston: Twayne, 1987), 264.

30. Our understanding of Mexican American working women during World War II is still in its infancy due to the paucity of primary sources. In 1990, Richard Santillán interviewed eighty-seven Mexican American women who worked in the war industries plants in the Midwest. Vicki L. Ruiz has interviewed women

whose wartime experiences were part of her book *From Out of the Shadows: Mexican Women in Twentieth-Century America*. Elizabeth Escovedo, a graduate student at UCLA working on her Ph.D. dissertation at the time of this writing, is collecting oral interviews and analyzing the experiences of Mexican American women during World War II. California State University at Long Beach has within its Rosie the Riveter Collection interviews with Hispanic women, and San Diego State University has seven interviews with Mexican American women who worked in San Diego during the war. The University of El Paso's Oral History Collection also has a number of interviews with women who worked in El Paso during World War II, and finally, the already-mentioned University of Texas Department of Journalism's Latinos and Latinas in World War II Oral History Project promises to build a more substantial collection than we presently have.

31. William H. Chafe, *The American Woman: Her Changing Social, Economic, and Political Roles, 1920–1970* (New York: Oxford University Press, 1972), 174–175.

32. Karen Anderson, *Wartime Women: Sex Roles, Family Relations, and the Status of Women during World War II* (Westport, Conn.: Greenwood Press, 1981), 7.

33. Santiago Solís Interviews (transcripts of oral interviews), SDSU Special Collections, 55.

34. Ibid., 70.

35. For an analysis of the role of women in the families of servicemen, see Rita Sánchez, "The Five Sánchez Brothers in World War II: Remembrance and Discovery," in Rivas-Rodriguez, *Mexican Americans and World War II*, 1–40.

36. Gluck, *Rosie the Riveter Revisited*, 88.

37. Solís Interviews, 33.

38. Ibid., 45.

39. Santillán, "Rosita the Riveter," 138–140.

40. Ibid., 137.

41. Solís Interviews, 21.

42. Gluck, *Rosie the Riveter Revisited*, 23.

43. Santillán, "Rosita the Riveter," 141.

44. Oral interview with Helen Sánchez, February 4, 2000, in R. Sánchez, "The Five Sánchez Brothers in World War II," 19.

45. Ibid., 20.

46. The classic critique of *pachuquismo* appears in Octavio Paz, *The Labyrinth of Solitude: Life and Thought in Mexico* (New York: Grove Press, 1961), chap. 1; For contemporary interpretations of this phenomenon, see Griffith, *American Me*, 15–28; G. I. Sánchez, "Pachucos in the Making," 13–20; Tuck, *Not with the Fist*; also see Turner and Surace, "Zoot-Suiters and Mexicans," 14–24.

47. See Elizabeth Escovedo's discussion of this in Solís Interviews, 34–35.

48. Ibid., 36.

49. Ibid., 64.

50. Ruiz, *From Out of the Shadows*, 83.

51. Gluck, *Rosie the Riveter Revisited*, 98.

52. Solís Interviews, 61.

53. Naomi Quiñonez, "Rosita the Riveter: Welding Tradition with Wartime Transformations," in Rivas-Rodriguez, *Mexican Americans in World War II*, 266.

54. Benjamin Heber Johnson, *Revolution in Texas: How a Forgotten Rebellion and Its Bloody Suppression Turned Mexicans into Americans* (New Haven and London: Yale University Press, 2003), 208.

55. See Richard Buitron Jr.'s argument in *The Quest for Tejano Identity in San Antonio, Texas, 1913–2000* (New York: Routledge, 2004).

56. See Charles Montgomery, The Spanish Redemption: Heritage, Power, and Loss on New Mexico's Upper Rio Grande (Berkeley: University of California Press, 2002).

Chapter Five

1. M. T. Garcia, *Mexican Americans*, 20.

2. For a discussion of *Del Rio Independent School District v. Salvatierra* and the community reactions, see Guadalupe San Miguel Jr., *"Let All of Them Take Heed."*

3. M. T. Garcia, *Mexican Americans*, chap. 9.

4. George I. Sánchez, *The Forgotten People* (Albuquerque: University of New Mexico Press, 1940).

5. Félix Almaraz Jr., *Knight without Armor: Carlos Eduardo* Castañeda (College Station: Texas A&M Press, 1999), 213–252.

6. Ibid., 237.

7. Ibid., 246. For a review of the FEPC investigations headed by Castañeda in New Mexico, Arizona, and southern Colorado, see Vargas, *Labor Rights*, 214–224.

8. Emilio Zamora, "The Failed Promise of Wartime Opportunity for Mexicans in the Texas Oil Industry," *Southwestern Historical Quarterly* 95 (1992): 324–349.

9. Almaraz Jr., *Knight without Armor*, 259.

10. Her birth name was Alicia López Rodríguez. When she became an adult, she changed her name to Luisa Moreno to honor the Mexican labor organizer Luis Moreno.

11. Interview with Bert Corona, July 26, 1995, Carlos Larralde Collection (private), Calemesa, California.

12. Larralde interview with Luisa Moreno, May 28, 1971, Carlos Larralde Collection. G. J. Sanchez, *Becoming Mexican American*, 244.

13. "For Clerk," Folder 53, Robert W. Kenny Collection, Southern California Library for Social Studies and Research, Los Angeles, California. See M. T. Garcia, *Memories of Chicano History*, 117. For the California period, see Ruiz, *Cannery Women, Cannery Lives*, 42. On UCAPAWA and Moreno, see Vicki Lynn Ruiz, "UCAPAWA, Chicanas, and the California Food Processing Industry, 1937–1950" (Ph.D. diss., Stanford University, 1982), 135.

14. "For Clerk," Folder 53, Robert W. Kenny Collection.

15. Carlos Larralde interview with Luisa Moreno, April 17, 1971; Carey McWilliams' leaflet "Luisa Moreno Bemis Biography," August 1949, Los Angeles, which was written for the "Provisional Committee for Luisa Moreno Bemis," Carlos Larralde Collection.

16. Carlos Larralde interview with Luisa Moreno, April 17, 1971; Carlos

Larralde interview with Bert Corona, April 25, 1980—both in Carlos Larralde Collection.

17. M. T. Garcia, *Memories of Chicano History*, 109, 113, 117. For further information on Moreno and the Congreso, see M. T. Garcia, *Mexican Americans*, 146–153.

18. Carlos Larralde interview with Luisa Moreno, May 28, 1971, Carlos Larralde Collection.

19. "W. T. Webber to Those Concerned," August 5, 1949, "Provisional Committee for Luisa Moreno Bemis," Carlos Larralde Collection; "Memo for Robert Morris on Character Witness," undated, Folder 54, Robert W. Kenny Collection.

20. Carlos Larralde interview with Luisa Moreno, June 2, 1971, Carlos Larralde Collection. See also Carey McWilliams, *The New Republic*, January 18, 1943.

21. M. T. Garcia, *Memories of Chicano History*, 143. For more information about the Zoot-Suit Riots, see Mazón, *The Zoot-Suit Riots*.

22. Address delivered by Luisa Moreno Bemis to the Twelfth Annual Convention, California CIO Council, October 15, 1949, 3–4, Folder 53, Robert W. Kenny Collection. Also quoted in G. J. Sanchez, *Becoming Mexican American*, 251.

23. Johnson, *Revolution in Texas*, 185.

24. Márquez, *LULAC*, 37.

25. Ibid., 40.

26. M. T. Garcia, *Mexican Americans*, 36.

27. Gladys Ruth Leff, "George I. Sánchez: Don Quixote of the Southwest" (Ph.D. diss., History Department, North Texas State University, 1976), 397.

28. G. I. Sánchez, "Pachucos in the Making."

29. Ibid., 20.

30. "Pan-Americanism Must Begin at Home, Sánchez Tells Parent-Teacher Congress," *Albuquerque Journal*, May 6, 1942, cited in Emilio Zamora, "Joining the Wartime Fight for Mexican Rights in Texas," chap. 3, unpublished manuscript used by permission of the author.

31. Zamora, "Joining the Wartime Fight," 11.

32. Ibid., 15–20.

33. *La Prensa*, May 9, 1945.

34. Zamora, "Joining the Wartime Fight," 40.

35. Ricardo Romo, "George I. Sánchez and the Civil Rights Movement," *La Raza Law Journal* 1, no. 3 (Fall 1986): 350.

36. Ibid., 356–357.

37. Ibid., 358–359.

38. Robert Alvarez Jr., "The Lemon Grove Incident: The Nation's First Successful Desegregation Court Case," *Journal of San Diego History* 22, no. 2 (Spring 1986): 116–135. See also his *Familia: Migration and Adaptation in Baja and Alta California, 1800–1975* (Berkeley and Los Angeles: University of California Press, 1987). *The Lemon Grove Incident* (San Diego, Calif.: KPBS, 1985), TV documentary produced by Paul Espinosa.

39. M. T. Garcia, "Americans All."

40. Ibid., 282.

41. Ibid., 286.

42. Enrique M. López, "Community Resistance to Injustice and Inequality: Ontario, California, 1937–1947," *Aztlan* 17, no. 2 (1988): 1–29. See also M. T. Garcia, *Mexican Americans,* chap. 4.

43. López, "Community Resistance," 14.

44. *El Espectador,* August 12, 1942.

45. Ibid., October 16, 1942.

46. Ibid., December 11, 1942.

47. Ibid., December 31, 1943.

48. *López et al. v. Seccombe et al.,* United States District Court for the Southern District of Southern California, Central Division 71 F. Supp. 769 (S.D. Cal 1944), February 5, 1944. For the full text, see http://sshl.ucsd.edu/brown/López .htm.

49. Ibid., August 10, 1945.

50. M. T. Garcia, *Mexican Americans,* 101.

51. J. Fierro de Bright to Manuel Ruiz, April 20, 1942, Manuel Ruiz Collection, Special Collections, Stanford University. The members of the organizing committee for the conference included liberal Anglos like Carey McWilliams and Guy T. Nunn, representing African American organizations like the Urban League, and labor union representatives like Bert Corona from the CIO.

52. Christine Marín, "Mexican Americans on the Home Front: Community Organizations in Arizona during World War II," *Perspectives in Mexican American Studies* 4, no. 4 (1993): 77.

53. Ibid., 86.

54. Julie Campbell, "Madres y Esposas: Tucson's Spanish-American Mothers and Wives Association," *Journal of Arizona History,* (Summer 1990): 167–170.

55. "Racial Conditions (Spanish-Mexican Activities) in Los Angeles Field Station," FBI Report, January 14, 1944.

56. Vargas, *Labor Rights,* 225–227.

57. Ibid., 233–234.

58. Ibid., 235.

Chapter Six

1. Texas House Concurrent Resolution 105, 48th Legislature, quoted in Everett Ross Clinchy Jr., "Equal Opportunity for Latin Americans in Texas" (Ph.D. diss, Political Science Department, Columbia University, 1954), 181.

2. 48th Texas Legislature, 1943, House Joint Resolutions and Senate and House Concurrent Resolutions, "House Concurrent Resolution 105," Texas State Archives, Vols. 100–1106.

3. In early 1945, the Spears bill was proposed in the Texas Senate to outlaw discrimination against Mexican or Latin American residents in public facilities, including restaurants, theaters, and hotels. For violation of the law, the bill stipulated a fine of $500 and/or imprisonment for thirty days. See Clinchy, "Equal Opportunity," 182–183.

4. Richard W. Steele, *Free Speech in the Good War* (New York: St. Martin's Press, 1999), 177.

5. Ibid.

6. See González, *Chicano Education*, 147–156, for a complete discussion of this case.

7. San Miguel Jr., *"Let All of Them Take Heed,"* 126.

8. Ibid., 133.

9. Ibid., 116.

10. Acuña, *Occupied America*, 280.

11. M. T. Garcia, *Mexican Americans*, 200.

12. Ibid.

13. Ibid., 202.

14. M. T. Garcia, *Memories of Chicano History*, 202–204.

15. Ignacio García, *Viva Kennedy: Mexican Americans in Search of Camelot* (College Station: Texas A&M Press, 2000), 93.

16. McWilliams, *North from Mexico*, 283.

17. M. T. Garcia, *Mexican Americans*.

18. G. J. Sanchez, *Becoming Mexican American*, 256–264.

19. Vargas, *Labor Rights*, chap. 5.

20. Some scholars have studied the formation of Mexican American identity in this century and shown how its evolution was a response to complex regional, economic, and cultural transformations. See Richard Buitron Jr., *The Quest for Tejano Identity in San Antonio, Texas, 1913–2000* (New York: Routledge Press, 2004); Gilbert González, *Labor and Community: Mexican Citrus Worker Villages in a Southern California County, 1900–1950* (Urbana: University of Illinois Press, 1994); De León, *Mexican Americans in Texas*; Montgomery, *Spanish Redemption*.

Appendix A

1. Tuck, *Not with the Fist* (New York: Harcourt, Brace, 1946), 197–222.

2. Ibid., viii.

Appendix B

1. "Fair Employment Practices Act Hearings," in Perales, *Are We Good Neighbors?*, 92–98.

Appendix C

1. Office of the Federal Register, *Code of Federal Regulations, Title 3—The President, 1938–1943 Compilation* (Washington, DC: GPO, 1943).

Appendix D

1. 48th Legislature, State of Texas, "Caucasian Race—Equal Privileges," *General and Special Laws of the State of Texas January 12, 1943, to May 11, 1943*, 119.

Appendix E

1. Manuel Ruiz Collection, Special Collections, Stanford University, M295, Box 1, Folder 6. Published in *Crime Prevention Digest* 1, no. 13 (December 1942). Reprinted courtesy of the Department of Special Collections, Stanford University Libraries.

Appendix F

1. Excerpts from Morin, *Among the Valiant*, 48–56, 94–103, 166–171, 277–280.

Appendix G

1. Alonso S. Perales, *En defensa de mi raza*, 2 vols. (San Antonio: Artes Gráficas, 1936–1937).

2. From Perales, *Are We Good Neighbors?*, 170–186.

Selected Annotated Bibliography

Allsup, Carl. *The American G.I. Forum: Origins and Evolution*. Austin: Center for Mexican American Studies, ⬛niversity of Texas at Austin, 1982. A general overview of the history of this early Mexican American civil rights organization formed after the war.

Camarillo, Albert. "Research Note on Chicano Community Leaders: The G.I. Generation." *Aztlan* 2, no. 1 (Spring 1971): 145–150. Makes the point that many civil rights activists were organizers in the 1930s, but that the war did spawn a new generation of activists.

Campbell, Julie. "Madres y Esposas: Tucson's Spanish-American Mothers and Wives Association." *Journal of Arizona History* 31, no. 2 (1990): 161–182. A study of how women were active in supporting the war effort and defining themselves as Americans.

Canales, J. T. *Personal Recollections of J. T. Canales*. Brownsville, Texas, 1945. Canales was a lawyer who was active in civil rights actions in South Texas. This book of recollections gives a personal insight into the conditions in Texas.

Cletus, Daniel. *Chicano Workers and the Politics of Fairness: The FEPC in the Southwest, 1941–1945*. Austin: University of Texas Press, 1991. A study of how this agency failed the expectations of Mexican Americans for justice in the workplace.

Driscoll, Bárbara A. *Mexican Railroad Workers in the United States during World War II/Me voy pa' Pensilvania por no andar en la vagancia: Los ferrocarrileros mexicanos en Estados Unidos durante la Segunda Guerra Mundial*. Trans. Lauro Medina. 1st ed. Mexico City: Consejo Nacional para la Cultura y las Artes; Universidad Nacional Autónoma de México, Centro de Investigaciones sobre América del Norte, 1996. A study using Mexican oral histories and documents of the struggles of the Mexican bracero workers on the railroads during the war.

Garcia, Mario T. "Americans All: The Mexican American Generation and the Politics of Wartime Los Angeles, 1941–45." *Social Science Quarterly* 65, no. 2 (1984): 278–289. An in-depth study of the Coordinating Council for Latin American Youth, headed by Manuel Ruiz Jr.

————, ed. *Memories of Chicano History: The Life and Narrative of Bert Corona*. Berkeley and Los Angeles: University of California Press, 1994. Personal recollections of a major civil rights leader, spanning the 1930s to the Chicano movement days.

————. *Mexican Americans: Leadership, Ideology, and Identity, 1930–1960*. New Haven and London: Yale University Press, 1989. A study of organizations and individuals who developed a Mexican American civil rights movement after World War II.

González, Gilbert. *Chicano Education in the Era of Segregation*. Philadelphia: The Balch Institute Press, 1990. The *Mendez et al. v. Westminster* case set within a larger context of colonialist and racist practices. Detail on the community organization after the war.

Griffith, Beatrice W. *American Me*. Boston: Houghton Mifflin, 1948. A series of oral interviews interspersed with sociological commentary by a wide variety of Mexican Americans in wartime Los Angeles.

Griswold del Castillo, Richard. "The Los Angeles 'Zoot Suit Riots' Revisited: Mexican and Latin American Perspectives." *Mexican Studies/Estudios Mexicanos* 16, no. 2 (Summer 2000): 367–392. A study of how the Mexican public and government reacted to the Zoot-Suit Riots.

Kibbe, Pauline R. *Latin Americans in Texas*. Albuquerque: University of New Mexico Press, 1946.

Marín, Christine. "Mexican Americans on the Home Front: Community Organizations in Arizona during World War II." *Perspectives in Mexican American Studies* 4 (1993): 75–92. Discusses patriotic organizations of Mexican Americans who supported the war effort at home.

Márquez, Benjamin. LULAC: *The Evolution of a Mexican American Political Organization*. Austin: University of Texas Press, 1993. The best overall survey of this important civil rights organization, but lacking detail for the World War II period.

Mazón, Mauricio. *The Zoot-Suit Riots: The Psychology of Symbolic Annihilation*. Austin: University of Texas Press, 1984. Advances an interpretation of the violence of these riots as stemming from popular cultural prejudices.

Montejano, David. *Anglos and Mexicans in the Making of Texas, 1836–1986*. Austin: University of Texas Press, 1987. A sweeping interpretation of how Mexican Americans in Texas have been changed by socioeconomic conditions. The World War II period is not emphasized.

Morin, Raul. *Among the Valiant: Mexican Americans in WWII and Korea*. Alhambra, Calif.: Borden Publishing, 1963. The only book thus far published telling the stories of Mexican American soldiers during these wars.

Perales, Alonso S. *Are We Good Neighbors?*. New York: Arno Press, 1974 (Orig. pub. San Antonio: Artes Gráficas, 1948). A series of documents, speeches, and testimonies illustrating that Mexican Americans suffered second-class citizenship in Texas.

Ruiz, Vicki L. *Cannery Women, Cannery Lives: Mexican Women, Unionization, and the California Food Processing Industry, 1930–1950*. Albuquerque: University of New Mexico Press, 1987. A study of the women who founded a militant agricultural union, UCAPAWA, during the 1930s.

Sanchez, George J. *Becoming Mexican American: Ethnicity, Culture and Identity in Chicano Los Angeles, 1900–1945*. New York: Oxford University Press, 1993. Interprets changing identities among Mexican Americans in this important city. Focuses on the Mexican American movement during World War II.

San Miguel, Guadalupe, Jr. *"Let All of Them Take Heed": Mexican Americans and the Campaign for Educational Equality in Texas, 1910–1981*. Austin: University of Texas Press, 1987. A detailed account of the various organized attempts to challenge segregation in the Texas schools.

Santillán, Richard. "Rosita the Riveter: Midwest Mexican American Women during World War II, 1941–1945." In *Perspectives in Mexican American Studies*, Vol. 2, *Mexicans in the Midwest*, ed. Juan R. García, 115–148. Tucson: Mexican-American Studies and Research Center, University of Arizona, 1989. Based on scores of personal interviews with women, this study shows the ways that the war challenged traditional expectations.

Takaki, Ronald. *Double Victory: Multicultural History of America in World War II*. New York: Little, Brown, 2000. A lively and engaging account of how minority groups lived through the war with protest and patriotism.

Tuck, Ruth D. *Not with the Fist: Mexican-Americans in a Southwest City*. New York: Harcourt, Brace, 1974. (Orig. pub. 1946.) A series of interviews with Mexican Americans in Los Angeles interspersed with social commentary. A classic in presenting the feel of life in Los Angeles during World War II.

Vargas, Zaragosa. *Labor Rights Are Civil Rights: Mexican American Workers in Twentieth-Century America*. Princeton and Oxford: Princeton University Press, 2005. An examination of the working-class movement, in particular within labor unions during the 1930s and through the World War II years, arguing that the modern civil rights movement owes a debt to these early organizers and leaders.

Index

Page numbers in *italics* refer to figures.

Acuña, Rudolfo, 2
African Americans: civil rights activism of, 15, 66; and discrimination, 11, 15, 29; and double-consciousness, 219–220n18; education of, 13; effects of World War II on, 4; and employment discrimination, 20, 143; employment of African American women, 67; injustices experienced by, 74, 98; integration of, 85; on juries, 123, 124; liberals' support of, 34; and limits of federal civil rights action, 97; and Mexico, 212n23; in military, 132; political power of, 22, 211n39, 212n16; pressure tactics of, 29, 32; and race riots, 42–43, 107; and racial classification of Mexican Americans, 12; relations with Mexican Americans, 61, 67, 116, 117–118; second-class citizenship of, 74; and Sleepy Lagoon case, 38; in Texas, 209n20, 211n39; and zoot suits, 41
agriculture, 11, 17–18. *See also* farm-workers; migrant workers
Aguirre, Andrew, 59–60
Alger, Horatio, 31
Alianza Hispano-Americana, 90, 105

American Council for Spanish-Speaking People (ACSSP), 85, 105
American Delegation of Labor, 78
American dream, 56, 58, 82, 106
American empire, 54
American GI Forum: civil rights activism of, 100–101; formation of, *103;* and Héctor P. García, 61, 101; and Gran Junta de Protesta flyer, *102;* and Morin, 159, 188; and George I. Sánchez, 85; women active in, 59
American Indians: and discrimination, 11; education of, 13; injustices experienced by, 74; liberals' support of, 34, 214n1; in military, 50
American Left, 39
American Southwest: attitudes towards Mexico in, 23; and civil rights activism, 97, 106; and discrimination, 14, 24; labor shortages in, 9; Mexican American organizations in, 93; as part of Mexican territory, 8–9; and public facilities desegregation, 105; racism in, 29; and reform movements, 34
Amor, Carlos, 178
Anderson, Karen, 63
Anglos. *See* white Americans

Anti-Nazi League, 79
anti-Semitism, and Fascism, 39
Arizona, 2, 103, 104, 137, 142
Arlee, Juan, 178
Arlington National Cemetery, 101
Arvisu, Joe, 178
Asian Americans: and discrimination,
    11, 12; education of, 13; relations
    with Mexican Americans, 116, 117,
    118–119; treatment as transitory
    workforce, 9. *See also* Japanese
    Americans
Asociación Hispano-Americana
    de Madres y Esposas (Spanish-
    American Mothers and Wives
    Association), 90, *91*
Asociación Nacional México-
    Americana (ANMA), 103–104
assimilation: and Mexican American
    identity, 60; and Mexican Ameri-
    can women, 67–68; of Mexican
    immigrants, 153; need for, 8; Prot-
    estant churches fostering, 210n28
Ávala Camacho, Manuel, 23
Axis alliance: and discrimination in
    U.S., 25, 74; and Good Neighbor
    Policy, 23; Mexico declaring war
    on, 51; and Zoot-Suit Riots, 47

Barron, Agustin, 173
Bell Town Improvement League, 105
Bemis, Gray, 80
Bernal, Manny, 170
Biddle, Francis, 97, 98
bilingual education programs, 86
Blocker, William P., 28
Bogardus, Emory, 15, 17
Bonsal, Phillip, 219n48
Bowron, Fletcher, 218n48
Bracero Program, 24, 95
Brown v. Board of Education (1954),
    86, 88

California: African Americans' orga-
    nizations in, 15; civil rights activ-
    ism in, 101, 103, 104; descendants
    of Spanish-speaking settlers in,

2, 8; education in, 12, 13; and em-
    ployment discrimination, 20–21,
    88, 138, 142; integration of Mexi-
    can Americans into Anglo society,
    9; and Mexican American iden-
    tity, 72; Mexican American labor
    organizations in, 21; Mexican
    immigrants settling in, 11; as part
    of Mexican territory, 8; and race-
    based legal distinctions, 11–12, 14;
    segregation fight in, 86–89. *See also*
    Los Angeles, California
California Congress of Industrial
    Organizations (CIO) Council, 81
California Portland Cement Com-
    pany, 88
California Un-American Activities
    Committee, 81
Campos, Antonio, 54–56
Canales, J. T., 72, 76
Cañoncito school, San Miguel
    County, New Mexico, *10*
Capp, Al, 43
Carrasco, Chive, *104*
Carrasco, Hortencia, 64, 65–66
Castañeda, Carlos Eduardo: and
    employment discrimination, 76–78,
    135–142; and FEPC, 25, 75–78, 94,
    135, 136, 141, 142; and League of
    United Latin American Citizens,
    27, 78, 136
Castillo Nájera, Francisco, 24
Central America, 23
Chafe, William H., 63
Chávez, César, 101, 103
Chavez, Dennis, 77
Cherin, William B., 214n47, 218n46
Chicana feminism, 70
Chicano, use of term, 68
Chicano movement, 1, 104, 107, 148
Citizens Committee for Latin-
    American Youth, 218n48
citizenship: and defense industry
    employment, 21; and League of
    United Latin American Citizens,
    82, 83; and Mexican American
    identity, 71; and middle-class

Mexican Americans, 72; military service accelerating process of, 211n1; for minorities, 99; and naturalization, 16, 119, 120–121, 210n31; promise of, to Mexican GIS, 56–57; questioning of, 58–59; second-class citizenship, 1, 4, 12, 14, 74, 95; Tuck on, 119–124

civil rights activism: of African Americans, 15, 66; and El Congreso del Pueblo de Habla Española, 21–22, 50, 79, 224n51; and Corona, 2; and home front, 75, 94; and League of United Latin American Citizens, 26–31; and Mexican American leaders, 1, 94, 99–101, 103–106; and World War II, 28, 29–30, 31, 32, 33, 94, 95, 96–99, 105, 106; and Zoot-Suit Riots, 48

civil rights consciousness: and Castañeda, 75–78; discourse of, 75; evolution of, 1–2, 4, 5, 6, 71–72, 75, 110–111; and Mexican American GIS, 57; and Mexican American identity, 49, 59, 61–62, 66, 71, 72, 73; and Mexican American organizations, 1, 2, 3, 86–89, 93, 94, 104–105; and Mexican American women, 62, 66–67, 70; of middle-class Mexican Americans, 18; and Luisa Moreno, 78–81; in post-World War II era, 1, 4, 99–101, 103–106; in pre-World War II era, 1, 15–18, 50, 61, 71, 74, 105; and George I. Sánchez, 81–86, 95, 96, 99; and Spanish-language newspapers, 16, 87

civil rights movement of 1950s and 1960s, precursors of, 1–2, 75, 94, 103, 104, 107

Club Cívico Latinoamericano, 88

Club Latino Americana, 90

colonias: and civil rights activism, 106; Mexican immigrants' settling in, 10; and political participation rates, 17; segregation in, 1; and support

of war effort, 93. See also housing discrimination

Colorado, 104, 138–139

Comité de Defensa Mexicanamericano, 88

Communist Party of the United States (CPUSA): and El Congreso del Pueblo de Habla Española, 21–22; and Luisa Moreno, 78, 81; and Sleepy Lagoon case, 38, 40, 215n14; and Zoot-Suit Riots, 39, 46

Community Service Organization (CSO), 101, 103, 188

El Congreso del Pueblo de Habla Española (The Congress of Spanish-Speaking People): and civil rights activism, 21–22, 50, 79, 224n51; establishment of, 89, 106; and Mexican American Political Association, 105; and opposition to racism, 72

Congress of Industrial Organizations (CIO), 94, 106

Cooley, Charles Horton, 108

Coordinating Council for Latin-American Youth, 86–87, 148

Corona, Bert: and civil rights activism, 2; and El Congreso del Pueblo de Habla Española, 224n51; and Fair Employment Practices Committee, 22; and Mexican American Political Association, 104; on Luisa Moreno, 78; photograph of, 104

Corona, Frank, 215n14

Cota, Norman D., 173

Coughlin, Charles, 39

Council of Inter-American Affairs, 138

Cramer, Lawrence, 25

Cranston, Alan, 37–38, 44, 151, 218n48

Cuellar, Catarino "Cato," 169, 170

Davies, Lawrence E., 217n35

Davila, Manuel, 178

defense contractors: and eligibility of aliens for employment, 21, 211n7; and employment discrimination, 20–21; and employment of farmworkers, 95; and FEPC hearings, 22, 138, 139, 142

De León, Arnoldo, 2

Delgado v. Bastrop Independent School District (1948), 100

Democratic Party, 14

Desma, Jimmy, 178

Despagne, Tony, 175

Detroit, Michigan, race riots in, 42–43, 216n26

discrimination: and African Americans, 11, 15, 29; and alienation of Mexican American youth, 36–37; and Axis alliance, 25, 74; Blocker's investigation of, 28–29; and Ignacio López, 87–89; and meaning of World War II, 49; and Mexican American generation, 75; and Mexican American GIs, 50, 54–55, 56, 57; and Mexican American identity, 58, 59, 62, 71; and Mexican Americans' exclusion from mainstream, 29; and Mexican American women, 64, 66; mobilization against, 83–85; national campaign against, 107; and George I. Sánchez, 81, 82; and Sleepy Lagoon case, 38; and stereotypes, 11, 31; Tuck on, 108, 109–119, 122; and Zoot-Suit Riots, 217n35. *See also* employment discrimination; housing discrimination; public accommodations/ facilities discrimination

double-consciousness, 57–62, 219–220n18

Du Bois, W. E. B., 219–220n18

Eastside Sun, 69

Echeverría, Rose, 69

education: as civil right, 106; and division of minorities, 116; and GI Bill, 54, 55, 57, 105–106, 186, 187; and League of United Latin American Citizens, 30, 82, 100; and Mexican American identity, 58, 59–61; and Mexican American women, 64, 66;

and middle-class Mexican Americans, 13, 18; and political participation, 16; quality of, 12–13, 14, 134; and George I. Sánchez, 81, 82, 83, 85, 86; segregation in, 12–14, 26, 29, 30, 34, 37, 74, 83, 100, 105, 107, 112, 152–153

Ellinger, W. Don, 77

employment: of African American women, 67; aliens' eligibility for, 21, 211n7; as attraction for Mexican immigrants, 9; effect of World War II on, 1, 20, 33, 98; and Great Depression, 10; and industrial mobilization opportunities, 22, 33; of Mexican American women, 22, 58–59, 62, 63–67, 70, 140, 220–221n30; and Mexican labor, 95; and reform measures, 37, 40, 46, 86, 94, 154–155, 156

employment discrimination: and African Americans, 20, 143; and California, 20–21, 88, 138, 142; and Castañeda, 76–78, 135–142; and Mexican American women, 64; and Luisa Moreno, 79; and poverty, 9–12; and racism, 9, 11–12, 20–22, 33; Manuel Ruiz on, 154; and unions, 76, 77, 94, 106

Escobar, Eleuterio, 76

Escovedo, Elizabeth, 65, 66, 69, 221n30

Esparza, Elvira, 67

El Espectador, 87–89, 94

ethnic identity: and melting-pot theory, 27, 31; and role of World War II, 4; and union movement, 212n11. *See also* Mexican American identity

Evers, Medgar, 107

Fair Employment Practices Committee (FEPC): and Castañeda, 25, 75–78, 94, 135, 136, 141, 142; creation of, 21, 143, 144; and division of minorities, 116; politics of, 25–26; public hearings of, 22, 138, 139, 142;

and reform programs, 30; Manuel
Ruiz on, 157; and unions, 93
farmworkers: and civil rights activism,
103; and employment in defense industry, 95; and Luisa Moreno, 79;
and political participation rates, 16–
17; protests against discrimination,
85; and women's employment, 64
Fascism: and anti-Semitism, 39; and
Mexican American organiza-
tions, 90–91; and patriotism, 74;
and Sinarquistas, 37; and Sleepy
Lagoon case, 39, 150
Federal Bureau of Investigation (FBI):
and Mexican American organiza-
tions, 90–93, 94, 104; and Sleepy
Lagoon case, 39, 40; and Zoot-Suit
Riots, 90, 217–218n36
FEPC. See Fair Employment Practices
Committee (FEPC)
Fierro de Bright, Josefina, 72, 79, 89,
215n14
15th Amendment, 97
Flores, Lorinda, 63
Flores, Moisés, 56
Flores, Raymond, 57
Ford, Henry, 39
14th Amendment, 97, 99

Galvan, "Chuy," 170
gangs: and press, 35, 39, 124; and
Sleepy Lagoon case, 35, 37, 39, 41;
and stereotypes, 215n7; and Zoot-
Suit Riots, 43, 44, 45
García, Héctor P., 5, 61, 101
García, Macario, 83–84
Garcia, Mario T., 1, 18, 75, 106
Garza, George, 82–83
Gastellum, Marcy, 69, 70
Germany, 23
GI Bill, 54, 55, 57, 105–106, 186, 187
Gluck, Sherna Berger, 62, 65, 67
Gonzales, Jaime, 215n14
Gonzales, Lupe, 178
Gonzales, Manuel C., 76
Gonzales, Manuel J., 27, 28
Gonzales, Vincent, 171

Good Neighbor Commission, 96, 145
Good Neighbor policy: and FEPC
hearings, 25; and racial bigotry,
150–151; and racial justice, 29;
and reform initiatives, 23–24; and
Texas, 95–96, 145
Gran Junta de Protesta (Big Protest
Meeting) flyer, 102
Great Depression, 10, 18, 58, 75, 78
Gutiérrez, David, 17

Hearst, William Randolph, 39
Hernández v. Driscoll Consolidated Independent School District (1955), 85
Hernández v. State of Texas (1954), 85,
101
Herrerías, Ignacio F., 212–213n24
Hitler, Adolf, 20
home front: and civil rights activism,
75, 94; contradictions of, 4, 74;
and munitions manufacturing, 20
Hoover, J. Edgar, 217–218n36
housing discrimination: and living
conditions, 12, 58, 112–113, 114, 115,
128; and restrictive covenants, 14,
113, 114; and second generation,
115–116; and segregation, 74, 113,
196–197, 206
Huck, Karen, 42
Huerta, Dolores, 103

Idar brothers, 72
immigrant groups: European immigrant groups, 2–3; exploitation of,
37; and Los Angeles, 151–152; and
melting-pot theory, 27; Mexican
immigrant groups, 2, 8, 9, 10, 11,
15–16, 110, 152–153, 209–210n27;
return to homelands, 10, 208n11
income. See poverty; wages
Incorporated Mexican American Government Employees (IMAGE), 59
Industrial Areas Foundation (IAF), 101
industrialists, antilabor activity of, 39
infant mortality, 12, 209n16
Inter-American Educational Foundation, 83

interest-group politics, and Sleepy
  Lagoon case, 38–39
intermarriage: and Mexican American
  identity, 73; and Mexican Ameri-
  can veterans, 132–133
International Ladies Garment
  Workers Union (ILGWU), 94
International Longshoremen's and
  Warehousemen's Union (ILWU),
  22, 94
International Union of Mine, Mill
  and Smelter Workers, 103, 105, 106
Italian Americans, 8, 20, 29
Italy, 23, 39

Japan, 23
Japanese Americans, 8, 12, 79, 118
Jewish Americans, 7–8, 20, 29, 34
Jim Crow policy, in Texas, 27
Johnson, Benjamin, 71–72, 82
Johnson, Charles S., 12
Johnson, Lyndon B., 101
juries: African Americans on, 123, 124;
  and federal civil rights actions, 97,
  98; lack of Mexican Americans on,
  14, 38, 85, 97, 98, 101, 123–124
juvenile delinquency: and arrests of
  juveniles, 125, 214n3; Mexican
  Americans associated with, 8; and
  Mexican American youth, 35–36,
  128, 215n9; and reform movements, 41; Manuel Ruiz on, 149–
  158; and George I. Sánchez, 83; as
  term, 35; and Zoot-Suit Riots, 43,
  46, 47
juvenile justice system, 38, 40, 46–47

Kennedy, John F., 105
King, Martin Luther, Jr., 107
Ku Klux Klan, 97

labor movement: and civil rights
  activism, 1, 94; and Luisa Moreno,
  72, 78–81, 94, 222n10. See also
  unions
labor shortages: in defense industry,

21, 141; and Mexican immigration, 9, 10, 120, 121, 153; and U.S.-
  Mexico relations, 95–96
Latin American relations, 3, 23–24, 31
Latinos and Latinas in World War II
  Project, 53, 64–65, 71, 221n30
League of United Latin American
  Citizens (LULAC): Americanism of,
  72; and civil rights activism, 26–31;
  education, 30, 82, 100; establishment of, 28, 76, 82, 106; leaders
  labeled as self-seekers, 27, 214n42;
  and Mexican American identity,
  59, 61; and Mexican American veterans, 99; Mexico's support of, 26,
  27, 28, 29; and national Mexican
  American constituency, 16; and
  Perales, 27, 76, 189; and George I.
  Sánchez, 76, 81–86, 94
leftist activists, and gangs, 35
Leyva, Luis, 56–57
liberal, support of American Indians,
  34, 214n1
liberals: and civil rights tactics, 29,
  32; and El Congreso del Pueblo
  de Habla Española, 224n51; and
  Coordinating Council for Latin-
  American Youth, 86; and minori-
  ties' civil rights, 34; and Sleepy
  Lagoon case, 38; and Spears bill,
  85; support of American Indians,
  34, 214n1; and Zoot-Suit Riots,
  42, 43
Lichtenstein, Nelson, 212n11
Life, 42, 43, 45
La Liga Pro-Defensa Escolar, 99–100
Li'l Abner cartoons, 43, 217n32
Lincoln School, El Modeno, Califor-
  nia, *100*
Lindbergh, Charles, 39
local governments, 31
Lockheed Aircraft, 22
Longoria, Félix, 101
López, Beatriz, 87
López, Emma, 65
López, Ignacio, 87–88, 108

López, José, 38
Lopez, Jose M., 179–180, *181*, 182–184
Los Angeles, California: and immigrant groups, 151–152; Mexican American organizations in, 91–93, 105; segregation in, 86; and Sleepy Lagoon case, 35–41; and Zoot-Suit Riots, 41–48
Louisiana, 141
Lozano, Mundo, 170
Lucey, Robert, 47
Lucio, Agustin, 171, *172*, 173
LULAC. *See* League of United Latin American Citizens (LULAC)

Malcolm X, 107
"Marcha for Justice", Corpus Christi, Texas, 5
marijuana use, 45, 69, 218n37
Márquez, Benjamin, 27
Marshall Trust, 85
Martinez, Frank P., 169
Martinez, Jess, 178
Martinez, Jose P., 160–161, *162*, 163–168
Mazón, Mauricio, 4, 217n32
McWilliams, Carey: and El Congreso del Pueblo de Habla Española, 224n51; on East Coast liberals, 34; on Mexican Americans, 17–18, 210n36; and Sleepy Lagoon case, 38, 40–41, 215n14; as West Coast correspondent, 214n2; on zoot suits, 216n28
melting-pot theory, 27, 31
Mendez v. Westminster (1946), 86, 99, 100
Mesa, Rudy, 173
Messersmith, George, 218n40
mestizaje, 56
Mexican American civil rights, pre–World War II struggles for, 1–2
Mexican American community: and civil rights consciousness, 6; and Coordinating Council for Latin-American Youth, 86–87; and

corporate sense of ethnicity, 2; on delinquent behavior of youth, 35–36, 215n9; mobilization of, 4, 84, 189; morale of, 37–38, 40; and Zoot-Suit Riots, 43, 217n30
Mexican American generation: adoption of American values, 18; emergence of, 5; leadership of, 107; and precursors to civil rights movement, 1–2, 75
Mexican American GIs: and Aleutian campaign, 160–161, 163–168; and Asociación Hispano-Americana de Madres y Esposas, 90; contributions of, 4, 51, 53, 56, 72–73, 159, 160–188; and D Day, 169–171, 173–178; and draft, 49–50, 54, 177, 217–218n36; drafting of, 49–50, 54, 177, 217–218n36; and education, 54; enlistment of, 19–20, 50, 54, 56, 60, 82; and equality, 50–51; Jose M. Lopez, 179–180, *181*, 182–184; and Mexican American organizations, 90; motivations of, 50; and organizations, 87; return from war, 185–188
Mexican American identity: and civil rights consciousness, 49, 59, 61–62, 66, 71, 72, 73; and double-consciousness, 57–62; effects of World War II on, 54–57, 106; formation of, 58, 225n20; and Mexican American women, 62–70; remembered identities, 71–73
Mexican American leaders: and Chicano movement's challenge to, 107; and civic involvement, 72; and civil rights activism, 1, 94, 99–101, 103–106; and desegregation lawsuits, 76, 86; and discrimination, 88; and division of minorities, 117–118; formation of, 18; and group consciousness, 15–16; labeling of as self-seekers, 27, 117, 214n42; and Mexican American veterans, 133–134; and military service, 50; U.S.

government's acknowledgement of, 19; and U.S. government's role, 2, 3; and voting rights, 122–123. *See also* League of United Latin American Citizens (LULAC)

Mexican American Movement, 50

Mexican American organizations: California labor organizations, 21; and civil rights consciousness, 1, 2, 3, 86–89, 93, 94, 104–105; and League of United Latin American Citizens, 26; in Los Angeles, 91–93, 105; and Mexican American women, 90, *91*, 93; and post-World War II activism, 99–101, 103–106; and segregation, 86–89, 94; and World War II, 89–94

Mexican American Political Association (MAPA), 87, 104, 188

Mexican Americans: classification as "white," 27, 109, 213n37; electoral campaigns of, 86–87, 89, 104; as ethnic minority, 2, 3, 4, 17–18, 19, 96, 107; national awareness of, 34; political power of, 2, 3, 4, 18, 89, 122–123, 211n39; population of, 8, 208n5, 214n3; racial classification of, 12; relations with African Americans, 61, 67, 116, 117–118; relations with Asian Americans, 116, 117, 118–119; repatriation of, 10–11, 18, 75, 210n36; and second-class citizenship, 1, 4, 12, 14, 74, 95; social-economic caste in 1940, 9–17; treatment of, 3, 8, 74

Mexican American veterans: and American GI Forum, 100–101; and civil rights activism, 99–100, 105–106; and civil rights consciousness, 4; and discrimination, 88; Morin on, 185–188; Tuck on, 131–134

Mexican American women: and Americanization, 66–68, 70; correspondence with servicemen, 65; employment of, 22, 58–59, 62, 63–67, 70, 140, 220–221n30; gender roles of, 69–70; and Mexican

American identity, 62–70; and Mexican American organizations, 90, *91*, 93; as pachucas, 44, 68, 69, 128, 129; part-time and occasional work of, 63–64; and social life, 65, 66, 70; Tuck on, 126; white women compared to, 63–64

Mexican American youth: and Americanization, 153; antisocial behavior of, 36–37, 47–48; arrests of, 35, 125–126, 149–151, 214n3, 215n6; effect of inequities on, 83; and policing policy, 35, 83, 125–126, 130; and press, 35, 128–129; and recreational facilities, 40, 46, 86, 125, 128, 155; and reform programs, 46; Manuel Ruiz on, 149–158; Tuck on, 124–125; violence of, 35–36; and Zoot-Suit Riots, 4, 41–48

Mexican Civic Committee, 105

Mexican Foreign Office, 24

Mexican GIs: contributions of, 51, 53; drafting of, 51, 54; effects of World War II on, 56–57; enlistment of, 56. *See also* Mexican American GIs

Mexican Revolution, 23

Mexicans: discrimination against, 83, 85, 87–88; as immigrant group, 2, 8, 9, 119–120; military contributions during World War II, 4; white Americans' perceptions of, 7–8, 17–18, 210n36

Mexico: and African Americans, 212n23; allegiance of progressives of, 104; and discrimination against Mexicans, 83, 85, 87–88; and repatriation, 10; right-wing nationalist political movements of, 23; support of League of United Latin American Citizens, 26, 27, 28, 29; and Texas' human rights record, 95, 96, 98, 145; and war on Axis powers, 51; and Zoot-Suit Riots, 218n40. *See also* U.S.-Mexico relations

middle-class Mexican Americans: and citizenship, 72; and civil rights reform programs, 30; education of, 13, 18; emergence of, 18, 210n38; and League of United Latin American Citizens, 82

migrant workers: McWilliams on, 17–18; and naturalization, 120; and poverty, 11; and women's employment, 64

military: and drafting of Mexican Americans, 49–50, 54, 177, 217–218n36; equality for Mexican Americans in, 1; Mexican Americans' enlistment in, 19–20, 50, 54, 56, 60, 82; preoccupation with efficiency, 33; racism in, 57

mines, Mexican Americans working in, 11, 25, 137, 139

minorities: antisocial behavior of youth, 36; and Blocker's investigation of discrimination, 29; dominant community's dividing of, 110, 116–119; Mexican Americans as ethnic minority, 2, 3, 4, 17–18, 19, 96, 107; and U.S. government policies, 3, 6, 31, 32, 97, 99, 214n47

Monroy, Douglas, 210n38

Montano, Joe, 173

Montejano, David, 2

Morales, David, *104*

Morales, Victoria, 51

Moreno, Luisa: and El Congreso del Pueblo de Habla Española, 89; and labor movement, 72, 78–81, 94, 222n10; photograph of, *80*

Morin, Raul: on Aleutian campaign, 160–161, 163–168; on contributions of Mexican American GIs, 4, 51, 159, 160–188; on D Day, 169–171, 173–178; on Jose M. Lopez, 179–180, *181*, 182–184; on military service, 50–51; on return from war, 185–188

movie theaters, 15, 61, 74, 87, 105, 190–191, 205–206

Muschinsky, Leonard, 175

Musick, Walt, 175

Mussolini, Benito, 39

mutualistas (mutual aid societies), 16, 79, 89–90, 93

National Association for the Advancement of Colored People (NAACP), 15, 143

National Catholic Welfare Council, 47

National Congress of Parents and Teachers, 83

national ideology, and self-help, 31

national security: and Good Neighbor Policy, 23; and treatment of Mexican Americans, 3, 8, 18, 19, 26

National Union of Mine, Mill, and Smelter Workers, 25

Native Americans. *See* American Indians

naturalization, 16, 119, 120–121, 210n31

Nazi Germany, and Fascism, 39

Nerios, Jose, 178

Nevada, 142

New Deal, 31

New Mexico: and civil rights activism, 94, 103; descendants of Mexican colonists in, 2, 9; employment discrimination in, 139, 141; and Mexican American identity, 72–73; Sánchez's study of Spanish-speaking community of, 17

New York Times, 217n35

Nunez, Bobby, 178

Nuñez, Manuel, 170

Nunn, Guy T., 224n51

Office of War Information, 37, 157

oil industry, 77, 139

Okies, 11

La Opinión, 51, 210n30, 217n30

Order of the Knights of America, 82

Order of the Sons of America, 82

Orendain, Antonio, 103

pachucos: as juvenile delinquents, 47; Mexican American women as pachucas, 44, 68, 69, 128, 129; Mexican American youth as, 36;

middle class rejection of, 72; older
Mexican Americans' response to,
43, 217n30; and press, 44, 69, 86,
124–125, 129; sailors' reaction to,
41, 48, 217n30; George I. Sánchez
on, 83; and stereotypes, 68–69,
148. *See also* Zoot-Suit Riots
pachuqismo, 68, 69
Pacific First, 39, 216n17
Padilla, Gil, 103
patriarchal authority, and Mexican
American women's employment,
63, 64, 65
patriotism: contradictions in, 75; and
double-consciousness, 57, 58; and
League of United Latin American Citizens, 82–83; and Mexican
American GIs, 50–51, 55, 56; and
Mexican American identity, 58, 71,
73; and Mexican American organizations, 94; Mexican Americans'
belief in, 1; and Mexican American
women, 66; pervasiveness of, 74
Peña, Charlie, *104*
Peña, Héctor, Jr., 60–62
Perales, Alonso S.: on assaults on
Mexican Americans, 193–194, 199,
205–206; and civil rights activism,
28; on denial of service, 190, 191–
192, 195–200, 202–205; on discrimination, 83, 189; and League
of United Latin American Citizens, 27, 76, 189; photograph of,
84; on segregation, 190–191, 196,
201, 205
Phelps-Dodge copper mine, 77
El Plan de San Diego, 72
police brutality: and Communist
Party, 78; and Community Service
Organization, 101; and Mexican
Americans, 14, 74, 209n23; and
Mexican American youth, 35; and
Zoot-Suit Riots, 41, 216n28
policing policy: and Mexican American youth, 35, 83, 125–126, 130;
Manuel Ruiz on, 149–150, 155–156;

Tuck on, 125–127, 130; and Zoot-
Suit Riots, 218n40
Political Association of Spanish-
speaking Organizations, 188
political power: of African Americans,
22, 211n39, 212n16; and Mexican
American organizations, 104–105;
of Mexican Americans, 2, 3, 4, 18,
89, 122–123, 211n39. *See also* voting
rights
polls, rating races of world, 7–8
poverty: and education quality, 12–13;
effect of Mexican Americans on
larger society, 17; and employment
discrimination, 9–12; and institutionalized racism, 19; and Mexican
American GIs, 50, 54; and Mexican
American identity, 58; and Mexican Americans' exclusion from
mainstream, 29; and Mexican
American women's employment,
64; and political participation, 16;
and World War II reform programs, 30, 31
prejudice: and Castañeda, 76, 77, 135,
138, 139, 140, 141; and civil rights
activism, 98; and civil rights consciousness, 75; education as protection against, 58; and employment
discrimination, 9, 11, 76, 139, 140,
141; and Mexican American generation, 75; Perales on, 189; and
Sleepy Lagoon case, 38; U.S. government recognition of, 29; and
Zoot-Suit Riots, 45, 46
La Prensa, 51, 83, 189
press: and delinquent behavior of
Mexican American youth, 35, 128–
129; and Fascism, 39; and gangs,
35, 39, 124; and pachucos, 44, 69,
86, 124–125, 129; Manuel Ruiz on,
150, 156; and Sleepy Lagoon case,
35, 37–38, 40, 79; Tuck on, 124–
125, 128–131; and Zoot-Suit Riots,
42, 43–46, 217nn30–35. *See also*
Spanish-language newspapers

El Primer Congreso Mexicanista, 82
Protestant churches, assimilation fostered by, 210n28
public accommodations/facilities discrimination: and denial of service, 15, 61, 66, 74, 83–85, 87, 88–89, 96, 112, 155, 190, 191–192, 195–200, 202–205; and division of minorities, 116; and League of United Latin American Citizens, 26, 28, 30–31; and liberals, 34; and Mexican American organizations, 105; protests against, 87–89; and public services, 64; and segregation, 58, 61, 74, 87–88, 190–191, 196, 201, 205; signs restricting access, 13, 14–15, 112; and Spears bill, 85, 224n3; and Texas' Concurrent Resolution, 95–96
public service organizations, 31

Quevedo, Eduardo, 87
Quiñonez, Naomi, 70

race, polls rating races of world, 7–8
race relations: friction as inherent in human condition, 32; and proposed U.S. government agency, 31, 214n47; in Texas, 29, 85; and Zoot-Suit Riots, 41, 42–43, 44, 45, 46
racism: and alienation of Mexican American youth, 36–37; effect of World War II on, 4, 99; and employment discrimination, 9, 11–12, 20–22, 33; as engrained human trait, 32; institutionalization of, 19; and League of United Latin American Citizens, 82; liberals' attitudes toward, 32; and Ignacio López, 87; and meaning of World War II, 49, 105; and Mexican American identity, 58, 67, 72; in military, 57; public awareness of, 99, 107; and George I. Sánchez, 82; and Sleepy Lagoon case, 38; systematic problems of, 77; U.S.

government opposition to, 74; and Zoot-Suit Riots, 4, 41, 46, 47, 217n35
radicals, 38, 72
railroads, 11
Ramirez, Gregorio, 178
Ramirez, Joe, 169, 170, 178
Ramirez, Jose T., 178
Randolph, A. Philip, 143
Reconstruction, 97–98
recreational facilities: and Mexican American youth, 40, 46, 86, 125, 128, 155; segregation of, 15, 58, 74, 87–88, 105
Red Cross, 90, 158
Republican Party, 31
Ríos, Tony, 101
Rivas-Rodriguez, Maggie, 4, 219n8
Rodríguez, María Elisa, 58–59, 64
Rodriguez, Tony, 178
Roman Catholic Church, 16, 115
Roosevelt, Franklin D., 21, 23, 25, 97, 143
Rosales, Raul, 169
Rosie the Riveter Collection, 221n30
Ross, Fred, 101
Rotnem, Victor, 97
Roybal, Edward, 86–87, 101
Rubio, Pedro, 171, 173
Ruiz, Manuel, Jr.: and civil rights activism, 94; and Coordinating Council for Latin-American Youth, 86, 87, 148; on juvenile delinquency, 149–158; on Sleepy Lagoon case, 148, 150
Ruiz, Vicki L., 69, 220–221n30

Sacco and Vanzetti affair, 40
Sáenz, J. Luz, 72
sailors: and press, 129, 130; and Zoot-Suit Riots, 41–42, 44–45, 46, 48, 216n28, 217nn30–35, 218n42
Salazar, Margarita, 65, 69, 70
Saldívar, Ramón, 54
Sánchez, Catalina, 68
Sánchez, Emiliano (Elmer), 52, 68

Sánchez, George I.: and civil rights consciousness, 81–86, 95, 96, 99; and League of United Latin American Citizens, 76, 81–86, 94; study of Mexican Americans, 17, 76; and U.S. government, 27, 47; on Zoot-Suit Riots, 47–48

Sanchez, G. J., 106, 210n38, 220n20

Sánchez, Helen, 68

Sánchez, John Edward (Eddie), 52, 68

Sánchez, Leonidas Nicolás (Leo), 52

Sánchez, Santiago (Jimmy), 52

Sánchez, Severo, 52

Sánchez Carpenter, Amalia (Molly), 53

Sánchez Mehl, Antonia (Tony), 53

Sánchez Miller, Angélica, 53

Santa Fe Railroad, 88

Santillán, Richard, 62, 65, 66, 67–68, 220n30

schoolhouse, Mathias, Texas, 30

second generation: alienation of, 36; and division of minorities, 117–118; and housing discrimination, 115–116; and juvenile delinquency, 125; and Zoot-Suit Riots, 46

segregation: in Boy Scout/Girl Scout troops, 55, 58; in California, 86–89; and Castañeda, 76, 78; and Communist Party, 78; and Coordinating Council for Latin-American Youth, 86; in education, 12–14, 26, 29, 30, 34, 37, 74, 83, 100, 105, 107, 112, 152–153; effect of World War II on, 4; in housing, 1; lawsuits against, 76; and League of United Latin American Citizens, 26, 78; and Mexican American identity, 71; and Mexican American organizations, 86–89, 94; in mortuaries and cemeteries, 101, 111; in public facilities, 58, 61, 74, 87–88, 190–191, 196, 201, 205; in real estate, 14; and George I. Sánchez, 81, 82, 83, 85

Selective Service Act of 1940, 211n1

self-help: and Mexican American

organizations, 93; and national ideology, 31

self-improvement: and League of United Latin American Citizens, 82; and Mexican American veterans, 188

Serna, Angel, 88–89

Servín, Manuel, 209–210n27

Sinarquistas: and Sleepy Lagoon case, 37, 39, 40, 150; and Zoot-Suit Riots, 47

Sleepy Lagoon case: and Cranston, 37–38; defendants of, 36, 38, 215n12; and delinquent Mexican American youths, 35–36; and gangs, 35, 37, 39, 41; impact of, 40; and lack of justice, 74; and Mc-Williams, 38, 40–41, 215n14; and morale of Mexican American community, 37–38, 40; Luisa Moreno on, 79; reversing of convictions, 39–40, 216n19; Manuel Ruiz on, 148, 150; and Sinarquistas, 37, 39, 40, 150

Sleepy Lagoon Defense Committee, 38, 39–40, 79

Smargeanian, Robert, 175

Smith v. Allwright (1944), 97

social class: and caste system, 14–15; and education discrimination, 12–13, 29; and employment discrimination, 9–12; and mobility, 3, 14; and promotion of cross-class unity, 212n11; and voting rights, 14

social clubs, 16

social-scientific thought, 36

La Sociedad Mutualista Porfirio Díaz, 90

Solís, Santiago, 65

South, and civil rights activism, 97–98

South America, 23

Soviet Union, 39

Spanish language: and discrimination, 58; in education system, 152–153; and job training, 155; and Mexican American identity, 60; New Mexicans' maintaining of, 9, 17; and

Office of War Information, 157; and segregation in education, 14
Spanish-language newspapers: and civil rights consciousness, 16, 87; and discrimination, 84–85; and FEPC, 25; and lists of those killed in war, 51; and segregation, 87; and war effort, 90
Spanish-speaking settlers, descendants of, 2, 8, 9, 15–16, 88–89, 209–210n27
Spears bill, 85, 224n3
Spencer, Herbert, 31
state government: and policies toward minorities, 2; and repatriation, 10; and World War II reform programs, 31
Steele, Richard, 6
Steinbeck, John, 11
stereotypes: and discrimination, 11, 31; and gangsters, 215n7; and general public, 7, 8; of Mexican American women, 68–69; and pachucos, 68–69, 148
Stevenson, Coke, 85

Tamayo, Andrew, 56
Tapia, Mike, 178
Taylor, Paul S., 17
Tejanos, 71–72
Tenayuca, Emma, 79
Tenney, Jack, 81
Terrazas, Guillermo "Memo," 169, 170, 173–174
Texas: and civil rights activism, 26–31, 94, 98, 100, 103; civil rights laws in, 85; Concurrent Resolution on the Good Neighbor, 48, 95–96, 145, 146–147; descendants of Spanish-speaking settlers in, 2, 8; and division of minorities, 117; education in, 12–13, 100, 209n20; employment discrimination in, 139, 141; and industrial mobilization, 22; integration of Mexican Americans into Anglo society, 9; and League of United Latin

American Citizens, 26–31, 100; and Mexican American identity, 71–72; Mexican immigrants settling in, 11; race relations in, 29, 85; racial caste system in, 11, 24; segregation in, 101, 107; treatment of African Americans, 209n20, 211n39; and voting rights, 14
Texas Council on Human Relations, 85
Texas Good Neighbor Commission, 85
Texas Rangers, 72
13th Amendment, 97
Time, 45–46, 218n40
tuberculosis rates, 12, 209n16, 218n36
Tuck, Ruth: on citizenship, 119–124; on discrimination, 108, 109–119, 122; ethnographic interviews of Mexican Americans, 108; on Mexican American veterans, 131–134; on policing policy, 125–127, 130; on press, 124–125, 128–131
Tucker, Pedro, 87

unions: and civil rights activism, 1, 106; and division of minorities, 116; and employment discrimination, 76, 77, 94, 106; lack of Mexican Americans in, 11, 93; Mexican Americans' involvement in, 94; and Luisa Moreno, 72, 78–81; pressure tactics of, 29, 32; and undermining of ethnic identity, 212n11; and war effort support, 89, 224n51. *See also* labor movement
United Cannery, Agricultural, Packing, and Allied Workers of America (UCAPAWA), 72, 79
United Farm Workers Union, 103
United Steel Workers of America (USWA), 94
Unity Clubs, 87
Unity Leagues, 89
Urban League, 224n51
U.S. Census Bureau, 213n37
U.S. Employment Service, 20, 213n37

244 World War II and Mexican American Civil Rights

U.S. government: and aliens' eligibility for employment, 21, 211n7; and civil rights compliance initiatives, 77, 99; and civil rights in wartime, 29–31, 96–99; and civil rights statutes, 97; and delinquency of Mexican American youth, 37; and League of United Latin American Citizens, 27, 28; limits of federal concern, 31–33; policies regarding ethnic minorities, 3, 6, 31, 32, 97, 99, 214n47; racism opposed by, 74; and repatriation, 10; reports on Mexican Americans, 8, 18; and Sleepy Lagoon case, 39; and terminology about Mexican Americans, 2, 3, 19, 106; and Zoot-Suit Riots, 47

U.S. Justice Department, 21, 97–98
U.S. Marine Corps, 60
U.S.-Mexican border, 71–72
U.S.-Mexican War, 71, 72
U.S.-Mexico relations: and Good Neighbor policy, 23, 24; and industrial mobilization, 22; and labor shortages, 95–96; and mistreatment of Spanish-speaking Americans, 3, 23–24, 26, 31; and pressure concerning discrimination, 29, 83, 85, 96; and Zoot-Suit Riots, 46, 47, 219n49

U.S. Navy: Mexican American recruits, 55; and Zoot-Suit Riots, 42
U.S. Office of Civilian Defense and Education, 83
U.S. State Department, 24, 25, 28–29, 32

Vargas, Zaragosa, 1, 5, 94, 106
Vélez, Lupe, 69
Veterans Administration (VA), 101
Veterans Clubs, 90
Victory Program, 89
vigilantism, 12
Villegas, Gilbert, 178
violence: assaults on Mexican Americans, 193–194, 199, 205–206; and

Mexican American youth, 35–36; and pachucas, 69; George I. Sánchez on, 83; and Tejano uprising of 1915, 72; and U.S. government's civil rights actions, 98; of World War II, 49, 54; and Zoot-Suit Riots, 41–42, 43, 44, 47, 48, 79

Viva Kennedy Clubs, 105
voting rights: and civil rights activism, 101, 105, 106; and court decisions, 97; and Mexican American leaders, 122–123; and Mexican American women, 66; and naturalization, 16, 210n31; and poll taxes, 14

wages: effect of World War II on, 20; equality of, during World War II, 1; and subordination of Mexican Americans, 8, 11, 12, 137; of women, 63, 64

Wallace, Frank, 29
Wallace, Henry, 32, 103
War Manpower Commission, 37, 88, 157
Welles, Sumner, 25, 28, 219n48
white Americans: as dominant population of American Southwest, 9; and education discrimination, 29; hostility towards Mexican Americans, 23, 211n39; Mexican Americans' equality with, 1; perceptions of Mexicans, 7–8, 17–18, 210n36; racism opposed by, 74; and Sleepy Lagoon case, 38, 40; and subordination of Mexican Americans, 12, 14

white supremacy, 27
women: employment of African American women, 67; and Luisa Moreno as labor leader, 78, 79; World War II experiences of, 63. See also Mexican American women
women's movement of 1960s, 62
World War II: and civil rights activism, 28, 29–30, 31, 32, 33, 94, 95, 96–99, 105, 106; conservation imperatives of, 44; evolution of civil

rights consciousness during, 1–2, 5, 6, 110–111; and Mexican American generation, 75; and Mexican American organizations, 89–94; and Mexican Americans as ethnic minority, 2, 3, 4; racism as damaging to war effort, 74; and reform programs, 3, 29–30, 31, 32, 33, 37; violence of, 49, 54

Zoot-Suit Riots: and Communist Party, 39, 46; and contradictions of home front, 4; and Cranston, 44, 218n48; and FBI, 90, 217– 218n36; and lack of justice, 74; lack of public sympathy, 43; and Mexican American women, 44, 69; and Luisa Moreno, 79; Morin on, 168; and preoccupation with zoot suits, 44, 45, 47, 217n33; and race relations, 41, 42–43, 44, 45, 46; and sailors, 41–42, 44–45, 46, 48, 216n28, 217nn30–35, 218n42; and U.S.-Mexico relations, 46, 47, 219n49

zoot suits, 41, 43–44, 45, 124, 216n28, 217n33